The Girl from Nip 'n' Tuck

PART II

The Girl from Nip 'n' Tuck

PART II

DIANNE H. LUNDY

PRIMIX
PUBLISHING
THE WRITE CHOICE

Primix Publishing
11620 Wilshire Blvd
Suite 900, West Wilshire Center, Los Angeles, CA, 90025
www.primixpublishing.com
Phone: 1-800-538-5788

Published by Primix Publishing: 09/14/2023

ISBN: 978-1-957676-95-1(sc)
ISBN: 978-1-957676-96-8(e)

Contents

Dedication

This book is dedicated to my husband, Richard L. Lundy, who has always supported me in my writing endeavors.

Chapter 1

Dianne H. Lundy was feeling both excited and a little scared. She had spent the first twenty-eight years of her life looking for two things: the perfect man and the ideal job. It looked as though her dreams had finally come true—or had they? She had spent the past seven years teaching at four different schools. Each school had a different student body with distinct personalities. She had made some mistakes along the way, but she had also learned a lot about teaching. Now she was about to begin her first year as a teacher at Pineville High School in Rapides Parish, Louisiana. She just hoped she was prepared for the job.

As the opening date of the school year approached, Dianne and her husband, Rick, began making plans on how to handle the situation. Rick, they decided, would return to Northwestern Louisiana State University in Natchitoches to complete his degree in Business Administration, as he needed only a few more hours of credit to finish. His education had been interrupted when he joined the Navy during the Vietnam war. He would stay in one of the dorms during the week and drive home for weekends. Otherwise, he would have to drive one hundred and twenty miles a day round trip in order to meet his classes.

After looking at other apartments, they decided to stay in Dianne's apartment on Payne Street in Pineville. It would be better, they thought, to save their money in hopes of being able to make a down payment on a house next year rather than splurging on more expensive living quarters. Besides that, it was right down the street from Pineville High, making it convenient for Dianne.

She soon headed to the school in order to get her room ready and to obtain the books she needed to make out lesson plans. Mr. Millet, the school's principal, took her down to the room that was assigned to her.

"We are going to give you room ten on the second wing of the school," he told her. "It's an empty room that nobody is using, and it's next to the home economics department. That room and room nine used to be the business department when the school was first built, so they are a little bigger than some of our other rooms. Second wing is one of the original wings of the school. I'll tell our head custodian, Mr. Kees, to find some student desks and a teacher's desk for you."

"What about a filing cabinet?" she inquired.

"I'll check with him about that, too. If we don't have any extra ones, we'll have to order one for you. Don't worry; we'll get you one somehow."

"What about books? I need to get a copy of the book used for each subject so I can start making lesson plans," she said.

"I'll tell you what I'm going to do. One of our assistant principals, Mr. Lemon Coleman, is in charge of the bookroom. He can get you a copy of the book you need for General Science. However, the home economics courses have so many different books that I have no idea what book goes with what course. So, I am going to have our secretary, Mrs. Jeffey Whitworth, give you the phone number of one of our home economics teachers who lives in Pineville. Her name is Mrs. Peggy Wakefield, and she can tell you which books you will need. When you get that information, check with Mr. Coleman, and we will get a copy of those books for you."

He ushered Dianne back to the main office and made introductions all around. In addition to meeting Mr. Coleman and Mrs. Whitworth, the main secretary, she also met the other assistant principal, Mr.

Ralph Kees, and the other two secretaries, Mrs. Edith Calhoun and Mrs. Helen Johnson. By that time all the names were whirling through her head, as she tried to keep them all straight.

A phone call to Mrs. Wakefield provided the necessary information about the books she would need, so Mr. Coleman obtained a copy of each of those for her. Armed with almost more information than she could absorb, she headed home to try to sort it all out.

I really need to get some materials for bulletin boards, she decided. Putting up bulletin boards has always been one of my favorite activities, and I need something to brighten up that drab room. I can use some of the bulletin board ideas I already have, but I need to get some bulletin board background paper from the parish media center.

———

She obtained the colorful paper the next day and headed back out to school to put up the bulletin boards, and also to see if she had received the promised furniture for her room. She was slightly taken back when she opened the door to her room to discover a mishmash of student desks and one teacher's desk that was in very sad shape. All the furniture was apparently discards that other teachers had not wanted. She was doubtful that some of the student desks would actually make it through an entire school year, but she had little choice in the matter.

Oh, well, beggars can't be choosers, as the old saying goes. I'll just have to make do with this furniture for the year and hope that I can get something better next year, she reasoned.

She proceeded to put up the bulletin boards, silently congratulating herself on how much cheerier the room looked when they were completed. *Nothing like a good bulletin board to pep up a classroom* was her thought on the matter.

Following that task, she tackled the arrangement of the student desks and the placement of her teacher's desk, debating on exactly what would be exactly the right spot for her to observe the class. The center of the room didn't seem right, as it would block the view of the chalkboard. She finally placed her desk in the front corner of the room next to the teacher's storage closet. That little area would be her personal space while she was in the classroom.

The pencil sharpener, which would then be behind her desk, would have to be moved, she decided. She didn't want students traipsing back and forth behind her desk whenever they needed to sharpen their pencils. The only logical place to put it was on the opposite side of the room by the door.

The wall between rooms nine and ten contained several large panes of glass, a remnant of the original business department setting. Room ten had been the typing room, and room nine had held the business machines. There was an adjoining door between the two rooms. She decided the door should be locked from both sides in order to prevent students from traveling back and forth between the two rooms. She made a mental note to confer with whatever teacher was assigned to room nine about that situation.

Someone had covered the glass panes with blue contact paper to match the blue walls of the room, but it was coming loose in some places, creating an untidy look. *Definitely a need for some kind of curtains to cover those panes,* she thought. *That's a project to tackle later in the year, hopefully when there is some money available to pay for the materials.* Satisfied she had done all she could to prepare the room for the first day of school, she headed home to the apartment.

The first day of school rolled around almost too soon. Dianne received her yearly letter from Mr. Millet instructing her on the times and dates of the teacher workshops that were always held before students arrived. Nervous about meeting so many new people all at the same time, she arrived early on the appointed day and headed down to room ten to deposit most of her belongings.

The first two people she encountered were her co-workers in the home economics department, Mrs. Peggy Wakefield, whom she had already met over the phone, and Mrs. Bettye Watkins.

"You must be Dianne," Peggy exclaimed when she noticed Dianne unlocking the door to her room.

"Yes, I am," said Dianne.

"I'm so glad to meet you. I'm Peggy Wakefield, and this is our other home economics teacher, Bettye Watkins," Peggy told her. "You don't know how happy we are to have another teacher in our department. We have been trying to get a third teacher for quite a few years."

"Nice to meet both of you. I just hope I can live up to your expectations. Teaching in a school this size will be a new experience for me," Dianne responded.

"Glad to meet you, too," said Bettye.

"Well, we're probably in for a long faculty meeting, but whenever we have a chance, we need to have a departmental meeting to decide how to go about sharing the rooms in our department," Peggy commented.

"Why don't you come and sit with us at the faculty meeting?" asked Bettye.

"Sure, I would be glad to. I don't know anybody on this faculty," said Dianne.

The trio headed to the library for the faculty meeting as soon as they left their materials in their respective classrooms. Dianne was about to be initiated into one of the annual events at Pineville High—the back-to-school faculty meeting, an event which always consumed a large part of the morning hours.

As they walked into the library, Dianne noticed several tables were covered with stacks of materials.

"You have to find the red folder with your name on it," Peggy told her. "That's how you know which stack of stuff belongs to you."

"They're usually in alphabetical order. That makes them easier to find," said Bettye.

They all managed to locate their folders. They picked up the materials and headed towards the chairs that had been set up for the meeting. Dianne felt all eyes upon her, and she knew she was being scrutinized by the other faculty members as she took her seat with Peggy and Bettye.

"Whatever you do, don't lose this red folder. You will have to turn it in at the end of the year," warned Bettye.

"Yes, and I don't know why, because they always print up new ones every year, One of our coaches, Walter Holsomback, had his stolen one year as a prank. They almost didn't let him check out," Peggy added.

"In that case, I'll be sure to keep it in a safe place," Dianne declared.

<hr />

The meeting began with a welcome from Mr. Millet followed by a short prayer, as was the custom for every back-to-school faculty meeting at Pineville High. Announcements were made about several new policies that were being instituted. Then came the introduction of the new faculty members.

Dianne stood when her name was called, noting to herself that she was now an official part of the largest faculty in her teaching career. She hoped she could measure up to Mr. Millet's standards. She was still not sure if she had made the right decision in changing from a small country school to a school with an enrollment of over a thousand students, almost equal to that of her alma mater, Harding College.

The meeting then began in earnest with Dianne's first experience in what would be a yearly event—the presentation of the material in the "Red Book," which was the teachers' handbook. Not a single page was omitted as each principal covered the part pertaining to his domain in the school's day-to-day operation. There was apparently no detail left out. It was the most organized plan for running a school Dianne had ever seen.

Several hours later, with stiff legs and aching backs, everyone was relieved when the meeting finally came to a conclusion. It was almost time for lunch, so Dianne, Peggy, and Bettye decided to wait until afternoon to hold their departmental meeting.

"There's no use of us starting a meeting and then having to stop right in the middle of it," said Peggy. "Why don't we meet in the clothing lab after lunch?"

Dianne and Bettye agreed that seemed to be the best plan of action.

———

Following their lunch break, they headed back to the clothing lab, as planned. A blast of cool air greeted them when Peggy unlocked the door. Each room in the school contained two floor air units on the back wall which were connected to a central system that provided either cool or warm air, as the weather dictated. It was a welcome relief to Dianne after being in an un-air-conditioned school for two and one-half years.

Being alone with her two co-workers finally gave Dianne a chance to really study them for the first time. Both ladies were attractive and well-dressed, as befitted anyone teaching home economics. After all, home economics teachers were always expected to set a proper example for the girls of the school she had learned.

Peggy was a trim-figured woman with blue eyes and medium-length, neatly-coifed brown hair. Her soft voice and gentle manner would have rivaled that of any Southern belle. It was obvious she was a very kind person. Dianne would soon learn she was also a very knowledgeable and talented teacher who was well respected in her field.

Bettye, a black teacher who had been transferred from Peabody High School during the desegregation order, was tall with a large frame. Neatness personified, she was impeccably groomed. She had a special talent for sewing and made almost all of her own clothes, she informed Dianne. Although she was more of a talker than Peggy, she had an air of gentle strength that had a calming effect on anyone who came into contact with her. Somehow, Dianne sensed that working with these two women would be one of the best things that had ever happened to her in her teaching career.

Peggy opened the discussion as they settled in for their meeting. "We need to take a look at all three of our schedules to see what labs we are going to need and how to divide up the time for sharing them. Dianne, you can probably stay in room ten except for when you need the lab for cooking or sewing with your Home Economics II class. That leaves me and Bettye to work out the rest of the labs. We are going to have to move some desks into the kitchen and have some of the classes in there. The students will just have to push them out of the way whenever we cook. We're also going to need to get some kind of portable chalkboard for that room."

"I see one problem that needs to be addressed," commented Bettye. "If Dianne is going to be teaching Handicrafts, she is going to need some tables in room ten for that."

"We have some of the sewing tables that came to Pineville High when they closed Slocum," said Peggy, referring Pineville's former black high school. "I think we can have some of those moved into room ten. The room is big enough for both desks and tables," she noted.

"What am I supposed to do about storage of student materials for the handicraft projects?" asked Dianne.

"You need to talk to Mr. Millet about that. Our head custodian, Mr. Kees, can probably build you some kind of storage cabinet," Peggy told her.

"What exactly do the students learn in Handicrafts?" Dianne inquired.

"Well, I'll tell you the history of it. It started with Mrs. Virginia Thomas, the teacher who is next to you in room nine. She is the reading teacher for this school, and she deals with students who need to improve their reading skills. She initiated a plan for having students make handicraft items that could be sold in a school store that was called 'Hand-Did.' So many students wanted to take the course they had to give some of them to us home economics teachers.

What you do pretty much depends on the students you have. Since Bettye is the one who has been teaching it, I'll let her tell you about what she has been doing," said Peggy.

"We try to teach them a lot of skills dealing with sewing and sewing materials. The first thing I usually have everybody do is make a sampler of all the embroidery stitches. We have the embroidery hoops, and we buy some fabric and thread and needles for them to work with. After that, they learn to knit and crochet, and they have to complete something like a potholder or granny squares that can be used to make an Afghan. We also do some macramé projects. Since we also have boys in the class, we have to find some other projects that will interest them. It just varies from one semester to the next, depending on the students you get," explained Bettye.

"Boy, it's a good thing I learned how to do all of that in college," Dianne exclaimed. "However, that was so long ago I will have to go home and practice before I can teach anybody how to knit or crochet, and my embroidery skills are pretty rusty, too."

The meeting ended shortly afterwards, with all three teachers satisfied that they had covered all the bases. Dianne had learned she would also be expected to help out with the Future Homemakers of America club. She had been an FHA member during her high school days at Farmerville High, but sponsoring FHA would be a totally new experience for her.

Well, I can see teaching at a larger school is definitely going to be a lot more work. Still, it's something I have always wanted to do. I'll just have to give it my best effort and see what transpires, she thought, as she locked up her room and headed back to the apartment. It was Friday, and she planned to use the weekend to prepare some lesson plans and activities for her classes. Still, most of the preparations would have to wait until she actually met with the classes and found out what kind of students she would be dealing with.

I have finally been assigned to a school of my own choosing. Once again, I will just have to put my trust in God to watch over me. I am charting an unknown course, and I will have to leave it up to Him to guide me in the right direction.

Chapter 2

*W*hen Dianne walked into Pineville High School early the following Monday morning, there was an atmosphere somewhat akin to a small metropolis, with the one-thousand plus students running everywhere and the sixty-five or so teachers trying to direct them on where to go. She took her books and belongings to room ten and then went to the teachers' lounge to sign in and check on her mail, as the teachers' mailboxes lined the wall directly above the counter that held the sign-in sheets.

Since Dianne did not have a homeroom, she was assigned to hall duty on fourth wing during the homeroom period. She thought this would be a good thing, but time would prove it to actually be a detriment. She managed to make her way through the crowded halls to the other end of the school, finally finding the correct wing. At least she was a little savvier than the unsuspecting freshmen, who were often directed by upperclassmen to go to the nonexistent "sixth wing" or "out back by the swimming pool."

Homeroom on the first day of school usually lasted for at least an hour, she soon learned. Her job during that time was to keep everybody in their assigned rooms on fourth wing. Mr. Millet personally paid her a visit as she stood on duty to provide her with such instructions.

"Don't let anybody out in the halls. I don't care what their excuse is. I want them to stay in homeroom," he told her.

Whenever Mr. Millet gave an order, nobody dared disobey. He was definitely the captain of the ship. His word was the law.

About halfway through the hour-long homeroom, Dianne's feet began to hurt. She was wishing she had worn some more comfortable shoes, but it was too late for that. There were no chairs about, so there was no hope of sitting down. Just when she thought she couldn't stand it any longer, she had an idea. The doors leading to some outside steps were right behind her duty spot. On each side of the concrete steps was a ledge that looked just about the right size for sitting. So, she took herself outside and plopped down on the ledge, leaving the doors standing open so she still had a view of fourth wing. It was a relief to get off her feet.

It was then she began to think about the situation. *What am I doing here? Do I really belong in a school this size? Maybe I should have stuck with the little country schools. After all, I'm a country girl from Nip 'n' Tuck!* All these thoughts raced through her mind. Finally, the bell rang, signaling the end of the homeroom period, and she headed back to room ten to face her first class of the day.

That class was Home Economics II, and it consisted of only eleven students ranging from grades ten through twelve. She went through the usual motions of the first day's activities with them, trying to find out what they had covered in their previous home economics classes and what they had hoped to learn by enrolling in Home Economics II. They were a quiet group, and Dianne began to think maybe being at Pineville High wasn't such a bad thing, after all.

The shortened period soon came to an end, and it was time for second hour. That was Dianne's planning period. With no class scheduled, her room had been assigned to the assistant principal, Mr. Coleman, who had a World Geography class at that time. That meant Dianne had to find somewhere else to go during that class period. Mrs. Wakefield had suggested she use the home economics living room, and she liked that idea. Staying in the teachers' lounge for an entire hour was definitely not her cup of tea.

Third period soon rolled around, and it was time for Dianne to face her next class of the day, Home and Family Living, a class for eleventh and twelfth grade students. This class was much larger, containing almost thirty students, and much noisier. It soon became evident she would have to be on her toes to keep one step ahead of them. Still, the study of family relations was something she felt confident in teaching, so she wasn't worried about being able to handle those students.

Then came the two classes she had been dreading—fourth-hour and fifth-hour General Science. Both classes were large with a mixture of students who appeared to have a wide range of abilities. Fourth hour was definitely restless, as it was the hour just before lunch, and the students were getting hungry by then. It didn't take Dianne long to figure out those two classes were going to be her most challenging.

The sixth hour class was Handicrafts. Of course, there was really not much for students to do on the first day, as they hadn't bought any materials or paid their lab fees. The class was pretty much a disaster on that day. She finished up the day vowing to have some sort of activity for them the next day, as trouble always started when students were left with too much idle time. She remembered the embroidery sampler Bettye had suggested, so she went next door to ask about using the embroidery hoops that belonged to the department. Bettye gave her a few suggestions and told her she had some white material that students could use to embroider on. All Dianne needed was some embroidery thread and needles.

"You can pick those up at the Hancock's Fabric Store right up the street from the school," Bettye told her. "Just keep your receipt, and you can get reimbursed if you turn it in to the office."

Dianne spent the next few weeks going through what would soon become a regular routine. She was gradually becoming more familiar with the school, the faculty, and her students. She still had high hopes that she had finally attained her goal of getting her dream job in a school where she had wanted to teach ever since first setting foot in Rapides Parish. Little did she know she was entering what would become one of the darkest phases of her life.

She became somewhat depressed because Rick wasn't around during the week. He left for his classes at Northwestern early on Monday mornings and didn't come back home until Friday afternoons. That meant she had nobody to vent her frustrations to, as she had not yet made any real friends with the faculty members at Pineville High. Her one source of consolation was her friend Margaret Paul, and she often phoned Margaret at night, telling her about the problems. Margaret lent a sympathetic ear, reassuring Dianne that things would soon get better and speculating that a lot of the depression was probably due to Rick's absence.

Still, it seemed that whenever Dianne turned around she was always getting into trouble. No matter how hard she tried, she just couldn't please the administrators. One morning she was sitting at her spot on hall duty when Mr. Millet approached. Before she had a chance to say anything, he was standing right in front of her, eyes blazing, as he glared down at her.

"Mrs. Lundy, are you aware that you missed your football duty assignment Friday night?" he asked.

"No, I don't think I had it last week. I found my name and circled it on the duty roster, and it was for another date," she replied.

"No, you had it last Friday, and you weren't there. You have it twice. Almost everybody on the faculty has it twice."

"Well, I'm sorry, but I was unaware of that. After I found my name, I didn't look for it anymore. There's not much I can do about that now."

"In the future, make sure you show up for duty whenever your name is listed. That's all I have to say on that matter," he instructed as he turned and marched back down the hall.

Well, so much for that. I guess he told me, she thought.

Mr. Millet, it seemed, was always on her case about something. She was beginning to think the situation was hopeless.

On another occasion, her Home Economics II class was completing the second day of a two-day lab. Most of the food had been cooked the day before, and the students were in the process of reheating it and preparing the bread and beverage to complete a meal. Dianne had gone around to all of the kitchens and checked the food and the table settings, leaving her with little else to do, as the eleven students were well behaved in lab.

Mrs. Wakefield had given her a long, detailed report from the state department, asking her to look it over and recheck some of the figures they had entered. The report was due to the school board office the next day. Mrs. Wakefield had suggested that Dianne might be able to look at the report during the lab period so that she could get it back to Bettye to check before the day was over. Dianne sat down at the teacher's desk in the lab and began to study the report while the students were waiting for their food to heat up.

Unbeknownst to her, Mr. Millet came up behind the door of the lab and stood there for several minutes. In his eyes, she was doing little to supervise the students in the lab setting. He called her into his office the next day and expressed his displeasure over her apparent lack of supervision, paying little heed to her protests that she had already taken care of the students before pulling out the report to go over it.

Chalk up another mark against my record. Somehow, it seems that the fates are against me, she pondered, as she walked slowly back to her room.

Although she rarely encountered problems in the cooking labs with such a small group, one day a major problem did occur. She had been collecting lab money from the students before the lab began, and she stuck the money into her wallet, leaving some of it sticking out of the top of the wallet. She always kept her purse on the teacher's desk during the labs, along with her books and the gradebook. There did not seem to be any reason for concern regarding this arrangement.

Later that day, after the lab was over, one of her students in the fourth hour General Science class asked to borrow fifty cents in order to eat lunch in the school cafeteria. Dianne pulled out her purse and began to search for her wallet, discovering it was nowhere to be found.

"I'm sorry, but I can't lend you the money. It appears that someone has stolen my wallet," she told the boy.

Almost in a panic, she walked down to the teachers' lounge and told Peggy what had happened. Some of the other teachers who overheard the conversation advised her to report it immediately to the office.

"Mr. Millet will have the janitors search all of the trash barrels for your wallet. You need to tell him as soon as possible," one teacher informed her.

The report was made, and Dianne recovered the wallet and all of its contents, minus the cash that was in it. Fortunately, she had only a little of her own money plus the lab money she had collected that day. The one thing she most regretted losing was a two-dollar bill Dolores had given her to carry for good luck. It hadn't brought her much luck that day.

"Well, that taught me a valuable lesson," she told Peggy. "I taught at two different all-black schools and never had anything stolen except a half-drunk cola. I come here to Pineville High School, which is supposed to be one of the best schools in the parish, and my wallet is stolen during cooking lab. You can be sure I will keep my purse and wallet under lock and key from now on."

The Handicrafts class was not proving to be one of Dianne's favorite ones to teach. For one thing, it was strictly a lab class with no type of printed materials or instructions except what Dianne could concoct. Also, she had to constantly stay one step ahead of the students in order to provide them with examples of the work they were expected to complete. There was also a lot of moving around as students got up to get their materials out of the cabinets, and also at the end of class when they had to stop and store their materials.

One day after the materials had been put away, Dianne looked around the classroom and discovered two of the students were missing. The classroom doors had been left open for sixth hour because by that time of day the room was beginning to heat up from all the body heat given off by the students during the day. Slipping out of class while the other students were up and moving around was an easy thing to do.

"What happened to Sally Blackmon and Earl Johnson?" she inquired.

Nobody seemed to have an answer to that question, so she walked to the door and looked down the hall, which was empty by that time.

"Well, they seem to have flown the coop. Guess I will have to report their disappearance to the office after school is out," she said.

After the bell rang to dismiss school for the day, she walked down to the office, but all the principals were out on bus duty. She decided to wait until the following morning to make her report, because the students had already left for the day.

The next morning she signed in and deposited her belongings in room ten. She was in the process of setting up her materials for the first class when one of the secretaries called her room over the intercom.

"Mrs. Lundy, Mr. Millet would like to see you in his office as soon as possible."

"I'll be right down," Dianne replied, wondering what could possibly be wrong this time.

She walked into the office and was surprised to see Sally and Earl sitting in the chairs outside the principal's office. Before she could sit down, the door to Mr. Millet's office opened, and they were all summoned inside.

After they were all seated, Mr. Millet opened the discussion.

"Mrs. Lundy, were you aware that these two students walked out of your class yesterday at sixth period?" he inquired.

"Yes, I missed them, and I came down to the office to report it, but all of the principals were out on bus duty," she replied.

"Well, Mr. Kees saw them leaving from his classroom window over on third wing. They apparently just walked out of your room with no problem."

"It wasn't her fault," Sally began to speak.

"Be quiet. When I want to hear from you, I will ask for your opinion," he interjected. "Now, Mrs. Lundy, I want you to come up with a plan so that this sort of thing doesn't happen again. You may go back to your classroom, and I will deal with these two students."

"I'll see what I can do about the situation," Dianne responded, as she rose to leave.

Oh, brother. What is going to happen to me next? she wondered, as she walked back to her room.

She solved the problem by making sure the doors were closed before students got up to put their materials away and having them get up only one desk row at a time to go to the supply cabinet. She never did learn what punishment was doled out to the two delinquent students, but they never attempted to leave class early again.

———

Being chewed out in front of two of her students was bad enough, but on one occasion, Dianne was humiliated in front of the entire student body. An assembly had been scheduled for the end of sixth hour in order to inform students about a tax the school board was attempting to have renewed for the purpose of raising the salaries of teachers and school personnel. The plan was to pass out handbills to the students and have them carry the papers home to their parents.

Teachers were to accompany their sixth hour students to the gym for the assembly. Dianne normally did not have to take students to assemblies because she did not have a homeroom, so it was a new experience for her. She decided to wait until they were already seated in the assembly to pass out the papers, reasoning that a lot of the students would probably just discard the papers on the way to the gym.

She managed to find the correct place for the students to sit and got them all seated before the program began. Then she and the teacher next to her, Mrs. Alma Jo Wilkerson, began handing out their papers and having students pass them back. Mr. Millet began speaking before they could complete the task.

After making a few opening remarks, he paused and began to address the two teachers, who were still handing out their papers.

"If you two ladies need me to come down there and help you hand out those papers, just let me know," he said, much to the amusement of the rest of the student body.

"Yes, sir," Mrs. Wilkerson replied, as she and Dianne exchanged glances.

Chalk up another red mark on the Lundy chart, Dianne thought as she blushed from the added attention.

"I was never so embarrassed," she told Mrs. Wilkerson after the assembly was over.

"I wouldn't worry about it. It just tickled me," said Mrs. Wilkerson.

———

Things weren't going very well on the home front, either. In December, Dianne unexpectedly lost her beloved Uncle R. V. to a heart attack. She had been by his house to visit just a couple of days earlier, and R. V. was in bed. According to Hazel, he had been there since the day before her visit.

"He just decided he wasn't feeling well and took to the bed," Hazel told her.

"Dianne, come back here and talk to me," he yelled through the hall.

She walked into the bedroom, not knowing what to say. Her visit seemed to cheer him up, though. She left a short time later.

Several days later, when she walked into the teachers' lounge at lunch, Billie Boone, one of her fellow teachers approached her.

"Aren't you kin to R. V. Fulton?" she asked Dianne.

"Yes, he's my uncle," Dianne replied.

"Did you know that he passed away?" Billie inquired.

"No, what happened?" Dianne exclaimed.

"He had a heart attack," Billie explained.

"Oh, my goodness. I'd better get over there right after school. Thanks for letting me know," said Dianne.

Somehow, she knew it was the end of an era. Her gruff but funny uncle was gone. She had been scared of him in her younger days. But after moving to Pineville and getting to know him, she had found him to be a man of sterling character, always true to his word.

"You know, your Uncle R. V. is a very wise man," Rick had once said to her. "He knows a lot about life. When he gives an opinion on something, he's usually right."

Yes, Uncle V. is gone, but he will never be forgotten, she told herself.

Health problems seemed to be running in the family. In the spring, she had a call from Dolores, informing her that F. D. had been taken to the hospital in an ambulance.

"I went into his bedroom to see why he had never gotten up, and he was still sitting in his chair," she told Dianne. "I couldn't wake him up, so I called Kelton Howard and Bessie and Bennie Freeman. They came rushing over, and we called the ambulance. At first they took him to the hospital in Farmerville, but Dr. Wadlington knew he didn't have the equipment needed to save him, so he had them take him on to a hospital in Monroe."

F. D., who had been smoking since age seven, had developed emphysema. According to the doctors, the ratio of his blood gases had gotten out of proportion, and the lack of oxygen had caused him to go into a coma. He was put on a breathing machine and life support systems in the intensive care unit. It was basically touch-and-go as to whether or not he would recover.

The family, friends, and community rallied round, and someone was at the hospital at all times. Many prayers were offered in his behalf. That was really all they could do—wait and pray for his recovery.

Then his strong constitution kicked in, and he began to rally. He was moved out of the intensive care unit and into a regular hospital room. His regular personality, it seemed, was also coming back to life.

He refused to let the hospital orderly shave him, and his beard had grown quite long and straggly. His cousin Josh Hollis came to visit and saw that F. D. needed a shave. He tried to use an electric razor, but the beard was too tough.

"I'm going to go home and get my razor. I'll be back in a few minutes," he told F. D.

True to his word, Josh returned with the necessary equipment, and F. D. consented to the shave. A short time later, on his way out of the hospital, Josh saw one of the orderlies on F. D.'s floor.

"I just shaved your patient for you," he informed the orderly.

"This I've got to see," exclaimed the orderly, as he took off, halfway running down the hall towards F. D.'s room.

After staying in the hospital over a month, F. D. eventually recovered enough to return home, but he would never be the same man he was before his illness. The breathing tube had damaged his vocal cords, and he was unable to speak above a whisper. Also, the lack of oxygen had damaged his brain, making it difficult for him to remember things. He was destined to spend the rest of his days as a semi-invalid, dependent on Dolores's care.

———

Despite the bad luck at school, there was a bright side to the story. Dianne had managed to make a few friends during her first year at Pineville High. Of course, the first people she always turned to were her co-workers, Peggy and Bettye. Mrs. Alma Jo Wilkerson, who taught science in a room just around the corner, offered to share her *Current Science* papers with Dianne. The chemistry teacher, Miss Emily Needham, volunteered the use of her lab facilities for experiment demonstrations. She and Dianne switched rooms several times when Dianne's science classes were in session. Dianne learned that one of the librarians, Mary Chaudoir, had been acquainted with Martha Bass. Mary was also the daughter of Ruth Hyde, one of Dianne's former co-workers at Ruby-Wise. Dianne frequently stopped by the library to chat with her. After school, she often visited with Mrs. Ginny Thomas, the reading teacher who was next door in room nine. Slowly, but surely, she was widening her circle of friends at the school.

Rick, who had been staying in the dorm at Northwestern during the week, decided to move back home at the end of November. The semester was almost over, and he had only a few classes left. That meant Dianne had someone to talk to at night, so she was a lot happier about the situation.

Rick needed only a few more courses during the spring semester to complete his degree. He was offered a job, once again, at the family business in Colfax, Central Louisiana Wholesale, when one of the salesmen, Patch Cockfield, died from a heart attack as he was making his sales rounds. When he managed to work out a schedule that allowed him to work and attend classes, that provided enough income for him and Dianne to start looking for a house.

At Hazel's suggestion, they contacted Hickman Realty. One of R. V.'s nieces, Sunshine Hickman, was married to a realtor named Jess Hickman, who worked for that company. Under Jess's guidance, they managed to find a house they liked. It was still under construction, so that meant they got to pick out all the colors and materials. Since Dianne was a home economics teacher, that task was right up her alley. Despite all the things that had gone wrong during the school year, she felt that things were beginning to look up.

———

As the year drew to a close, she reminisced about her experiences. There had been a lot of bad days, and a lot of students she had rather not remember. Still, there were some good times, such as the mock wedding reception that her Home and Family Living class had sponsored. Her Home Economics II class had been the most enjoyable one, and their lab experiences had been fun. Working with the FHA club had been a learning experience, but it, too, had proven to be rewarding. Yes, Pineville High did have its good points, she was forced to admit.

There were a few good students she would never forget. The

most outstanding students in her General Science classes were Jackie Sharbano, Robin Nugent, John O'Neal, and Greg Jones. In Home and Family Living she taught Carol Jeukins, who was the FHA Sweetheart. In Home Economics II the most outstanding student was Kathi Cox, who served as the FHA treasurer and was voted Campus Queen. She also taught Leah Baden, who was the daughter of Pineville Mayor Fred Baden. Lori Barker, the FHA president, was an excellent student and a joy to work with. She was delighted to learn that Michelle Coleman, her most outstanding black student from her days at Ruby-Wise, had been well-received at Pineville High and had been elected vice-president of the Student Council. Yes, there were definitely some very good students at Pineville High, she reflected.

During the final week of school, Dianne was initiated into the checkout procedure, an annual ritual all the teachers had to endure. It was a long and tedious process that included reporting the final grades of each and every student to their homeroom teachers who then wrote them on the report cards. These were filed in the guidance office, to be checked against the final report cards which were printed out by computer and mailed to the students.

There were many other things that had to be turned in, all of which were documented on a checkout sheet that was required to be signed by different office personnel. It reminded Dianne of her college days, where she had spent many hours standing in line to register for classes. The final destination was the principal's office. Nobody could leave until he had signed their form.

Nobody dared to leave early because they had not received their paychecks. It wasn't until after the final teacher was checked out that a faculty meeting was announced over the PA system that everybody headed for the library. After a short speech, Mr. Millet began handing out the checks individually, after which everyone was free to go.

Dianne breathed a sigh of relief when she finally held her check in her hand. She had made it through a long and difficult school year and had encountered many doubts about her teaching abilities. Pineville High had both good and bad points. Did the good outweigh the bad? Should she stay at Pineville High, or should she look for other work? Was this really her dream come true, or had it become a nightmare? These were questions she would have to think about before making a decision. For the time being, she still had a job, and that was what really mattered at this point. Whether or not she would be happy with that job remained to be seen.

Chapter 3

*A*ll thoughts of school were quickly banished from Dianne's mind during the early summer months. She and Rick had been working feverishly to finish the selection of materials for their new house. They also had to buy furniture, as their apartment was furnished, and they possessed very little furniture of their own. Dianne was somewhat familiar with the furniture stores of the area, having taught a unit on home furnishings in her home economics classes.

"Let's go to Clark–Dunbar and look at their furniture," she told Rick. "I believe they have some of the best quality furniture in town."

So, the trip was made one Saturday afternoon when Rick was off from work. They ended up selecting a dining set, living room furniture, and a bedroom suite for the master bedroom. They also went to Tony's Furniture and Appliance Store and picked out a GE refrigerator. The rest of the kitchen appliances came with the house.

Mrs. Lundy gave them matching twin beds for the second bedroom. They decided to turn the third bedroom into a combination study/radio room for Dianne's desk, books, and filing cabinets, and Rick's ham radio station. Overall, they were pretty satisfied with their choices.

Their builder, Eddie Parker, was determined to have the house completed by the end of June. That meant they could move in by

July 1st. They went to Louisiana Savings and Loan and signed the papers the last week in June. Dianne gave notice to their landlord, Mr. Clayton Price, that they would be moving the first week in July. They could hardly wait to become homeowners.

When the big moving day finally arrived, Rick secured assistance from his friend Bruce Shockley and his cousin Buddy Tumminello, both of whom owned pickup trucks. Although they didn't own a lot of furniture, he and Dianne still had several large items which could not be transported in a car. Dianne had managed to pack most of the small items in boxes. Those were loaded into the trucks, along with their freezer, a washer, a dryer, several bookcases, Dianne's filing cabinets, and a metal storage cabinet. Dianne and Rick hauled their clothes and linens in their cars.

Their furniture wasn't scheduled to arrive until the following day, so they had to spend one last night in the apartment Dianne had called home for the past five years. It was a bittersweet moment for her because that little apartment held a lot of memories. Still, she was glad that they were moving to a larger and more comfortable place. It would be nice to have a house with central heat and air conditioning, she reasoned.

One of the last things they moved was Dianne's cat, Boo. Dianne had kept an extra close eye on him as they were moving things out of the apartment, because Boo wasn't above sneaking out an open door or window whenever he got the chance. On their last day in the apartment, Rick removed the little window air conditioner Dianne had bought for the living room. As soon as Boo spotted the open window, he was up there like a flash, and Dianne barely managed to grab him before he started to jump out.

"Boo, you bad cat. Where did you think you were going?" she scolded, as she loaded him into his carrier.

She wasn't sure how Boo would adjust to a new house. The little apartment was the only home he had known ever since she had rescued him from the parking lot at the Ruby-Wise school five years earlier. After arriving at the new house, she and Rick decided to leave him shut up in the utility room for a while until he got used to his new surroundings.

Later that night, they decided to out to get some hamburgers, since they were tired from unpacking. Dianne was worried that Boo might be able to get out through the dryer vent, as their dryer had not yet been connected.

"That cat can't get out there. He'll be fine," Rick reassured her as they locked the door and left. When they returned about an hour later, Boo was nowhere to be found. Dianne was beside herself and was about to burst into tears.

"He's gone! He's really gone! I told you he could get out through that vent," she told Rick.

"There's no way he could have fit through that little opening. That cat has to be in this room somewhere," Rick declared.

A further and more thorough search found Boo lodged beneath the freezer. How he managed to fit into that little space, Dianne would never know, but she was happy to learn that her beloved pet was not lost.

"Well, Boo. I guess it's about time we let you out to explore your new domain. This is going to be your new home from now on," she said.

Moving into a new home the first week in July had not changed one annual event in Dianne's life. F. D. was still planning on having his annual Fourth of July fish fry. This time he had real cause for celebrating, as he had just recently been released from the hospital. Dianne and Rick knew there was no way they could skip that gathering.

When they drove up into the Hollises' yard, Dianne was astounded at the number of cars that were already parked.

"Wow, where did all of these people come from?" she asked Rick.

"I don't know, but your dad outdid himself this time," Rick noted.

They walked into the kitchen, which was bustling with activity as Dolores was working diligently to get the food prepared. F. D.'s sisters, Corrie and Berdelle, were helping her, along with Donald's wife, Euline. Dolores, who had a tendency to run in circles when she was overwhelmed, greeted Dianne with a plea for help, rather than with a hug or a kiss.

"You'll have to make some hush puppies," was all the greeting Dianne received.

"I don't have my recipe," Dianne exclaimed. "Let me think. Maybe there's one in your *Mildred Swift Cookbook*."

The recipe was found, and the hush puppies were made, much to Dolores's relief.

F. D. was frying the fish out on the patio, using a new fish fryer he had recently bought.

Most of the men were out there with him, while the women who weren't assisting with the food preparation were visiting in the living room.

Dianne managed to get Dolores aside to ask her one important question in private.

"Why in the world did Daddy invite so many people?"

"He was so happy to be out of the hospital he invited everybody he could think of. They were all scared not to come, because they didn't want to make him mad," Dolores explained.

"Well, you ended up with quite a crowd. I estimate there must be at least sixty or more people here. That's the most this house has ever seen, except for when you had your housewarming party," Dianne commented.

The food was finally ready, and everyone was fed. They declared the fish to be some of the best they had ever eaten. It was the last time F. D. would be able to entertain on such a large scale, as his health was continuing to decline.

Dianne and Rick returned to their new home, and they continued to work throughout the summer to get things just the way they wanted them to be. Dianne spent a large part of the time in the yard clearing up debris and planting grass. Unfortunately, they had moved in during the rainy season, so a large part of their new dirt washed away before the grass seeds could take root. Dianne resorted to placing rows of leftover bricks on the hill beside the driveway to try to slow the flow of water. She wore shorts and boots as she tromped around in the mud.

"I got the biggest laugh when I saw you out there in those boots," Billie Boone told her later.

They decided to wait until fall to plant shrubs, as the summer was not the right time for planting. Their main objective was to get some grass to grow on their sloping lot. Finally, it took root and got tall enough to mow. It was beginning to resemble a hayfield.

Hazel offered them the use of her lawn mower, as she was no longer using it since R. V. had passed away. Dianne hated to see the grass cut after she had worked so hard to grow it, but Rick insisted it would be thicker and grow better after it was cut.

The back yard contained a lot of vines and poison ivy. Dianne worked long and hard to get it cleared and leveled. She accidentally came into contact with the poison ivy when she was working out there, and she developed a very bad rash.

"I never had poison ivy in my life. I used to reach into it all the time to retrieve a ball when Sallie and I were playing outside," she told Rick.

"Well, you've got a good case of it now," he observed.

#   #   #

The rest of the summer passed all too quickly as they continued to work on both the house and the yard. Before Dianne knew it, her vacation was over, and it was time for her to start thinking about school again. She decided to go back to Pineville High School for another year, reasoning that the first year in a new school was always the hardest.

"Mr. Millet wasn't too sure I should continue teaching," she told Rick. "He advised me to consider going into another profession."

"What do you want to do?" Rick asked.

"Well, I've thought about it, and I'm going to give it one more shot. I've already invested eight years of my life into teaching. I tried to get a job with the Extension Service, and that didn't work out. I also thought about going into dietetics and even went to LSU one summer and took some courses in advanced nutrition. Then I found out it would take me at least two years to get certified as a dietician, so I just went back to Northeast and got my master's degree in secondary education. Teaching is all I know. I just have to try it one more year."

Thus, the decision was made, and Dianne headed back to the Pineville High campus. Little did she know she was about to begin a journey that would take her through the next twenty-five years of her life.

Chapter 4

Somehow, Dianne knew things were going to be different when she started the new school year. Rather than having hall duty, she was assigned a ninth-grade homeroom. In her eyes, that meant she was now considered a regular faculty member, rather than just someone who had been added to the roster at the last minute. Her Home Economics II class was replaced with a second class of Home and Family Living. She still continued to teach two classes of General Science and one class of Handicrafts, her least favorite subjects. But she felt the new schedule was one that she could live with.

Reflecting on some of the discipline problems she had encountered during the previous year, she decided that the best way to solve them was to resort to her old stand-by method of punishment by assigning five-hundred-word reports to students who acted up in class. The more serious offenses would have to be reported to the office, of course, but assigning the extra work seemed to be the way to go. She made a special corner on the front board to list the names of students who were assigned the reports. Their names could not be erased until the punish work had been completed. Those who refused to do the work would be sent to the office, she resolved.

Making out lesson plans was also easier because she had already been through the courses once the year before, using the same textbooks. That gave her more free time to plan out little extra things to do to make the classes more interesting. Yes, the second year at Pineville High was promising to be more rewarding, she decided.

———

Although some problems did occur, things went a lot smoother as the school year progressed. Dianne successfully completed her second year at Pineville High School and made the decision to remain there for what became an additional twenty-four years. During that time she encountered many obstacles, as well as having many rewarding experiences. Dealing with over one hundred students per day in the classroom, in lab experiences, on field trips, on hall duty, and in the FHA club continued to reshape her teaching personality as she completed her teaching tenure. The memories of those times remained firmly implanted in her brain for years to come.

Some of the most memorable experiences occurred in the classroom setting. Room ten continued to be Dianne's home base as long as the original Pineville High School building was intact. Her list of five important classroom rules for success continued to grow over the years, as students sometimes complained they did not know a particular action was a violation of classroom policy. Many of the rules were permanently posted on laminated yellow poster board in the front of the room. Then when a student complained about not being previously informed of an infraction, Dianne merely had to point to the list of rules clearly in their line of vision. This eliminated a lot of arguments and saved a lot of time in the long run. It also provided some amusement to students who had already taken classes under Dianne in previous years. They had learned the rules were there for a reason and the rules were expected to be obeyed.

Some newcomers always had to learn the hard way. One five-hundred-word report was usually enough punishment to solve most discipline problems with a student. However, there was always at least one student in every class who vowed they were not going to write a report, no matter what. Dianne calmly informed them they would be sent to the office the following day if the report were not completed. The unbelievers were quickly converted to believer status when a trip to the office provided them with a choice of either writing the report or being suspended. Mr. Kees took particular delight in tacking an additional two hundred and fifty words onto the original five hundred total. It didn't take long for the news to get around that Dianne's punish work was nothing to be taken lightly. Word also filtered down to her students in later years, as she began to encounter the younger brothers and sisters of students she had previously taught.

"We already heard about those five-hundred-word reports of yours, Mrs. Lundy," they often informed her on the first day of school.

Being on time for class was one thing that was stressed at Pineville High. Mr. Millet's motto was "Seats on seats when the tardy bell rings." Dianne solved the problem of students trying to sneak into class late by closing the door herself, just after the tardy bell rang. The door was also kept locked from the outside, so no one could enter unless it was opened by someone who was already in the room. Students were not allowed to open the door to let other students in without permission. Students who were tardy were given detention slips and had to report to a detention room known as KIR before school within three days after the slip was issued.

Getting a detention slip was one of the worst fears of most students because an automatic suspension was assigned if they were issued four detentions in one semester. Some students resorted to extreme measures to try to make it to class on time. On one occasion, Dianne was startled when she stepped outside to close the door, just as one of the students dove into the room headfirst, making a valiant effort to reach his seat just as the bell rang, but landing on the floor beside his desk instead.

"That will be a tardy slip for you," Dianne informed him, much to his disappointment, as he ended up with both a sore noggin and a detention slip to boot.

Collecting detention slips once they were assigned was also a tricky chore. Students were very good at delaying handing in the slips in hopes that the teacher would totally forget they had been assigned. Then when the teacher did finally remember to ask for the slips, they would conveniently have "lost" it among their other papers. After several such experiences, Dianne solved that problem by making a list of who got the slips as soon as they were handed out. She then collected them before class work began, eliminating the excuse that they had been misplaced.

Keeping students in their assigned seats was another problem. Dianne always gave them a couple of days of freedom to sit where they chose at the beginning of school. Then she assigned seats in alphabetical order, making adjustments for height or vision problems as needed. It didn't take her very long to figure out which students were clamoring for a seating change just to be near their friends so they could talk during class. For that reason, seating changes were limited, once the seating chart had been made out.

Seating charts also helped Dianne to learn student names, something she was not very good at remembering. She would go over the charts daily, as the students were working on assignments or taking tests, trying to place faces and names together. The only problem was when they got up out of their seats, she didn't know who they were for the first six weeks.

Of course, there was always at least one student in every class whose name she learned on the first day of school. It didn't take long to spot the troublemakers, and they were usually the first ones she could positively identify, even if she met them in the hall. Sometimes they weren't with her long, though. Some of them were gone before the end of the first week, and most of them were gone before the end of the first semester. It wouldn't be the last she heard of them because she often saw their names, sometimes years later, on the police blotter in *The Town Talk,* the local newspaper.

The younger students Dianne had taught at Ruby-Wise had worked their way through the system by the time she reached Pineville High School. During her first few years there, she was delighted to, once again, teach students such as Marlene Quattlebaum, Rhonda McLauren, Bridgette Herrington, JoAnne Ryland, Pam Cupp, Robin Cannon, Lane Cripps, and Danny Beaubouf. Having them in class again brought back old memories and she was able to see how they had grown and matured into young ladies and young men, rather than the children she had known at the junior high level. It also helped to ease her transition into a new school, seeing a few familiar faces.

Letting students go to the restroom or get a drink of water was another problem that often required a lot of teacher discretion. Some teachers solved the problem by simply refusing to let students out of their room for any reason whatsoever. Dianne was a little more sympathetic, but she soon discovered a few students were trying to take advantage of the situation by asking to go every day. She solved that problem by creating a checkout sheet which had to be filled out whenever a student left the room for any reason, so there was a record of it.

Still, there were a few instances where she discovered the students would have been better off staying in her classroom. One such student was a boy named Jonas Marks. Jonas had been with Dianne for several years, taking every home economics course the school offered. He was a handsome athlete, an FHA member, and a very pleasant student to work with, so he was one of Dianne's favorites. She let him go to the restroom quite often, probably more than she should have. He always seemed to be gone a long time, and she was beginning to get suspicious.

One day one of the assistant principals, Betty Tumminello, appeared at the door with Jonas.

"I'm bringing Jonas back to your class, and don't let him out again," she told Dianne. "He was down in the lunchroom, eating lunch with the first lunch shift."

"Okay, I guess that takes care of his trips for the rest of the year," Dianne commented laughingly, as Jonas sheepishly made his way back to his seat, among guffaws from the other students.

"Jonas, do you have anything to say for yourself?" Dianne inquired.

"I was hungry," Jonas replied.

Students who had taken up the habit of smoking often tried to get out of class to sneak a cigarette in the restroom. They weren't hard to spot, as they usually returned to the classroom smelling like a chimney. Girls were worse about it than the boys. Once Dianne determined that was their reason for leaving class, they were not permitted to go anywhere else. Some students, however, were quite the con artists, putting on a convincing act about needing to go to the restroom. One day, against her better judgment, she let Katie Douglas, a ninth-grade girl from her sixth-hour class, leave, supposedly to go to the restroom. The girl never returned to class, so Dianne had to go to the office after school to find out what had happened to her.

"Well, I have quite a story to report to you about Miss Katie," one of the assistant principals informed Dianne. "It seems that Katie and another girl were caught smoking in the men's restroom out by the auditorium."

"Who caught them?" Dianne inquired.

"It was one of the JROTC instructors, and he wasn't too happy about having the men's restroom invaded by girls."

Dianne later learned the JROTC instructor was quoted as saying, "A guy can't even take a piss around this school anymore."

The girls were suspended for three days for smoking on campus, and, unfortunately, they did not make it through the entire school year. In fact, they didn't even last the first semester before being permanently expelled to the Redirection Academy, the school of last resort in Rapides Parish. Somehow, Dianne saw that one coming.

Students were not supposed to be out of a teacher's room without a hall pass, and the school went through several forms of hall passes over the years. Some teachers created their own hall passes by using staplers or some object off their desk. The principals decided some sort of uniform hall pass was needed, so the head custodian made the first ones from six-inch pieces of plastic. Each hall pass was engraved with the teacher's name, and they were supposed to be turned in at the end of the year when teachers checked out.

That project proved to be a complete flop, as most teachers never knew where their hall pass was. Some hall passes were stolen from teachers' desks, while others were lost when students laid them down and forgot to bring them back to class when they returned. Many teachers failed to turn them in at the end of the year. So, the next year one of the shop teachers volunteered to make a larger wooden hall pass that was easy to spot when a student was walking down the hall and almost impossible to lose. Dianne faithfully kept up with her pass, issuing it to a student each time they left the room. One day shortly after midterm, she had to attend an FHA parish officers' meeting at the school board office during sixth period. When she returned the next day, the hall pass was missing.

"I can't find my hall pass anywhere," she told her co-worker Bettye Watkins.

"While you were gone yesterday, a student used somebody's hall pass to beat up another student out in the hall. The principals came around to all the rooms and collected everybody's hall pass," Bettye informed her.

"Well, that explains the mystery. I guess they'll have to come up with a new system for hall passes," Dianne observed.

"Either that, or we just don't let anybody out of class," Bettye added.

The school officials eventually solved the hall pass problem by creating a standardized paper hall pass slip that had to be completed by a teacher each time a student left their classroom. Students who were caught out in the hall during class time without a paper hall pass were subject to KIR or suspension.

———

Pineville High School was built in the 1950's when it was believed a lot of natural light was conducive to good instruction. The rooms on the older wings had a row of windows above the ceilings, as well as windows going all across the back of the rooms. This made it very hard to show any type of visual aids on the projection screens, even with all the lights in the room turned off. Showing filmstrips that went with the lessons was difficult, at best, while the use of transparencies fared only a little better. Using sixteen-millimeter films that were available for the science classes required the use of the film rooms that were located next to the library.

Dianne dreaded every trip to the film rooms, as they were completely darkened when the movie began, and students had no assigned seating there, making supervision difficult. She had always enjoyed showing films to her classes but using them at Pineville High was becoming a real headache.

Since she usually remained in her room for some time after school was dismissed, working on her lesson plans and getting materials ready for the next day, she was often in the room when the janitor came in to sweep and tidy up. She made friends with him, and he agreed to paint the outside of the top windows with black paint if Dianne furnished the paint and a brush for the job. She wasted little time acquiring the necessary materials, and the windows were soon painted. However, that still didn't block out enough light, so she had the janitor also cover the inside of the windows with bulletin board paper that matched the room.

Mrs. Wakefield and Mrs. Watkins were having problems with too much light in their rooms, also, so they decided to use some of their vocational money to order material to make curtains for the two lab rooms and Dianne's room next door. They ordered the fabric from Hancock Fabrics, and when it arrived, the advanced sewing classes made the curtains. The yellow-checked curtains in the home ec. kitchen brightened the lab considerably, as did the pale blue sheers they had chosen for the sewing lab. Dianne's room was decked out in curtains made from a heavy yellow material in order to block out as much light as possible. All in all, the three teachers were satisfied with the results and felt that it was money well spent.

Dianne was particularly happy because she could then show her films and filmstrips in room ten without having to go to the film rooms during class. This saved a lot of class time and also allowed her to keep better control over the students, as they remained in their assigned seats during the viewings. She had learned over the years the less students moved around during class, the better it was. Such was the case at Pineville High.

———

As the years progressed at Pineville High, the enrollment in the home economics classes continued to increase to the point where Dianne was no longer required to teach science classes, as there were enough students in the department to allow her to teach home economics all day long. Part of the increase was due to changes in the curriculum requirements for graduation, which left students with more electives. Some of the increased interest, however, was due to the fact that a home economics teacher was allowed to accompany the guidance counselors to the junior high schools to explain what the home economics program was all about.

The most successful year of recruitment occurred when Bettye came up with the idea of making a giant cardboard hamburger as a prop, using the Burger King motto "Have It Your Way." Dianne took three of their most outstanding students, who were also FHA officers, Faith Ford, Tonya Kees, and E. Hope Ryland, to make a presentation.

Faith, who was supposed to model a red jacket she had made in Home Economics III, was late arriving for the trip. She rushed in at the last minute, breathlessly exclaiming she had accidentally backed her car into a tree as she was exiting her driveway. The next year they ended up with so many students they had to turn people away at the doors, because their classes were becoming overcrowded.

"You did too good a job of recruiting," said Mr. Homer Crouch, the principal at that time.

———

Teaching home economics all day long meant Dianne was more involved in teaching cooking and sewing, something that she definitely enjoyed more than teaching science. There were many humorous and sometimes dangerous situations that occurred during the lab classes.

The cooking lab was especially crowded with the desks that had been moved in so it could serve as a lecture room, in addition to being used for cooking activities. The air-conditioning system wasn't the best, and the room was often hot. Dianne sometimes left one of the doors open in an effort to try to make it cooler.

One morning a cat wandered into the building before school started. When all the outer entrance doors were closed as school began, the cat became trapped. It ran helter-skelter up and down the halls, jumping onto windows in a desperate attempt to escape.

As a final resort, it spotted the open door to the home economics kitchen and ran into the room where Dianne was conducting class.

The girls began to scream as it shot over their legs and headed straight to the washer and dryer, taking refuge behind those appliances. One girl, Tracy Murray, jumped up out of her seat and approached the cat.

"Leave that cat alone, Tracy," Dianne instructed.

"Oh, he won't hurt me," Tracy protested, as she reached out to try to pet the frightened creature.

Thoroughly confused and disoriented, the cat responded by trying to protect itself the only way it knew how—scratching and biting. Seconds later, Tracy drew back her hand, exclaiming, "It bit me!"

"I told you to leave it alone," Dianne scolded.

Just at that moment, the city's animal control officer appeared in the doorway, accompanied by Miss Needham, who was reputed to have a love for animals, especially cats.

"Did a cat run in here?" she inquired, directing her remark to Dianne.

"Yes, it's behind the washer and dryer," Dianne informed her. "And it bit one of my students, too."

"Poor little thing, half-scared to death. Now they'll probably put it to sleep," Miss Needham lamented, as the animal control officer made his way to the spot where the cat was holed up. He managed to snare it with a choke collar that was attached to a long pole. The cat was dragged out from its hiding place, hissing, spitting, and twisting, as it tried to loose itself from the collar.

"You had better send your student to the office to report the injury," said Miss Needham.

"Yes, that would be a good idea," Dianne agreed. "And from now on, I think I will keep my doors shut."

———————

The cooking labs with the Home Ec. I classes were always the most amusing. A few of the students had taken home economics in junior high, but the majority of them didn't have the foggiest notion of how to cook. Although Dianne always covered topics such as cooking terms and equipment, along with measuring techniques, some students had to learn the hard way.

The first cooking lab for Home Ec. I was always chocolate chip cookies. Dianne traditionally made her little speech about how everybody had the same recipe, but everybody's cookies wouldn't turn out the same. Then she just waited for her prediction to come true.

Inevitably, there would be one or two groups whose cookies would turn out perfectly, much to the envy of the other students in the class. Some groups would forget to sift their flour, resulting in the cookies being too dry. On one occasion, however, one group had cookie dough that resembled cake batter, rather than cookies. Dianne suggested they try pouring it onto a cookie sheet with raised sides and baking it as a single layer.

While they were waiting for it to bake, she began to quiz the students in the group.

"Are you sure you added the right amount of flour?" she asked.

"I put in one-half cup of flour," the cook commented.

"I believe you misread the recipe. It calls for one and one-half cups of flour. I hate to tell you this, but the cookies won't be any good without the right amount of flour," Dianne told them.

Just about that time, black smoke began to billow out of the stove, as the hapless cookies met their fate and burned to a crisp, much to the amusement of the other students in the class.

"At this rate, we may need to use the fire extinguisher," Dianne observed.

Most of the students learned from their mistakes and vowed to do better on their second lab, which was always biscuits in the Home Ec. I classes. By then they had learned to read the recipe, follow the directions in order, measure correctly, and, most importantly, sift their flour before measuring.

During one lab, however, a group of boys still hadn't mastered the measuring techniques. They worked really hard making their biscuits and bragged to the other students how good their product was going to be. Dianne was a little skeptical when she saw the biscuits as they were removed from the oven.

"Those biscuits look a little overdone to me," she commented.

"Aw, ain't nothin' wrong with them. They'll be just fine," insisted the cook.

The boys proceeded to serve themselves, cutting the biscuits and putting butter and jelly inside. Then they took their first bite and almost choked trying to swallow the nearly inedible rock-like product.

"Let me see one of those biscuits," Dianne instructed. She took a biscuit off the cookie sheet and threw it at the floor. The biscuit bounced up to the top of the table. "Yep, I'd say they are a wee bit hard. I told you they were overcooked. You probably put in too much flour and over-kneaded them, too," she said laughingly.

The study of quick breads in Home Ec. I continued with labs on muffins and cornbread. With muffins, the students had a choice of making plain muffins, blueberry muffins, or surprise muffins, which had a spoonful of jelly baked into the middle of each muffin. Blueberry was the favorite flavor.

Some students failed to heed Dianne's warning not to over mix the batter, and their muffins resembled miniature Pike's Peaks, with long tunnels running through the middle when they were cut open. One group forgot to drain the blueberries and dumped them into the batter, juice and all. When they were done, the muffins were bright blue.

"It's not a mistake, Mrs. Lundy. We made Smurfberry muffins," they declared.

Other groups were not satisfied that the muffins were not sweet like cupcakes.

"You can use up to one-half cup of sugar to make them sweeter," Dianne told the students. "But don't add any more than that, because it will upset the balance of ingredients in the recipe."

Some students figured if one-half cup of sugar was good, a whole cup would be better. Without telling Dianne, they proceeded to "doctor" the recipe to their own satisfaction. It all caught up with them when they put the muffins into the oven to bake. The extra sugar caused the muffins to bake too rapidly, and they exploded, resulting in burned batter being flung all over the inside of the oven.

"Maybe next time you'll believe me," Dianne chided, as she surveyed the disastrous experiment.

Cakes were always a favorite with all levels of the home economics classes. The Home Ec. I classes made layer cakes with butter cream frosting. Dianne tried to schedule the cake labs to coincide with the holiday season so the students could decorate them with a holiday theme. Through the years, she had collected many recipe ideas for decorating cakes. The Christmas season brought the cakes that resembled Christmas trees, Santa Clauses, or reindeer heads, while Easter featured bunnies and Easter basket cakes.

Students frequently requested food coloring to tint the frosting. One year a group of girls making a Christmas tree cake decided to tint it pink, rather than green.

"That's the strangest-looking Christmas tree I've ever seen," Dianne commented. "Whatever possessed you to color it pink?"

"Oh, we just decided to be different," was their reply.

She was equally surprised when a group of boys wanted to tint their frosting light blue at Christmas time.

How cute. They want to make some kind of snow scene. That will certainly be something different, she thought.

Cakes were displayed at the end of the lab, and students voted on which cake they thought was the most original. When the blue cake was displayed, Dianne was horrified to see it had been decorated in a gang-like theme with the word "Cripps" spelled out in blue frosting.

"I can't believe you guys. A gang cake! What were you thinking?" she exclaimed.

The students in Home Ec. II were a little savvier regarding cooking procedures. However, they, too, were not immune from making mistakes, often with humorous results.

Their first lab was some type of yeast bread, usually cinnamon rolls. There was always at least one group that got their liquid too hot and killed the yeast, resulting in dough that failed to rise. Other groups generously spread too much sugar and butter on their dough, and the rolls burned when they cooked. Somehow, they never seemed to believe Dianne when she cautioned them about the overuse of certain ingredients.

Those students were a little more careful about choosing who would be in their lab groups because by then they knew who could and could not cook. The boys always tried to include at least one girl in their group, rationalizing that should ensure them of having a decent product that was at least edible. One exception to this rule was a group of girls who picked one lone boy, Richard Carter, to be in their group. Theirs was the reverse situation because Richard was an excellent cook, while the girls had never seemed to master the art.

Home Ec. II students made Bundt cakes, rather than layer cakes, in order to learn different cooking techniques. Richard was absent on the day his class was scheduled to make cakes, so the girls had to muddle along without his help. Their cake, along with several others, did not get done by the time the bell rang. Dianne had to go back down the hall to room ten for another class, and she didn't want to leave students unsupervised in the lab. She told each group to write on a piece of paper what time their cake should come out of the oven, and she would come back down and take it out for them.

As she conducted class the following hour, she had the pieces of paper in front of her to remind her of exactly when the cakes would be done. As the hour progressed, some of the students in the class began to announce they smelled something burning.

"Mrs. Lundy, those cakes are burning up," they insisted.

"No, it's not time to take them out yet. I'll go down when it's the time listed on the papers," she replied, not wanting to interrupt class any more than necessary.

Finally, it was time for the first cake to come out of the oven, so she left her class with an assignment and walked back down the hall to the home ec. kitchen. As she opened the door, smoke began belching out of the stove belonging to Richard's group.

She walked over and pulled the cake out of the oven. It was as black as a piece of coal and just about as hard.

What could be the problem? she wondered. When she checked the stove, she solved the mystery. The girls had set the oven temperature twenty-five degrees higher than the recipe called for.

Poor Richard. He's going to be really disappointed. Now I see who's been doing all of the cooking in that group! She had to chuckle about the situation.

The next day Richard returned, and the class went down to the lab to make the glaze for their cakes, which had been wrapped in foil and stored overnight.

"Well, Richard, I'm afraid I have some bad news for you about your cake," she told him.

"I already heard something happened to it. What y'all did to our cake?" he inquired.

"Here it is," she said, as she unwrapped the offending piece of evidence.

"Oh, man. I can't believe it," he said, as he picked it up and rolled it down the aisle toward the cabinets at the end of the lab. The cake hit the cabinets, bounced off, and headed back toward Richard, who barely managed to jump out of its path.

"You know, if we had some bowling pins, you could have knocked them over with that cake," teased Dianne. "I'm going to call it the bowling ball cake."

———

The Home Ec. II classes included a cooking lab on salads and also one on vegetables in order to provide the students with some different experiences from those they had in Home Ec. I. Dianne figured it was a sneaky way to get them to try things such as broccoli and stuffed mushrooms, which most of them had never even seen, much less eaten.

In order to conserve money during those two labs, each group was assigned a different dish to prepare. Then the dishes were served buffet style, giving all students a chance to taste everything.

Dianne had found a broccoli casserole recipe she especially liked, so she decided to prepare two dishes of it for the class Richard was in. When the time came to sample the dishes, she put her casseroles out on the table alongside those that had been prepared by the students.

Everyone eyed the casseroles doubtfully, uncertain if they wanted to take a chance on trying them or not. Finally, a few brave souls, Richard among them, decided they didn't want to hurt Dianne's feelings.

"Let me have just a small spoonful of that broccoli casserole you made, Mrs. Lundy, since you worked so hard to make it," Richard said, as he passed down the buffet table.

"It's really good. Trust me," Dianne said, as she dished it up.

Other students soon followed suit, and pretty soon most of the first casserole had been served. A few minutes later, Richard sauntered back up to the table, plate in hand.

"I got to have some more of that broccoli casserole, Mrs. Lundy. It's really good," he informed her.

Almost before she knew it, the rest of both casseroles had disappeared, as the other classmates had also come back for seconds.

"I told you it was good," said Dianne.

The following week, some of the students asked for the recipe, so Dianne made up a recipe booklet featuring all of the salad and vegetable recipes they had made in the labs.

"I'm going to make some of these dishes for the holidays," declared Alicia Jones, one of her most outspoken and talkative students in that class.

That wasn't the last Dianne heard about her broccoli casseroles. The students were still talking about them the next year.

By the time she had taught the same students for three years, Dianne was quite familiar with both their good and bad points. Most years the class contained quite a few boys. Once they started taking home economics, they tended to stick with it for an elective. One such group consisted of Clydale Burns, George Simmons, and Kerry Whitehead. Kerry had a twin brother, Terry, who had been with Bettye for his first two years of home economics.

"You'll be getting Kerry's brother, Terry, next year in Home Ec. III. He's even worse than Kerry," Bettye told Dianne.

"Oh, brother. Just what I need," Dianne exclaimed.

To her surprise, the boys had matured and were fairly well behaved in class when their junior year rolled around. They wanted to be in a lab group together, along with Clydale and George. During their three years of taking home economics, all four boys had managed to learn how to cook. They took pride in their accomplishments and enjoyed taunting the girls of the class, always claiming their dishes had turned out better.

In Home Ec. III, students studied more advanced cooking techniques. They made chiffon or angel food cakes and cream pies. They also studied foreign foods and Louisiana cooking.

When the time came for the lab on Louisiana foods, the four boys decided they wanted to make red beans and rice, something that Dianne had never tried to cook.

"You guys would have to pick something I haven't actually made. Are you sure you don't want to try something else, maybe some etouffee, jambalaya, or gumbo?" Dianne inquired.

"No, we want red beans and rice," Clydale declared. "You're a home ec. teacher. You should be able to teach us how to cook anything."

"True, but red beans and rice has never been one of my favorites," she admitted.

She located a recipe, and the next day the boys put all of their energies into making the dish. They measured, stirred, and simmered, following the recipe directions. The dish was then stored until the following day when the foods would be eaten.

During the follow-up lab while their food was re-heating, they cooked some rice and whipped up a pan of cornbread to go with their dish.

"Boy, it sure smells good. I can't wait to eat some of that," Clydale exclaimed.

"Just don't burn your cornbread," Dianne warned.

"Oh, don't worry about that. We're not about to let it burn," said Kerry.

A few minutes later, the food was ready, and they began to dish it up.

"Man, talk about good! This is gonna be some great food," Terry announced.

"Yeah, you girls can just keep your etouffee and gumbo," added Kerry.

"Y'all had Mrs. Lundy helping you. That's why your food turned out so good. We did ours all by ourselves," the girls responded.

"Don't matter how it got cooked. It's cooked, and we're about to eat it," Clydale shot back.

George, the only quiet one in the bunch, had filled his plate during the argument. He sat down at the table and began sampling the red beans and rice.

"Well, George, how is it?" Dianne inquired.

"Good, really tasty," he replied, smiling as he bit off a chunk of cornbread.

"We should have made some pralines to go with this," Kerry commented.

"Or some pecan pie," added Terry.

"Maybe next time, guys. For now, just enjoy what you cooked in this lab," said Dianne.

Mishaps in the lab were not unique to her classes, Dianne learned. One group of girls in Peggy's class put their taco shells in the oven to warm. Instead of turning the oven on low, as instructed by the package, they put it on broil. A few minutes later, flames shot out of the oven as they opened it to discover the taco shells were on fire. They were unable to get the fire extinguisher off the wall, so someone had to run next door to the chemistry lab to get Miss Needham to come over and use the extinguisher to put out the fire.

Bettye, too, had some problems in lab. She was the one who was assigned the special education students who were mainstreamed into home economics classes. They required special attention to detail, and sometimes they got into trouble if they were not closely watched. One day one of the girls attempted to remove a cookie sheet of biscuits from the oven without using potholders. As soon as she got them out of the oven, the pain from the hot pan hit her, and she threw the whole sheet of biscuits straight up into the air.

On several occasions, the lab was shut down completely. One day when Peggy's Advanced Foods class was making seven-minute frosting, a bomb threat was called in to the school. The whole school was evacuated, and nobody was allowed to go back into the building. Finally, hours later, a few teachers were allowed back in. Peggy and Bettye had to clean up the mess and throw the whole batch of frosting out.

Another time Dianne's class was in the middle of a cooking lab when the fire marshal came around to inspect the gas hot water heater located in the lab. He and the head custodian, Mr. Scallan, examined the heater, and it was declared unsafe.

"We're going to have to cut off the hot water heater, Mrs. Lundy," Mr. Scallan told her.

"What? We're right in the middle of a cooking lab!" Dianne exclaimed.

"There's nothing I can do about it. The fire marshal says it has to be shut off until we can fix a safety valve on it," Mr. Scallan replied.

"Okay, I guess we'll just have to heat up some water on the electric stoves," Dianne decided.

That wasn't the only time the lab was without hot water. During another cooking lab at sixth hour, the students suddenly began complaining that there was no hot water. By that time, the gas hot water heater had been replaced with an electric one. Dianne walked over to the heater and felt it. It was warm, so that meant hot water should be available. There was just none coming out of the heater. Once again, the students had to heat the water on top of the stoves to wash their dishes.

She sent for Mr. Curtis Simmons, the head custodian at that time. He did not arrive until after school had been dismissed.

"Did you find out what's wrong with the hot water heater?" Dianne inquired, as she was tidying up the lab after school.

"There's nothing wrong with the water heater. Somebody cut off the valve that lets the water run out of it," he replied.

It didn't take Dianne any time to figure out who the guilty culprits were. There was a group of boys in that class who had caused nothing but trouble since the day they walked through the door. They were the ones who were assigned to the kitchen located by the hot water heater. Undoubtedly, they were the ones responsible for the problem.

They had also caused problems in the classroom. Someone had been throwing pieces of pencils during class. Dianne kept finding them on the floor after school was out. She was pretty sure she knew which boy it was, but she could never catch him in the act. It was always the same kind of pencil, so she came up with a plan to identify the guilty party.

The students needed a number two lead pencil to complete their answer sheets for each test. Dianne always had a few extra pencils on hand to check out to students who didn't have one. On the day before their next test, she announced to the class they would have to provide their own pencils for the test.

The next day, as she passed out test papers and monitored the test, she walked around the room, hoping to spot whoever was using that particular brand of pencil. Sure enough, the boy she had suspected was the only one who had the pencil matching the pieces she had been spotting on the floor. She just smiled to herself, knowing she would soon be able to catch him in the act.

A couple of days later, she managed to catch him throwing a piece of a pencil, watching him out of the corner of her eye. He was promptly written up on a disciplinary form and sent to the office.

And that takes care of that little problem, she thought.

Injuries to students during cooking labs was a common event, despite Dianne's demonstrations on correct cooking techniques and warnings about possible hazards. Cuts and burns were the usual problems, but most of them were not serious. Inevitably, someone always got burned during the labs on candies when they made popcorn balls and candied apples. The hot syrup would stick to their skin whenever it dropped on their hands or arms. Dianne usually had them run cold water over the burns and then applied an antiseptic spray to the area.

Two of the most serious incidents occurred with the use of the electric mixers. Dianne always cautioned students to be sure to unplug the mixer before removing the beaters. One year a girl named Georgia Merinevitch failed to heed the warning. She got her fingers caught between the beaters of the mixer. Dianne rushed over to the group and unplugged the mixer. She began tugging on the beaters and finally managed to get them out of the mixer. Georgia was sent to the office for first aid treatment.

"They made me go to the hospital to get a tetanus shot," she informed Dianne the next day.

Although Dianne used that story as an example of what not to do, there was a repeat incident a few years later.

About halfway through a cake lab, Dianne was called to one of the kitchens by a boy named Geoffrey Litton.

"Mrs. Lundy, you had better come quick. LaTonya Haynes has her hand caught in the mixer," he said.

"You've got to be kidding. After all of my warnings, somebody else got their hand hung in the mixer beaters!" Dianne exclaimed, as she rushed over to aid LaTonya.

After unplugging the mixer, Dianne began to tug on the beaters in an attempt to release them. They wouldn't budge, and every time she tugged, LaTonya began to yell, "Ouch! Ouch! That hurts!"

"I can't get them loose," Dianne declared. "Somebody had better go and get one of the principals."

By that time, LaTonya's fingers were starting to turn purple, and Dianne was getting really concerned about the circulation to the fingers being cut off for too long. The entire class had come to a standstill as they watched the event unfold.

Several minutes later the principal, Mr. Homer Crouch, entered the room. He was halfway grinning as he walked in.

"I hear you have a problem," he said.

"LaTonya's hand is hung in the mixer, and I can't get it loose," Dianne told him.

He walked over and attempted to pull the beaters out with much the same results Dianne had experienced.

Then he got serious about the matter, as he took off his coat and draped it across the back of one of the lab chairs. A few more attempts also proved unsuccessful, with LaTonya's fingers beginning to swell and turning even more purple with each passing minute.

"Mrs. Lundy, I can't get her hand loose, either. I guess you are just going to have to call 911," he announced.

Dianne decided she had better go to the office herself, as the secretaries might not believe a student. She hurried down the hall and almost burst into the main office where Irene Allgood, one of the secretaries, was sitting.

"You're not going to believe this, Mrs. A., but we have to call 911," Dianne exclaimed.

"What's happening?" Irene inquired.

"We have a student whose hand is hung in a mixer, and we can't get it out. Mr. Crouch sent me down here to tell you to call them," Dianne replied.

The call was placed, and as Irene was describing the situation to them, Christy Carter, another one of Dianne's students from that class, came running through the door.

"You can cancel the call," she said. "We finally got her hand loose."

"Thank goodness! But how did you get her hand to come out?" Dianne asked.

"We greased it with some Crisco," Christy answered.

"Well, that's one for the record books. Maybe we should write the company and tell them we have a new use for their shortening," Dianne noted.

Students were sometimes apt to pull pranks during the cooking labs. The boys liked to tease the girls, so Dianne always tried to put the worst behaved groups in the end kitchens, separating them from the rest of the students. The only problem with that was they were closer to the refrigerators, and they often tried to sneak around and steal some of the girls' Kool-Aid when the girls weren't watching.

On one occasion, Dianne had some extra grape soda left over from another class, so she decided to let the students in one of her Home Ec. I classes drink it during cooking lab. That turned out to be a mistake because one group of boys quickly guzzled down their allotted supply and then began harassing the other students, trying to get their soda. After correcting them several times, Dianne informed them that they were all being written up for disciplinary action.

"When the bell rings, go straight to the office. Don't go anywhere else, not even to your lockers," she told them.

After the bell, she walked down to the office and discovered the boys were not in there.

"Where's Mr. Kees?" she asked the secretary.

"He's in the teachers' lounge," the secretary replied.

Dianne walked into the lounge and spotted Mr. Kees sitting at one of the tables.

"I just sent some students to your office for disturbing lab class. They were running around trying to grab other students' grape sodas and Kool-Aid," she told him.

"You told them to report to the office, and they didn't come? I'm going to suspend all of them," he announced, as he arose from his chair and headed to the office.

Well, guess I won't be bothered with them for three days, Dianne thought, as she headed back to her next class.

———

Students also weren't above stealing food if they thought they could get by with it. At first, Dianne left the unrefrigerated food in grocery bags that were stacked in the department's grocery cart. She took out the food for each class as it was needed.

The problem with that was some food tended to disappear. One day at sixth hour she was missing a bag of chocolate chips. She had to divide the five bags among six lab groups. The next day she learned that a boy in her fifth-hour class had taken the chips, although there was no way to prove it.

The packages of Kool-Aid also had a tendency to go missing. The boys' groups liked to try to swipe an extra package and make themselves an extra pitcher, if they thought they wouldn't be caught.

It didn't take Dianne very long to wise up to those tactics, so she began keeping the food not used during each lab under lock and key. However, when she brought the groceries back to school on the day before the lab, the unrefrigerated items were often left in the grocery cart until the next morning, when she stored them away before her first lab class. One year she kept coming up one package of Kool-Aid short during her last lab class. She was positive she had bought the right number of packages. No matter how often she checked and rechecked and double-counted, one package was always missing.

She finally started buying one or two extra packages, just to make sure she would have enough to go around.

One day she commented about the problem to Mrs. Dorothy Burise, the female custodian who sometimes cleaned up the home economics kitchen.

"It's those janitors who be taking your Kool-Aid," said Mrs. Burise. "They see you come in with that cart of groceries. Then after you leave, they go down there and make themselves a pitcher of Kool-Aid."

"Well, I know how to stop that problem. From now own, I'll just lock up all the food before I go home," Dianne declared.

"And that's not all," Mrs. Burise added. "One of them has been taking naps on the couch in the home ec. living room."

"Okay, I can fix that problem, too," Dianne said.

She bought three locks and hasps from Wal-Mart that very afternoon. The next day she installed them on the three doors leading to the living room, locking the door to the hallway from the inside.

When she came back to school the following morning, she went to inspect the doors to see if the locks had held. All three locks were still in place, but the hasp inside the hall door had been bent, as if someone had tugged on it with all their might trying to get the door open.

Thank goodness for Master Lock, Dianne thought, as she surveyed the damage.

As far as she knew, that was their last attempt to use the home ec. living room as their lounge.

Scheduling labs for complete meals was a real problem because an hour lab was not enough time to prepare and eat a complete meal. Dianne solved the problem by having students pre-prepare some foods on the first day and reheat them while cooking foods that required the least amount of time during the second day's lab. The results were not always satisfactory.

On one occasion, the Home Ec. II students were planning to cook pizzas. Dianne had learned the homemade pizzas never got done on the first day, so she suggested the students partially cook the crust on the first lab day. Everything seemed to be going according to plan until they came into the lab for their second session.

"Mrs. Lundy, our pizza crust is hard as a rock. We won't be able to use it," they informed her.

"Well, I'm sorry. I guess we shouldn't have cooked it quite so long," Dianne told them. "The only thing to do is to make another crust and hope the pizza gets done by bell time."

On another occasion, one group of boys decided to cook fried chicken as their main dish. Dianne instructed them to cook the chicken on the first day and warm it up on the second day. She walked by their group just as they were dishing up the perfectly-fried chicken onto a serving platter.

"It looks really good, guys," she told them.

A few minutes later she came over to check on the group, and the chicken was gone.

"What happened to the chicken?" she inquired.

"We ate it already," they told her.

"Ate it! You were supposed to save it for tomorrow's lab," she exclaimed.

"We didn't want to be eatin' no warmed-up chicken," one boy told her.

"Well, I guess you will just have to make do with biscuits and gravy and your vegetables tomorrow because that's all you have left," she said.

Dianne always tried to plan so that every class had at least one or two cooking labs during the year, even if it was a class that didn't study cooking as its primary topic. One such class was Home and Family Living. During the second semester they studied about snacks, microwave cooking, and party foods, and she included a lab with each of those lessons.

Since it was a non-prerequisite course, many of the students had not taken Home Ec. I, so they did not know much about correct cooking techniques. In fact, some of them had never cooked anything in their entire lives.

One senior girl named LaWanda Jacobs told her, "I don't know anything about cooking. My mama won't even let me turn on the stove."

"That's going to backfire on you whenever you get married," Dianne noted.

During the lab on party foods, each group was assigned to prepare a different food on the first lab day. Then on the second day, the foods were served buffet style so everybody could sample them.

Dianne tried to select recipes that weren't too complicated. One thing they always liked to make was Rice Krispie Treats. One group assigned to make them included one of her favorite students, Dale Winegeart, who was the son of one of the counselors Dianne had worked with while at the Ruby Wise School. She was sure the group could handle the job.

Her instincts proved to be wrong on that occasion when Dale came up to her in the middle of lab.

"Mrs. Lundy, I have something bad to tell you about our Rice Krispie Treats," he said.

"What? Don't tell me. Let me guess—you scorched the marshmallows!" she exclaimed.

"No, worse than that. We were stirring them with a rubber spatula, and the spatula melted into the marshmallows," he admitted.

"I can't believe it. You are supposed to stir hot ingredients with a wooden spoon, not a rubber spatula," she chided, as she hurried over to view the damage. "Well, there's nothing to do but to throw it out. We don't want to be eating part of a rubber spatula. I'll try to scrape up some more ingredients and be more careful the second time."

Keeping outside students from invading the cooking labs also proved to be a problem at times at Pineville High. As soon as the food began to cook, the smells drifted down through the halls, tantalizing students in nearby classrooms. The main interruptions occurred during the times when different lunch shifts were held at the same time as the cooking classes. Dianne always instructed students not to let anyone in without her approval.

On one occasion, the opposite problem occurred. Instead of having to keep outsiders from invading the lab, Dianne had to deal with a lab student sneaking out without permission.

At the end that lab she was going around to check the kitchens to make sure they had been properly cleaned and all the equipment had been put away. When she got to one of the back kitchens that was located by an outside window, she noticed one of the girls was missing.

"Where is Debbie Edwards?" she inquired.

"She's outside," replied one of the other students in her group.

"What do you mean 'outside'?" Dianne asked.

"She jumped out the window, and now she's outside walking around. She says she lost a ring when it fell out the window."

Dianne peered through the window, and sure enough, there was Debbie, wandering around like she was lost, in the enclosed space between the first and second wings of the school. Knowing there was no way for Debbie to get back into the school unless somebody opened a door and let her in, Dianne made a quick decision.

"Well, she's outside, and that's where she's going to stay," she declared, as she closed and locked the window. "Don't anybody let her back in. I'm going to report her to the office when the bell rings."

As soon as the class was over, Dianne made a beeline for the office and reported the student for leaving class without permission.

"Where is she now?" inquired one of the principals.

"As far as I know, she's still meandering around between first and second wings, and she can stay there as far as I'm concerned," Dianne retorted, as she turned on her heels to exit the office.

Wow, I've had some strange things happen in cooking labs, but that has to be one of the weirdest. I'll say one thing—No matter how long I live, I'll never forget some of the experiences I've had with the cooking labs while at Pineville High School, she reflected, as she headed back to class.

Chapter 5

Until Dianne came to Pineville High School, the most students she had to deal with in a sewing lab were twenty to twenty-five at one time. But with the legal limit in high school classes being thirty-three students, the principals and guidance counselors at Pineville felt it was only fair that the home economics department carry its share of the load. So, having thirty students in a sewing lab became a reality Dianne had to face.

She soon learned organization was the key to success in teaching sewing to that many students at the same time. Despite her best efforts, it was impossible to keep everybody together on the same step because students always progress at different rates. The best thing was to let them work at their own pace, while trying to keep the slower students from falling too far behind.

During the early years, she had the students put their names on the help list written on the chalkboard. Each student's name was erased after they received help, and she went on to the next student, moving around the room from one sewing machine to another. Although this seemed like a good plan, it had its drawbacks. The students were a sneaky lot, with some of them trying to write their names in between two other names to skip a turn. Others simply erased one name and substituted their name instead.

Dianne soon caught on to such antics and learned to keep a close eye on the list as the period progressed. That actually wasn't hard because the students delighted in telling on each other if someone tried to break in line.

She also let students choose their own sewing machines for the first few years. But she found that the noisy students tended to congregate in one area, while other students who couldn't get along ended up beside each other. So, she devised an alternate plan. Each student picked a lab partner, and those two students were assigned sewing machines next to each other. If a student was absent, it was their lab partner's job to inform them of what they had missed and to help them catch up with the rest of the class. Since there was not enough room for all of the students to cut out their projects at the same time, the lab partners took turns, with each helping the other one with the cutting.

When Dianne first arrived at Pineville High, vocational money for schools was readily available and students rarely had to pay any type of fee for their home economics courses. But much of the funding was discontinued, and teachers were no longer allowed to use the remaining money to pay for food for cooking labs or materials and patterns for sewing labs. The only alternative left was to charge each student a lab fee for every home economics class they enrolled in.

Many of the students came from disadvantaged backgrounds and were unable to come up with the money for the entire lab fee all at one time, so Dianne had to initiate a plan with an incentive for paying. Those who were taking classes in foods and nutrition had to pay at least one dollar before each cooking lab until the entire fee for the semester was paid. In the sewing classes, patterns were ordered through the school, and students had to pay a portion of the fee before they could receive their patterns. Although it required a lot of time and careful bookkeeping, that plan seemed to work.

Getting the students to bring their materials for sewing projects was another problem. Even though Dianne carefully explained the course requirements on the first day of each semester and gave students ample notice about what materials would be needed for sewing, there were always some students who didn't have their materials on the first day of sewing.

Traditionally, the first project for Home Ec. I classes was a pillow that was completed just before Valentine's Day. It required only one yard of fabric, plus some thread, lace, and Polyfil stuffing. Through the years, Dianne carefully saved leftover fabric donated to the department by students. Also, there were always some students who bought more than enough fabric for their pillow. They usually volunteered to share with another student. Between those two factors, she managed to scrape up enough material for the students who could not get their pillow supplies.

Most of the time the students did manage to get the material for the remaining projects. Inevitably, though, there would always be one or two students in a class who simply could not or would not bring the materials they needed for additional projects.

Some of them told Dianne they had the money for their supplies, but no way to get to the store. They asked her if she would get the materials for them if they gave her their money. She agreed, seeing that there was no other choice. She took notes on what kind and color fabric they wanted and then purchased the materials.

Other students resorted to more desperate measures. One girl brought her mother's discarded living room curtains to use as material, while another student brought an old bed sheet. Their classmates found these tactics highly amusing, but Dianne reminded them that at least the students were trying.

One boy named Alex Cole never bought any materials for his project, but he always seemed to come up with the supplies he needed. Whenever he asked for help, Dianne would tell him what he needed for the next step. He always said, "I'll be back in just a minute."

Then he would saunter around the lab and come back with exactly the right supplies. Strangely enough, some other student would soon discover they were missing those same items. But they could never prove Alex was the culprit who took their materials.

Dianne went the extra mile in trying to help the underprivileged students. Each student was required to have a sewing kit that contained all of the small equipment such as scissors, a tape measure, a seam ripper, pins, and needles. As the years progressed, she began to collect the discarded kits at the end of the year in order to recycle them to needy students. Each kit was numbered, and all of the equipment in it was labeled with a matching number. Students could check out the kits to use for the semester and turn them back in when the sewing unit ended.

Keeping students supplied with pins was another problem. Dianne acquired a wand with a magnet at the end and used it to pick up the pins off the floor every day before the janitor came around to sweep the room. Most days she collected the equivalent of one or two boxes of pins. They were reissued to students who had lost most of their pins.

Several rolls of red-and-blue plaid fabric were donated to the department by the Louisiana State University at Alexandria school (LSUA). The fabric was originally intended to be used as uniforms for its student nurses, but when they decided to go with a different design, they elected to give the fabric to some of the area high schools.

Dianne carefully guarded the fabric because she knew if the students were aware it was available they would have little incentive for buying their own. It was reserved for students who were in dire need of financial help.

One year a group of girls in Home Ec. II chose patterns for hooded parkas and a pair of shorts. Some of them were unable to buy their fabric, so Dianne gave them enough of the plaid fabric for both garments. Some of the teachers commented about seeing the girls wearing them around school.

"I saw a couple of your girls with their plaid parkas, and they looked really cute," commented Terri Juneau, the French teacher, as she and Dianne met in the teachers' lounge when they checked their mailboxes.

The following year, a girl in another class needed some material for a pair of shorts, so Dianne gave her some of the plaid fabric. As the semester progressed, the girl sat at her sewing machine every day, but never asked for help and never appeared to be working. Dianne questioned her about it several times, and the girl always assured her she was going to have her shorts finished by the deadline.

Day after day, it was the same story. The girl simply did not seem to be making any progress on her project, and Dianne had serious doubts it would ever be finished. On the last day of lab, the girl came up to the front desk and handed in a completed pair of shorts.

"Told you I would finish on time," she boasted.

Dianne gave her a score sheet to fill out and told her to put the shorts on the desk in the stack of garments to be graded.

After school that day, she began to examine the shorts more closely. Then she noticed they were faded and had obviously been washed. Remembering the shorts from the previous year, she concluded the student was trying to pass off someone else's project as her own.

The next day she called the girl down for it.

"This is not your work. I remember these shorts from last year. They have obviously been washed several times because they are faded. You are not getting a passing grade for this project, and that means you have failed the course, because you have not met the course requirements. Furthermore, I am keeping the shorts as evidence, so you will not be getting them back."

———

She told the students it was best if they went to the store to buy their own materials, rather than sending their mothers, because it was part of the learning process. Nevertheless, there was always one student in every class who didn't heed those instructions. Usually when mothers went to the store for the students they bought the wrong kinds of materials. Students in Home Ec. I classes were not supposed to buy knit materials or plaids. When they showed up with the wrong kind of material, Dianne had to make a decision on whether or not to let them proceed with the project, and that decision was not always an easy one. Some students did not have the money to buy any more fabric, so she usually let them go ahead and sew.

On one occasion, a boy named Travis Anderson learned the hard way that sending his mother to buy his fabric was not a wise move. He showed up for class with a bag of supplies in hand and a sheepish look on his face. His mother had bought him pink material for a shirt he was going to make in Home Ec. II.

"You're going to look awfully funny in a pink shirt, Travis," Dianne teased.

"I got to make it with this material. I got no choice," was his reply.

When the time came for the next project, a pair of shorts, he decided to pick out the material himself. He chose a cotton print fabric with little black Scottie dogs. But he didn't fare much better on that project.

When he cut out the shorts, he didn't pay attention to how he laid the pattern out on the fabric. After the shorts were completed, Dianne discovered the little Scottie dogs were all upside down.

"Well, Travis, you've given me two good stories for my future classes," Dianne told him.

Travis wasn't the only student who encountered problems in the sewing lab due to careless errors. One girl who was making a pair of white pants kept cutting up pieces of material to test stitch her machine every day. A few days later, she discovered she had been cutting up one of the pants legs as scrap material, and there wasn't enough fabric left to salvage the project.

Several students lost pieces of their garment when they threw it away as excess material. Although Dianne always cautioned them to leave the pattern pieces on their fabric until they were actually ready to use each piece, some students didn't listen. One boy threw away the entire left front of his shirt, and several other students threw away their sleeves or facings. Dianne finally resorted to checking the lab trashcan every day at the end of school, just to make sure nobody else had thrown away any important part of their project.

⎯⎯⎯⎯

LaTonya Haynes, who had gotten her hand hung in a mixer during cooking lab, didn't have any better luck with sewing. Her class decided to make vests as one of their projects in Home Ec. I after they finished their pillows. LaTonya faithfully brought her project up to the front for Dianne to check after each step. Dianne always commented, "It looks fine, but did you backstitch?"

LaTonya always replied in the affirmative, so Dianne took her word for it. That particular year, the department had acquired a camcorder, and Dianne decided to have the students model their projects in front of the camera. As LaTonya proudly showed off her completed vest, Dianne captured the image for future classes to view.

A few days later, LaTonya made a confession, "Mrs. Lundy, I have something to tell you about my vest. I decided to wash it, and it fell apart in the washing machine. I had to take it out piece by piece. I was so mad!"

"Well, LaTonya, all I can say is one word—backstitch. That's what holds the seams together," said Dianne.

⎯⎯⎯⎯

Some students brought their materials on time, but they didn't buy enough fabric for their projects. One such student was a girl in Home Ec. III named Belinda Doyle.

Belinda had selected purple corduroy fabric for a lined jacket. Not realizing corduroy required the pattern to be laid out all in the same direction, she miscalculated the amount needed and didn't have enough to make the sleeves. When she went back to the store to buy another yard of material, the fabric had all been sold. The department manager informed Belinda that some more fabric had been ordered and instructed her to come back in a week. After waiting the allotted time, Belinda returned to the store only to find the new fabric didn't match her original color. She ended up making a purple jacket with lavender sleeves, giving Dianne quite a laugh when she viewed the finished product.

———

Other students brought their material for the first project but had trouble getting what they needed for additional projects. One of those students was a boy named Andres Sanchez. Andres was an athlete, and he was actually one of Dianne's brightest students. He had big plans for his future.

"I want to be a brain surgeon, Mrs. Lundy, and I want to operate on you some day. I'll even give you a discount," he said.

"Andres, I truly appreciate the offer, but I hope I never have a need for your services," Dianne replied laughingly.

After over a week of not having his materials, he informed Dianne he was going to buy his materials after school. Then during the same class period, Dianne received a call over the intercom to come to the office when the bell rang because his mother had brought some fabric for him to use.

"I know what kind of fabric she brought, and I'm not using it," he told Dianne.

"Well, Andres, you know the old saying, 'Beggars can't be choosers,'" Dianne reminded him.

When the bell rang, Dianne stopped by the office and met Mrs. Sanchez, who had a large bag of assorted fabrics with her. Dianne doubtfully eyed the colorful array of floral, plaids, and other designs.

"I'm not sure if any of that will work for Andres," she said. "He told me he's not using any of the fabric you brought up here because he doesn't like it."

"He may not like it, but he will use it. He will use it," said Mrs. Sanchez.

Dianne took the bag of materials as she commented, "Okay, let me take these down to the lab, and I'll have Andres check them over to see if he likes any of them. Thanks so much for bringing them up here."

Dianne never got the chance to ask Andres about the fabric because he showed up for class the next day with some material of his own choosing. Dianne sent the bag of fabric back to his mother, relieved that she didn't have to watch Andres model some brightly colored floral shorts.

When the students in Home Ec. I made their pillows, it usually took them several days to complete the projects. Once the pillows were stuffed, they did not fit into the students' sewing trays, so Dianne stored them on the couch in the home ec. living room which was located between the cooking and sewing labs. Students were supposed to pin their names on the pillows for identification, but after assisting each student with their pillow project, Dianne could pretty much identify which pillow belonged to which student.

Students would walk into the living room after roll check and pick up their pillows to work on them until they were finished and graded. On one occasion a girl named Charlotte Hickman went in to get her pillow, and it was missing.

"I can't find my pillow anywhere, Mrs. Lundy," the student said.

"Are you sure? It has to be here somewhere," Dianne insisted. But the pillow was nowhere to be found.

The next hour some students came to Dianne with a strange report.

"Mrs. Lundy, we know where Charlotte's pillow is," they told her. "Kensrea Tolbert has it. She has been showing it off to all of her teachers and telling them that she made it."

"Where is Kensrea now?" Dianne inquired.

"She's in Mrs. Keitha Cleveland's class."

Dianne sent a note to Mrs. Cleveland that read, "Please send Kensrea Tolbert and her pillow to see me as soon as possible."

Towards the end of the class, Kensrea appeared at the doorway, pillow in hand.

"Kensrea, what are you doing with that pillow? You know it isn't yours," Dianne scolded. "Your pillow is still in the living room." She promptly rescued the pillow and returned it to its rightful owner the next day.

Kensrea made some of the best grades in the class, but she definitely had a mind of her own. Dianne had learned over the years it was best to limit the Home Ec. I classes to just a few simple patterns to select from when the time came to make their garments.

Kensrea informed Dianne that she didn't like any of the pattern choices.

"I have a pattern of my own at home for a sleeveless dress. That's what I want to make," she said.

"Okay, Kensrea. You may bring the pattern tomorrow, and I'll take a look at it and see if it's suitable for a Home Ec. I project," Dianne responded.

The following day, Kensrea brought the pattern up to the front as the students began to work on their projects in the sewing lab. Dianne took the pattern and began to examine it. Although it didn't look too complicated, when she turned the pattern over, she discovered it called for a twenty-two-inch zipper in the back of the dress.

"I'm afraid you won't be able to use this pattern, Kensrea. It has a long zipper, and we don't do zippers in Home Ec. I any more."

"But that's the only dress I like," Kensrea insisted.

"I'm sorry, but the answer is 'no,'" Dianne replied.

"Well then, I just won't make a damn thing," Kensrea retorted, shouting as she spoke.

The rest of the class came to a halt as the students listened in on the conversation.

"That does it! I'm going to have to write you up for the use of profane language in the classroom," Dianne calmly informed her, as she proceeded to drag a discipline referral form out of the desk drawer.

Kensrea never got the chance to make anything else in Dianne's class because she transferred to another school the following week.

And I guess that solves that problem, but good luck to her next teacher, Dianne reflected.

———

Students were just as apt to pull pranks in sewing labs as they had been in cooking labs. Most of the time the pranks were harmless. One of the favorite jokes for the boys was to unthread other students' machines or change someone's machine tension when the students weren't looking. Some students also tried to cause problems by leaving the irons plugged in and turning them on the highest setting in hopes that the next person to use it would burn their fabric. A few of the boys tried to cut holes in some of the girls' fabric, while others delighted in sticking pins into the sewing machine stools and waiting for someone to sit on them.

One year someone kept stringing thread across the paths everyone had to walk through to move around in lab, hoping to trip someone. It was wrapped around the machine legs and sewing stool legs, and it took quite some time to untangle it. Dianne thought it was an accident at first, but one day she finally caught a boy in the act. After she warned him he would be written up for disrupting class, he never tried it again.

A more serious incident occurred during a lab demonstration. Dianne always showed the Home Ec. I students how to sew up their pillows. One day students in her second hour class gathered around her machine for the demonstration. They were one of her most cooperative classes, so she did not suspect that anything was amiss.

Later that day, during the lunch period, she was visited by one of the assistant principals, Mr. Roy Prestridge.

"Are you aware that one of the boys in your second hour class set a girl's hair on fire today?" he asked.

"No, I don't know anything about it. You've got to be kidding!" Dianne exclaimed.

"While you were giving a demonstration, Gerald Hughes took out a lighter and held it up to the back of a girl's hair. It actually scorched her hair. She came down to the office and reported it."

"Well, I can't understand why the girl didn't say anything to me about it."

"I checked with Mrs. O'Banion," he said, referring to the teachers' aide who came to class with the special ed. students. "She confirmed what happened."

"Okay, I guess that's one for the record books. I hope he gets suspended," Dianne declared.

"Oh, yes. I think he will be spending several days at the detention center," Roy replied.

─────

After she began teaching all levels of home economics at Pineville High, Dianne found that the same students tended to stick with the courses, year after year, some of them taking every class that was offered. In many cases, the boys who took the courses voluntarily were actually better than the girls at cooking and sewing.

Such was the case with the class Richard Carter was in. The boys came up to Dianne and asked for help on almost every step, but the girls often sat at their machines and gabbed while they worked. The result was the boys ended up making "A's" on their projects, while most of the girls made "C's."

Richard was particularly proud of his outfit that year. He had made a shirt and a pair of pants from red satin material. He was one of Dianne's favorite students, but he did tend to be on the mischievous side at times. She sent him to the office to show off his work to the principals. As he walked out the door, she thought to herself that a pair of horns, a tail, and a pitchfork would have completed the outfit nicely.

─────

Keeping an eye on all of the students during lab was not an easy task. Dianne found that the only way to make sure they didn't sneak out the door was to keep it closed at all times. On several occasions, though, some of the students did manage to slip away.

One day Dianne gave a girl in her third hour class permission to go to the restroom. Several minutes later, she noticed that a boy who was dating the girl had disappeared. Since there was no way to call the office on the intercom, she decided to wait until class was over to report the incident.

She didn't have to wait that long. About halfway through the class period assistant principal Betty Tumminello came into the room with the two students in tow. She had a paper hall pass in her hand.

"Is this your handwriting?" she inquired of Dianne.

Dianne peered at the badly scribbled document. "No, it's not."

"I didn't think so," Betty commented. "These two students were brought to the office by Miss Jackie LaBorde. She found them kissing down in the alcove by the water fountain on this wing. Don't worry. They will be coming down to the office with me."

Dianne was at a loss for words after that incident. But an even stranger incident happened on another occasion.

At the end of lab every student was supposed to put their sewing machine away because not all machines were used every hour. One day after all the students had stored away their materials and put their sewing machines back into the cabinets, one machine was still out.

"Whose sewing machine is that?" Dianne inquired.

"It belongs to Otis Hardy," one of the students replied.

"Where is Otis?" Dianne inquired.

He was nowhere to be found, so Dianne could only conclude he had slipped out the door when students got up to put their materials away.

She reported him to the office as missing and later learned he was seen running down the back hall at top speed. He never returned to class, and she never saw him again.

Well, that's one less student I have to worry about, I suppose, she reasoned.

Students who did not finish their projects by the end of each semester had to stay for after-school labs. These were held from the time school was dismissed until 5:00 p.m. several days a week until all the projects were completed.

Dianne quickly learned she had to come up with a set of guidelines to maintain order in the labs. For starters, no outsiders were admitted. Only the students actually enrolled in home economics could attend. Students were also supposed to have their own transportation home.

"Remember, I'm not running a taxi cab company," she often reminded them.

Still, there were times when students couldn't find a ride home. Many of them rode the city bus, but often needed money for it. Dianne found herself loaning out quite a few quarters for them to make the fare so they could catch the bus that stopped at the corner of the school grounds.

She also ended up taking a few students home in her own vehicle on several occasions. One time she gave a boy a ride home to the Karst Park subdivision, a black neighborhood in Alexandria.

"You might want to just let me out at the corner store," the boy told her. "We had a shooting down here last night."

On another occasion, she gave a girl a ride home to another black neighborhood near Alexandria's north traffic circle. She dropped the girl off and headed back out, or so she thought. After driving over a few streets, she realized she had taken a wrong turn.

There were quite a few black people out on their front porches, and they all stared as she drove past their houses.

After passing the same yard with a spotted dog sitting in the front of it several times, she was beginning to get a little worried. It was getting late. It was also beginning to get dark, and the houses were all starting to look alike.

Okay, stay calm, she told herself. Pay attention to where you are going and stop making the same turns over and over again. The next time you see the spotted dog, turn a different way, and maybe you'll get out of here. The technique worked, and she soon found herself back at the subdivision entrance, much to her relief.

She made an exception to her rule of not bringing food into the lab one day during the after-school labs. One of her foods classes had cooked pizzas earlier in the day. Some of the students didn't want to take the extra pizza home, so they gave it to Dianne. She decided to let the students who stayed after school eat the pizza, along with some extra cokes she had bought.

The students couldn't believe their good fortune in actually getting to eat in the lab. The only catch was they had to finish the food before they began sewing. They wasted no time in devouring the unexpected feast.

One boy who stayed that day was Freddie Hall. He hadn't even started making his second project, a pair of shorts, and there was only one more day of after-school labs left. He was an athlete, and he had after-school practice every day.

"The coach said I could stay today, but it's the only day he'll let me out of practice," he announced.

"Boy, you can't finish a pair of shorts in one day," said one of the girls.

"Bet you I can," he shot back.

"I think we can do it if we work together," Dianne interceded. "You sew, and I'll help you press."

True to her prediction, Freddie finished putting the hem in the shorts just as 5:00 p.m. rolled around. She didn't know who was more relieved, her or Freddie.

The next day she was confronted by some of the other students in the class.

"We heard you helped Freddie and he finished his shorts in one day," they said.

"Sho' did," Freddie retorted. "And she fed us, too. We got pizza and cokes."

"Man, that's not fair," complained one of the boys.

"Well, that's life, and life isn't always fair. That's something you'll have to learn as you grow older," Dianne replied.

Chapter 6

*L*ab classes were not the only source of humorous events Dianne encountered during her teaching tenure at Pineville High. Parenthood Education also proved to be a source of interesting and amusing incidents.

Students enrolled in Parenthood Ed. were required to carry a boiled egg that was known as an "egg baby" for three days. The eggs were numbered and stamped with the year they were issued to prevent students from simply using another egg if they broke theirs. The purpose of the project was to demonstrate that babies are delicate creatures who require a lot of special care and attention.

Although the students thought it would be an easy project to complete, they soon found they were mistaken. Many students never made it through the first day without breaking their egg. Some eggs were accidentally dropped, while others were stolen and smashed by students from other classes. One girl reported that a boy stole her egg baby and ate it.

There weren't a lot of boys who took the class, but those who did were often athletes. One such boy was a robust and talented football player named Kenneth Mixon.

He was also a fairly good student, so he had a good chance of getting a scholarship.

"Stay on Kenneth and make sure he makes good grades," advised the senior guidance counselor, Mollie Mount.

Kenneth did his part and successfully completed the egg baby project, as well as passing the course. He won a football scholarship to LSU and was later drafted into the NFL to play for the Miami Dolphins.

———

A boy named Paul Gilbert, who was also an athlete, didn't have such good luck. Paul had enrolled in the class late. When he came to the door with his enrollment slip, Dianne discouraged him from taking the class. She had taught him Home Economics I the previous year, and she was pretty sure he was not the type to take Parenthood Ed.

"Paul, you really don't want to be in this class. If you take it, first you'll have to carry around an egg baby and later an electronic doll," she warned him.

"I can do it," he assured her.

"Okay, but if you take the class, you will have to complete both projects in order to pass," she said.

Against her better judgment, she agreed to let him enroll in the course. On the day the egg babies were passed out, his baby rolled off his desk five minutes later.

"Can I get another one?" he asked.

"No, Paul. If you kill your baby, you can't just go to the hospital and get another one. You should have been paying more attention when you got it," she informed him.

———

The students had to provide the egg babies with a face, hair, clothes, and a carrier. They also had to turn in a booklet that recorded all of their experiences with their baby. On the third day, when the babies were turned in, the class voted on which baby was the most original, and that student got bonus points added to their six-weeks' grade.

They had to make a brief report to the class about their experiences. Some of them had sad tales to relate when they explained why they didn't make it back with their baby in one piece.

"I was taking really good care of my baby," one girl reported. "I had it in a little shoe box bed. I put the box right beside my bed when I went to sleep. When I got up the next morning, I stepped in the middle of the box and completely squashed the baby."

"I put mine on top of the TV set, and it rolled off and cracked," another girl told the class.

"I had mine in my locker, and some books fell on top if it," said one of the boys.

"My mama put mine on the countertop, and our cat jumped up and knocked it off," lamented another girl.

Some of the girls didn't want to give up their babies. "Do we have to turn them in? I was really getting attached to mine," one girl declared.

The school eventually acquired four electronic dolls known as "Baby Think It Over." The dolls were battery-operated and could be programmed to cry at specific intervals to simulate that they needed "tending." Tending consisted of giving the baby a pacifier key that was inserted into a keyhole in its back. After a certain length of time, the baby would signal it no longer needed tending by giving a short cry and the pacifier had to be removed.

Students were required to carry the babies around school for one complete day. They had to check the baby out before school started and bring it back during the last ten minutes of sixth hour. The babies had electronic controls that indicated abuse such as shaking, hitting, or letting it cry too long without tending.

Most of the students were eager for the experience, although they were often teased by teachers and students. Those who got the most laughs were the males, especially the athletes. One such boy was a student named Larry Quinney.

Larry was enrolled in two home economics courses during his senior year, and he was actually one of Dianne's most entertaining students. He liked to make up rap songs, and he could do so on short notice, instantly making up a song or poem about any topic given to him. He also made fairly good grades, which gave him a good chance of getting an athletic scholarship.

Larry couldn't wait to get his hands on Baby Think It Over. He was really excited about the project. When he walked into the gym carrying the baby, he was an instant hit, with everybody rushing over to see it. He made it through the day without mishap and successfully completed the project, much to Dianne's relief.

At least I know it won't be Parenthood Ed. keeping him from getting a scholarship, she thought.

Some girls ran into problems with the dolls. One year a girl named Tammy Peters was the first person to receive Baby Think It Over. Dianne had selected her to be first because she was one of the most reliable students. On the morning she picked up the doll, there was an assembly with a guest speaker. Dianne did not have a first-hour class, so she stayed in her room to complete some paperwork.

About the middle of the hour, Dianne heard some strange sounds coming from the hall. It sounded like a baby crying. In fact, it sounded very much like Baby Think It Over.

No, it can't be. It's got to be my imagination, she thought.

Then she heard a knock on her door. She opened it to find Tammy, accompanied by Betty Tumminello.

"Your doll was disturbing the assembly," Betty told her.

"I can't get it to stop crying. I don't know what's wrong!" Tammy exclaimed. She was holding the doll with the pacifier in its back.

Dianne reached over and removed the pacifier, and the crying immediately ceased.

"It wasn't hungry," she said, shaking her head.

———

Most of the time the dolls were fairly indestructible. One of them even survived being kidnapped and kicked down the hall by an unidentified assailant. Others were beat upon by students and some teachers in an attempt to make them cry. Dianne had to resort to having an announcement read over the intercom describing the project to the entire student body and stating that anyone who interfered with the care of the dolls would be subject to disciplinary action.

On one occasion a girl named Amanda Strother did manage to break her doll. She came back to see Dianne two hours after she had received it.

"Mrs. Lundy, I think there's something wrong with this baby. I've had it for two hours, and it hasn't cried yet," she said.

Dianne took the baby and turned it over. There was no response. She shook it gently, and it still didn't cry. She checked the battery box, and it appeared to be intact. She tried inserting fresh batteries, but the baby still wouldn't cry.

"I think it's dead," she told Amanda. "What did you do to it?"

"I didn't do anything. I swear!" Amanda insisted.

"Well, you killed it somehow, so you will be receiving a zero on this project," Dianne informed her.

Dianne later learned from some of the students that Amanda had forgotten all about the baby in her science class. She had put it down in her desk and then sat on it, squashing the electronic voice box, which had to be replaced. That was the only time one of the dolls was actually broken.

———

Students in Parenthood Ed. also came up with some interesting questions. Dianne was prohibited by state law from discussing those classified as sex education, but she did the best she could. On one occasion a girl named Jennifer Monk asked a question that Dianne would not soon forget.

"Mrs. Lundy, I've been wondering about something," Jennifer told her in the middle of a class discussion.

"Yes, Jennifer, what is it?" Dianne inquired.

"When the woman is pregnant and gets so big, how does the couple have sex?"

"Well, Jennifer, all I can say is where there's a will, there's a way," Dianne replied.

On another occasion Jimmy White, a boy Dianne had been teaching for several years, knocked on her door one morning before school started. He had been dating a girl who had also been in home economics classes for three years.

"Mrs. Lundy, I wonder if I could borrow one of your little booklets about pregnancy," he said.

"Sure, Jimmy, I'll get you one out of the cabinet," Dianne replied.

She loaned him the booklet, and he brought it back the next day. She was highly suspicious that the girlfriend, Merlinda Fields, was probably pregnant, but she didn't let on. Her instincts proved right, as the girl became noticeably pregnant before the school year was over.

The couple got married, and the next year Merlinda brought the baby by for Dianne to see.

"He's cute. What's his name?" Dianne inquired.

"Oh, we just call him Lil' Jim," Merlinda told her.

"How would you like to bring him by the Parenthood Ed. class for a demonstration?" Dianne asked. "You could show them how to feed him and tell us about some of your experiences with a baby."

"Yes, I guess can do that," Merlinda agreed.

A few days later she arrived at the appointed time with the baby. All the girls "oohed" and "aahed" over how cute he was.

"He really is cute," said Dianne, as she bent down to take a closer look at the Afro-American child.

Lil' Jim burst into tears, and the entire class burst out laughing.

"Aw, this baby is scared of white people. What have you been telling him?" Dianne teased.

———

Another class that would prove unforgettable was Home and Family which was eventually split into two semester courses, with the second semester being labeled Adult Responsibilities. The first semester course delved into topics on human and family relations, while consumer education was the main focus during second semester.

One of the favorite topics during the first semester was the study about weddings. Dianne often arranged for guest speakers during that time. The featured speakers included Mrs. June Lambard, a florist, who spoke on selecting flowers for the wedding. She always gave some sort of demonstration during her speech and gave the finished product away to one of the students. Mrs. Aileen Birge, the owner of Aileen's Bridal Boutique, talked to the students almost every year about how to plan a wedding and gave pointers on how to select the right wedding attire. One year Mr. Carl Carstens from Schnack's Jewelry came to the class and explained how to select a diamond, bringing with him some samples of diamonds from their store. Dr. Glen Bryant, a renowned speaker and marriage counselor, spoke to them about love and relationships between couples.

The highlight of the wedding unit was a mock wedding reception that featured a bride and groom and the wedding party, all of whom were voted on by their fellow classmates. Aileen donated a wedding dress and matching veil to the school, so the choice of brides was limited to someone who could fit into the dress.

One of the couples, Hank Tabor and Debbie Setnicky, ended up getting married in real life. Other couples were not as compatible. One year the bride actually hated the groom. "If he tries to kiss me, I'm gonna slap him up-side his head," she threatened.

During the first few years, Dianne always tried to find a class member's mother who knew how to decorate cakes. The school furnished the supplies, and Dianne sent them home by that student. One such mother was Mrs. Juneau, whose three daughters, Susan, Debbie, and Patricia, enrolled in the class over the years.

One year one of the boys in the class, Gary Vercher, volunteered for the job. He assured Dianne she had nothing to worry about. Then on the day before the reception, he made a disturbing announcement.

"Mrs. Lundy, I have something to tell you about the cake. I cooked it last night, and then I decided to go to the mall with some friends. I left the cake in the pans, and when I got back, it was totally stuck to the bottom of the pans. I had to go out and buy all new ingredients and start all over again."

"Gary, are you sure the cake will be ready?" Dianne asked doubtfully. "Maybe we shouldn't have assigned you to make the cake, since you are supposed to be the groom, too."

"Man, you gonna ruin our cake," complained one of the boys in the class.

"Yeah, Gary, don't mess up *our* cake," exclaimed Vicki Freeman, who had been selected to be his bride.

Dianne's faith was restored the next day when Gary showed up with a beautifully decorated cake that featured pale pink roses.

"Told you I would finish it," he said, as Dianne breathed a thankful sigh of relief.

But it became harder and harder to find anybody who was willing to take on the chore. So, Dianne took a class on cake decorating from Atwood's Bakery, giving her insight in how to make, assemble, and decorate a wedding cake. That information proved invaluable, year after year.

The students were divided into groups to prepare the food for the reception. Dianne always tried to pick the students who actually knew how to cook to make the wedding cakes. Other students were assigned tasks according to their abilities. Everyone had to do something to prepare for the reception, the least favorite job being washing dishes.

Dianne assured them that none of her students had expired while washing dishes, but that didn't make the job any more popular.

In addition to the cake, the food array also included sandwiches, chips and dip, and punch. Dianne made sure there would be enough food to have leftovers. There were usually at least two trays of sandwiches, and sometimes three. Without fail, students would always leave the last tray uneaten.

On the day after the reception, the students had to clean up all the dirty dishes. Every group got some of the dishes to wash. Only after everything had been cleaned and stored away did they get to eat the leftovers. Anything not eaten that day was wrapped up and taken home by the students, leaving only a table scattered with crumbs.

With the exception of the first year, all the receptions were held in the school library. The school had acquired several video cameras, so Dianne arranged for the library assistants to film the receptions. The students looked at the tapes while they were eating the leftovers. This allowed them to see what had actually transpired during the event, often with unexpected results.

Most of the students were camera shy and tried to hurry by the spot where the camera was stationed. One year, though, several boys decided to interject their own version of a rap song onto the tape, posing and performing in front of the camera while Dianne was otherwise occupied across the room. It all caught up with them the next day when the tape was played.

"Very funny, guys. Very funny," Dianne said, as she viewed their act, thinking it was just a sign of the times.

On another occasion the tape actually helped unravel a mystery. That year the class had made only two trays of sandwiches, but the trays were extra-large in size. Dianne took both trays down to the library, fully expecting the second tray to be uneaten.

At the end of the reception when the students were wheeling the remains of the food back to the kitchen, Dianne discovered the second tray was still sitting on the bottom shelf of one of the serving carts, but almost all of the sandwiches were gone.

"What happened to all of those sandwiches? How did they

disappear when we didn't even put that tray onto the table?" she inquired.

Nobody seemed to know, or else they weren't telling.

The next day, as the class was viewing the tape, the question was answered. In the very corner of the frame, one of the boys was seen sneaking behind the cart and helping himself to the sandwiches—not once, not twice, but three times.

"Well, I guess we know where all those extra sandwiches went," Dianne exclaimed.

———

Field trips were used as an additional teaching tool in many of Dianne's classes. For several years the students enrolled in sewing made a walking field trip to the Hancock's fabric store that was located in the shopping center just down the street from the school. They looked at the types of fabric that were suitable for their projects, and those who brought their money could actually buy their sewing supplies on the spot.

Other trips were longer distances and required some type of transportation. For the first few years Dianne depended on students who had cars to provide transportation for the rest of the class. Some problems resulted with that arrangement. A boy named Matt Hughes who had a sizable car informed her he couldn't carry anyone in his back seat.

"Why not?" Dianne inquired.

"That's where I have the speakers for my stereo," he told her.

"Do your speakers take up that much room?" Dianne asked unbelievingly.

"Have you ever seen his speakers?" interjected one of the classmates.

"No, but how big can they be?" Dianne wondered.

"I promise you, they take up my whole back seat," said Matt.

On another occasion, a girl got a ticket for running a red light when she was trying to keep up with the car caravan. She and her group never made it to the assigned destination, Aileen's Bridal Boutique, before Dianne and the rest of the class headed back home. The next day, Dianne quizzed her about the incident.

"By the time we got there, you were all gone," the girl told her.

Dianne checked with the establishment and verified that the group of girls did actually arrive later.

"They came in about twenty minutes late and looked around. They found your wedding picture on the wall. One of them said, 'I guess she really is married.' They all giggled and then they left," Aileen reported to Dianne.

The trip to Aileen's was always a favorite with the class. Aileen allowed the girls to try on any wedding dress and veil in the store. Some of them also tried on the bridesmaids' dresses. For them, it was almost as much fun as getting ready for a real wedding.

So the guys wouldn't feel left out, that class also made a trip almost every year to Randall's tuxedo and formal wear shop. Mr. Lee Rubin was a most gracious host and gave the students pointers on how to select the right tuxedo for a wedding or prom.

Later the school board began requiring teachers to use busses for field trips, so Dianne resorted to scheduling the Rebel bus as an alternative. Anyone who drove the bus had to be a certified driver, so she had to depend on the assistant principals to make sure someone was available. One of the drivers often used was Mr. Whitworth, who was the husband of one of the school secretaries. Eventually, the school stopped hiring outside people to drive the bus and used either coaches or JROTC instructors. Some of the most frequent bus chauffeurs were Sergeant Charles Wilson, coach Ronnie Kaiser, and Colonel Robert Tanaka. Some of those drivers sacrificed their lunch period in order to transport the students, going above and beyond the call of duty.

The Housing and Interior Design class toured places that featured materials used for building, decorating, or furnishing homes such as Downs Furniture, Carroll Furniture, J. C. Penney's, Sherwin Williams, and Hill-Harris. Several realtors, including Ron Noles, took them to see new homes that were under construction.

One year the students set a record by making eleven field trips during the eighteen-week semester course. Before students got off the bus, Dianne reminded them of two important rules.

"Okay, remember—don't break anything, and no shoplifting," she told them jokingly.

After the housing class was discontinued, Dianne began to include a unit on home furnishings in the Adult Responsibilities class. She incorporated several field trips into the unit, including places such as The Retreat condominiums, Tanglewood Apartments, and Pine Highland Apartments in Pineville. One of the favorite places to visit was a mobile home lot. The students were most impressed with their treatment at Ed's Mobile Homes in Alexandria when the owner furnished them with free Cokes.

In the later years, Dianne began to encounter problems with a few of the students. One year at the mobile home lot, some of the boys were caught playing hide-and-seek among the trailers rather than touring them and filling out their questionnaires. That year someone also decided to use the bathroom in one of the trailers. The only problem was the sewage line wasn't connected.

"Honestly, I can't believe high school students didn't have any better sense than to use an unconnected toilet. That pretty much concludes the field trips for that class," she reported to one of her fellow teachers.

Another class that included field trips was Parenthood Ed. They traditionally made two trips every year. The first trip was to tour and evaluate a day care center. Those they visited included Sylvia's, First Baptist, and Peggy's, all located in Pineville. Then they went back for a second time just before the Christmas holidays to give the children a Christmas party. The class was divided into groups, and each group got to pick what age children they wanted to work with. They had to furnish food and entertainment appropriate for that age. It was something they always looked forward to.

Things went pretty well most years, but one year there was a slip-up. One of the groups wanted to have pizza as the main food for their children. Janice Monet, one of the girls in their group, volunteered to leave school early in her car to pick up the pizzas. She checked into class and then said she was leaving to get the pizzas.

The bus arrived at the day care center, but there was no sign of Janice.

"I'm sure she'll be along shortly. Why don't you go ahead with the games, and maybe she'll get here with the pizzas," Dianne told the group.

They waited and waited, but Janice never came. Some of the other groups had to share their sandwiches so there would be enough food for the children.

Later when they got back to school, Dianne reported the incident to assistant principal Roy Prestridge.

"Lost another student! I don't know what we're going to do with you. If this keeps up, you won't have any class left," he teased.

Although the field trips were fun, and Dianne enjoyed most of them, they were also a lot of work. When the class periods were shortened and the trips became more expensive, she was gradually forced to discontinue them.

Chapter 7

One of the most fulfilling experiences Dianne encountered during her tenure at Pineville High School was working with the Future Homemakers of America club, also known as FHA. Dianne's membership in FHA under the direction of Mrs. Lucille Stewart at Farmerville High School had given her valuable insight in knowing exactly how the organization worked.

As long as there were three home economics teachers at the Pineville school, they all took turns working with the organization, although Dianne eventually became the main adviser. The club was quite large during the 1970's, with the membership swelling to one hundred and twenty at one point, making it the largest club on campus. At that time, it outgrew the home economics facilities and had to meet in the choir room. Eventually, though, the membership began to decline as other types of clubs were organized and, at the same time, the enrollment in home economics classes dropped.

Over the years, the club members participated in quite a few activities. One of the oldest and most popular contests was the Golden Yam Contest that was sponsored by the state yam growers' organization. It began at the local level and progressed through the parish, district, and state levels, with one winner being selected at each level.

Students who entered had to prepare an original yam or sweet potato dish, demonstrate a table setting for serving that dish, make a speech, and answer judges' questions regarding facts about yams. The home economics teachers often enlisted help from faculty and staff members for judging the school's yam dishes. It was something they always looked forward to. Some of those who assisted included Mrs. Diane Cripps, Miss Mary Frances Crump, Dr. Mary Edwards, Miss Emily Needham, Mrs. Elizabeth Roy, Mrs. Donna Reed, Mrs. Betty Tumminello, and Mr. Jerry White.

Entries ranged from Tina Campbell's yam puff orange shells to Jecole Roland's yam-beef-vegetable stew and Tina St. Andrie's yam-and-cranberry cornbread. Other students chose more traditional dishes such as yam cookies, biscuits, cakes, and pies. Several students won at the parish level and advanced to the district contest at Northwestern Louisiana State University. Two students who made it that far were Robin Cooley, who made a yam pound cake, and Dana Miller, who created a recipe for Yummy Yam Bars. Another student, Tracy Richardson, came up with an original dish she called Tangy Yam Surprise Cake. Then, to everyone's surprise, she won at both the district and state levels, making her the only state winner from the school.

The home economics teachers in the parish decided to reactivate the parish FHA organization in the 1970's. Pineville High played a major role by sponsoring a number of parish officers. The first girl to serve as a parish officer under Dianne's guidance was Denny Tuma, who was the Pineville FHA president in 1976. She was elected parish historian during 1977. Another student, Tina Nalley, who was Pineville's FHA vice president, ran for and won the seats as both parish and district secretary the following year.

During the parish meeting, several contests were held each year. All the clubs entered the sign contest in which each school displayed a sign depicting the theme for the meeting, along with their school's name. The Pineville students were excited when they won first place in that category in 1976. The theme for the meeting was "FHA Steps Forward." Their sign consisted of a giant cardboard foot accented with red toenails and plastered with the theme and their school's name.

Another competition was the program cover contest. All schools submitted in advance of the meeting an entry that illustrated the theme for the year. The following year, Pineville won first place in that category with Lori Lollis's entry. The theme was "Up, Up, and Away with FHA." Lori drew a Ziggy character who was holding a rising bunch of balloons inscribed with "FHA." They also won several other years with entries drawn by Patricia Fairley.

The badge contest was the one that gave them the most trouble. Each member was supposed to wear a badge that contained their name and an illustration about the theme. Every year they were sure they had the best entry, only to be beaten by some other school. Finally, in 1987-88 they won with a badge using the theme "Spotlight on You." It featured a girl who was wearing an apron and holding a tray of cookies as she stood in a spotlight.

Clubs could also enter a scrapbook contest by completing a scrapbook that recorded their club's activities for the year. Pineville never won first place in that contest, but they did manage to snag several second and third place entries. Some of the most outstanding scrapbooks were made by Kerrie Drott, Teresa Compton, Robin Cooley, Brenda Masson, and Alis Perkins, all of whom served as Pineville High's club historians.

The most coveted award was the Ideal Club Award, which was based on merit points. Each club's adviser had to complete a score sheet that listed all of the club's activities for the year. The club that won the most often was Rapides High. Dianne was just about to give up hope of Pineville ever winning when her club shockingly beat out Rapides High by one point. She proudly carried the silver tray for the award back to Pineville High and rushed in to show it to Peggy and Betty after school. They were incredulous that Pineville had finally managed to pull off a victory.

The talent contest provided the entertainment for the afternoon session. Pineville rarely entered that one, but the year they did featured a most unusual participant. E. Hope Ryland, who also served as one of Pineville's FHA presidents, performed a tap dance routine to the tune of "Tuxedo Junction."

Eventually, the talent contest was replaced by entertainment provided by local high school choirs, the selection depending on the meeting's location. Some of the favorites with the students were the choirs from Rapides, Pineville, and Oak Hill high schools. One year Pineville provided the sole entertainment using one of their male students who played the guitar and sang. He was so popular the girls all rushed the stage afterwards to get his autograph.

Sometimes the afternoon session also featured a style show. For several years, each school sponsored one or two students who modeled garments they had made during their home economics classes. At other times, local stores such as The Clothes Closet and The Limited agreed to provide the apparel. The most impressive attire was the formal wear that came from Aileen's Bridal Boutique. The girls who modeled the formals and wedding dresses were escorted by boys who wore tuxedos from Squire's.

In 1984-85 the parish activities were expanded to include the FHA STAR contests. The initials stood for "Students Taking Action with Recognition." Those contests included the Golden Yam Contest, the Job Interview Contest, the FHA Fact and Parliamentary Procedure Test, and the Energy Conservation Contest. With the exception of the yam contest, all of the competitions contained a junior level for ninth grade students and a senior level for students in grades ten through twelve.

That particular year, Pineville High had the parish president, Teri Brown, so it became Dianne's responsibility to set up the first competitions. Because they had to be held at a separate time than the parish meeting, she arranged for Pineville to host the event. She had to contact and secure judges for all of the contests, as well as providing facilities. It was quite a chore, but together she and Teri managed the arrangements. Dianne was rewarded for her efforts later that year at the parish meeting when she was presented with a silver tray as a "thank you" present from the FHA members and the other advisers.

The Pineville club also participated in a slew of activities at the local level. These varied from year to year, depending on club finances and students' interests. Among the most memorable events was their participation in the homecoming parade. One of their most outstanding entries was a float that was on a trailer owned by Suzanne Mizell's dad. Their theme was "Stew the Bears." They made a huge black pot using wire mesh and crepe paper with a big cardboard Bolton Bear inside it. Students who rode on the float wore aprons and chef's hats and wielded various cooking instruments such as wooden spoons and rolling pins. That year they won honorable mention.

Another year they borrowed a speed boat that was pulled by a pickup truck. The boat was decorated with blue bulletin board paper and blue and white crepe paper chains to resemble ocean waves. It sported a paper sail that read "Sail to #1 Rebs." Students who rode in the boat and the back of the truck wore sailor hats that Dianne borrowed from Rick. That float also won honorable mention.

Aside from those two large entries, the other years they used cars or trucks. Eventually, Dianne stopped asking other people to furnish the vehicles. For several years they used Rick's red Chevy Citation and then his red Chevy S-10 truck. Although the entries were smaller and didn't win any prizes, the students always had fun working on them, riding in the parade, and throwing candy to the crowd.

The club also participated in a number of school and community service projects. One event they always assisted with was preparing and serving refreshments on Parents' Night. For the first few years the Advanced Foods classes made the food, usually cookies, cakes, sandwiches, and punch. The FHA members would set up and serve it. When the date was moved closer and closer to the opening of school, alternate plans had to be made. For several years, the Home Ec. II classes made Bundt cakes and punch. Finally, when the event was scheduled before the home economics kitchen was even cleaned up for its yearly usage, they had to resort to ordering large sheet cakes from Harlow's Bakery in Pineville.

Over the years Dianne learned how to provide specific instructions to the FHA members who volunteered to help serve the food. She had them pretty well trained so they could carry the food to the library and set it up by themselves while she remained in her room to meet with parents. Things usually went off without a hitch. One year, though, was stamped into her memory. That year Faith Ford, Tonya Kees, and E. Hope Ryland were among the volunteers. Dianne had decided to wear a dress she had made that featured an unusual design. It had a fake vest that was fastened to the neck in the back. It came around under her arms and tied in the front. She was describing the sewing techniques to the girls when E. Hope decided to try to disassemble it in front of everybody to see just how it was put together.

"What are you doing?" Dianne exclaimed, as E. Hope began tugging on her garment, lifting up the hem in the back.

"I just wanted to see how it was made," replied E. Hope.

"Watch out! You're about to expose me to the world," Dianne joked, as she jerked the dress back down behind her.

The club also contributed to a number of service organizations in the community. The Red Cross always sponsored Cookie Day for the veterans at the VA Hospital in Pineville at Christmas and Easter. The FHA members baked cookies for those occasions for several years.

The Salvation Army provided dolls and toys for needy children at Christmas. They held Dress-a-Doll and Dress-a-Bear competitions in which people selected dolls and stuffed bears and made clothes for them. Dianne asked the students to sign up for the number of dolls or bears they wanted to be responsible for, and then she picked them up. The students did excellent work, and several of them received certificates of recognition for having the most original outfits at the Salvation Army's "Thank-You" luncheon.

Dianne usually made a few outfits for the dolls and bears, too. One year she decided to dress two sets of twin bears. She made matching dresses for the girl bears and jokingly named them "LaTasha" and "LaTonya" after two of her favorite students, LaTasha Williams and LaTonya Haynes. The boy bears were outfitted with vests, pants, and little caps, all made from blue material. She named them "Jeff" and "Jon" after Geoffrey Litton, who declared himself her adopted son, and her real son, Jonathan.

One year the club sponsored a family for Christmas through The Shepherd Center in Alexandria. They requested a family with a single mother and several children. It was one of their biggest and most important projects ever undertaken. Dianne wasn't sure if they could do it, but the members, as always, came through. They furnished toys, clothes, presents, and food for the entire family. After the items were boxed up by club members, Dianne delivered them to a very grateful family just before Christmas.

Another year the members decided to do something for the children at the Huey P. Long Hospital in Pineville. They made valentine baskets and filled them with treats for the children. Then they personally delivered the goodies to the hospital, visiting with the children and reading stories to them.

One of the favorite activities of the club for a number of years was their annual bus trip to the Masonic Children's Home in Alexandria. They sponsored parties at different times of the year, sometimes at Christmas, and other times at Valentine's Day or even May Day. During every visit they furnished food for the children and played games with them. When Tina St. Andrie was the club president, they made each child a personalized Christmas stocking filled with goodies. They always received "Thank You" notes signed by the children and their housemothers. It was a rewarding experience for both Dianne and the club members, knowing they had done something to brighten an underprivileged child's day.

The club always observed National FHA Week, which occurred the second week in February. They planned for a different activity every school day of that week, and those who participated could earn merit point towards being selected as outstanding FHA member for the year. Monday was Publicity Day. FHA members made posters illustrating the national FHA theme for the year and displayed them around the school. Tuesday was Badge Day. Members had to wear badges with their name and the FHA theme. Wednesday was Red-and-White Day. Those members wearing red-and-white, the official FHA colors, got merit points for doing so. Thursday was Teacher Appreciation Day. They provided refreshments for the teachers, either with a tea after school or food in the teachers' lounge for teachers to eat at their break time. Friday was School Spirit Day. Since the boys' basketball team always got so much attention, the FHA members decided to do something for the girls' team, the Lady Rebs. Some years they provided each team member and coach Jackie LaBorde with a small basket of goodies, and other years they decorated the girls' lockers on game day.

"Mrs. Lundy, you have no idea how excited the girls were to get those goodies. They thought it was Christmas. It really meant a lot to them," Jackie told Dianne.

National FHA Week always resulted in a lot of extra work for Dianne. Not only did she have to coordinate the activities, but she had to keep up with the students' merit points. She felt it was worth the effort, though, because the students were learning leadership skills and developing a sense of responsibility.

Whether by bus, van, or car, the FHA members loved to travel, and travel they did. They attended every parish FHA meeting, almost every district meeting, and some state meetings while Dianne was the adviser. Although most of the trips went smoothly, some problems did develop.

The parish officers and everyone taking part in the program were expected to attend a practice session on the day before the actual meeting. Dianne would usually carry all of the Pineville participants to the practice session in her car. One year there were too many people going to fit comfortably in a car, so she signed up for the Rebel van. When she went to collect the keys at lunch time, they were nowhere to be found.

"Coach William Broussard was the last person to use the van yesterday, and he didn't return the keys. He's not here today, and I don't have a spare key. This is not the first time he's done this," said assistant principal Ralph Kees.

"What am I supposed to do? We have to be there," Dianne declared, almost in a panic.

"All I can tell you is to take your car. Will all of your students fit into it?" he inquired.

"I don't know, but we'll give it a try. It will be a tight fit," she told him.

Dianne informed the students of the situation and got the response she expected.

"You've got to be kidding! How will ten people fit into your car?" they exclaimed.

"Well, it's either that or don't go, so we have to give it a try. My car is pretty big," she replied, hoping she wasn't being overly optimistic.

They gathered their materials for the meeting and headed out to Dianne's 1978 brown Pontiac Grand Prix. Everyone eyed the car doubtfully.

"Okay, climb in and let's see if we can shut the doors," Dianne instructed.

Six students squeezed onto the back seat with some sitting in other people's laps. That left four more students plus Dianne for the front seat. Someway, though she never figured out just how, they managed it.

"Let's just hope we don't meet any cops on the way, because this is definitely illegal," she commented, as she started the car and put it into gear. She eased onto the street slowly, with the car's under carriage barely clearing the curb.

Dianne had been to Oak Hill High, the place where the meeting was being held, on several occasions. She was pretty sure she knew how to get there. But when they hit Highway 28 West out of Alexandria, she began to have doubts.

"Does anybody know how far we're supposed to go before we turn off this road?" she inquired.

"No, we don't. You're the teacher. You're supposed to know," was the reply.

"There's a convenience store up ahead. Let's stop there, and one of you get out and ask them if they know how to get to Oak Hill High from here," she said.

One of the girls managed to extract herself from the pile and came back with a report.

"They said to keep going until you come to an intersection. Turn left there," she told the group.

They drove for a few miles and found the intersection. Dianne, who had been highly nervous about driving so many students, relaxed a bit. Before long, she realized she didn't know how far to go on the new road before turning again to find the school.

They drove until it seemed as if they had been going forever, with the school nowhere in sight. Then Dianne spotted a small grocery store.

"We're going to stop here and ask for directions again. Otherwise, we might end up somewhere in Mississippi," she said.

"Take the next road on the left," reported another girl who had been drafted to ask for directions.

They arrived at the school shortly afterwards. Two boys were waiting as they pulled up by the front entrance. The girls, who were a little stiff and sore from the cramped conditions, climbed out of the car one by one.

"Wow, y'all look just like one of those little clown cars at the circus where people just keep comin' and comin' out of nowhere!" one of the boys exclaimed.

And we pretty much feel like a bunch of clowns at this point, Dianne thought, as they hurried towards the auditorium.

They were greeted by cheers as they entered the facility.

"There they are," exclaimed Gerry Craft, the Rapides High adviser.

"Where have y'all been? We called the school, and they said you left at noon," said Sandra Melder, the adviser from Oak Hill.

"We were worried about you," added the Glenmora adviser, Wanda Johnson.

"We got lost," Dianne replied.

They made it through the practice session and headed back to school, arriving just minutes before the final bell to dismiss classes. The front parking lot was full, as usual.

The only parking spot left was one at the end of the student parking section at the corner of Line and Payne Streets. Dianne managed to maneuver her car into the tight space.

"I'm not too crazy about parking way down here. I just hope nothing happens to my car," she commented.

"Oh, Mrs. Lundy, nobody's going to mess with your car," said Tonya Kees.

"I hope not," Dianne replied.

When she came out later to head home, something didn't look right about the car. Closer examination showed that someone had stolen one of the protective vinyl strips off the right side.

Well, that makes the perfect end to a perfectly crazy day! Dianne thought, as she climbed into the car and headed home, tired to the bone.

———

Trips to the district meetings in Natchitoches also proved to be memorable. On one occasion the club decided to sit in the middle of the auditorium just underneath the edge of the balcony. Jane Middleton, one of the members, peered upwards towards the balcony.

"Mrs. Lundy, there's somebody sitting right over you with their feet propped up on the edge of the balcony. They have their shoes halfway off, too. If one of those shoes comes off, it's going to hit you right in the head," she said.

"Tell you what—you keep an eye on it, and if it starts to drop, let me know, and I'll duck," Dianne replied.

Jane couldn't get that shoe out of her mind the whole meeting. She kept looking up and nearly burst out laughing several times. Fortunately, the shoe never dropped, and Dianne managed to keep her cool.

During the time the club's enrollment was quite large, they used the Rebel bus to provide transportation to the district meetings. But when their numbers declined, they began sharing a bus with other schools. One year they went with the Bolton FHA, which was under the guidance of Mrs. Nancy Bradford. About halfway to Natchitoches, Dianne's bra came unhooked when she leaned forward. She compensated for the problem by sitting up straight in her seat for the rest of the trip. Since there were boys on the bus, she had to wait until they got to Northwestern to fix it. Another year they teamed up with Tioga's FHA whose adviser was Mrs. Barbara Johnson. That year the bus driver broke the bus mirror when he hit a tree limb as he swung the bus around the narrow streets on the Northwestern campus.

"At least I didn't hit a car," he cheerfully informed his passengers.

Although Dianne was perfectly content to sit back and let someone else do the driving, the decreasing membership in the club eventually made it financially impossible for them to afford a large bus. Dianne drove the group herself in the Rebel van for several years. When it was put out of commission due to age, she had to find other means of transportation.

She began renting a van from some of the local car dealerships. One year a serious problem occurred after they reached Natchitoches. She parked the van to let the students out and went in to pick up the registration packet. Then she went back outside to move the van because the parking space was restricted, and she didn't want to get a ticket. When she turned the key, the van wouldn't start. She went in and told the girls what had happened.

"My brother goes to Northwestern, and he knows something about engines. I'll see if I can call him to come over and take a look at it," said club member Tia Wysinger.

Dianne and Tia walked to the student center to make the call. Dianne also called the car dealership to let them know about the problem.

"I'm stranded up here with ten girls. If I can't get it started, we have no way to get home," she informed them. After further consultation, Dianne found out the van had been giving them trouble, but they thought they had the problem fixed. The dealer told her to call him if they couldn't get it running, and he would make arrangements to send another van to pick them up.

Fortunately, the boy managed to fix the problem, which turned out to be a loose battery terminal. Dianne ended up missing half of the morning session, but she didn't care. The main thing was to be able to get the students back to Pineville safely.

That was her last trip driving a van. After that, she decided to take only a few FHA members in her car. Those who earned the most merit points had the first choice of attending. Since the students viewed any day off from school as a holiday, she didn't have any trouble finding volunteers.

Eventually, the Rapides Parish School Board began requiring anyone using a private vehicle to transport students to school events to have at least a million dollars' worth of liability insurance.

"A million dollars' worth of insurance. You've got to be joking. There's no way we can afford that!" Rick exclaimed when she told him about the new policy.

Salvation appeared through the Louisiana Vocational Teachers'

Association. Dianne discovered they offered such a policy to their members for only seventy-five dollars a year. She joined the organization and was covered for the one-million-dollar liability.

"I never thought I'd be taking out that much insurance," she observed to some of her fellow teachers.

———

The club also made several pleasure trips at the end of the year. One year they toured the French Quarter in New Orleans and then went to the fun park at Lake Pontchartrain Beach. Another year they voted to go to the beach at Galveston, Texas. The most popular trip, however, was the one to Astroworld in Houston.

The students earned money to pay for the trips through fund-raising events. They sold everything from magazines to Christmas cards, but they soon discovered the easiest and fastest way to make money was through candy sales. Students at Pineville High School were always hungry, so the candy went quickly. They didn't particularly care what kind of candy it was, as long as it was food.

Most of the trips went off without a hitch. Sometimes, though, problems did occur. One year Dianne got wind that a student who was not in FHA planned to sneak on the bus and hide in the restroom until they were too far out of town to put her off. She nipped that plot in the bud by announcing to all of her classes that the bus would be searched for intruders before they left town. Her plan evidently worked because there was nobody hiding on the bus when she followed through with her search plan before the bus pulled out of the parking lot.

They always carried several ice chests filled with cokes for students to drink during the trip. Since they had to leave Pineville High at 4:30 in the morning, Dianne had to get up extra early to ice down the drinks and put them into her car trunk. One year she was out on the carport loading the ice chests into her car when the neighbors' dog began barking. The dog knew everybody in the neighborhood and considered it her duty to try to protect all of the houses in that vicinity. Dianne wasn't too worried until the dog came closer and closer, barking loudly the whole time. Before long, it was halfway up her driveway.

Great, I hope I don't get bitten by a dog before I even get started on the trip, she thought. In desperation, she called the dog's name loudly. "Taffy, stop all of that barking," she yelled. The dog immediately ceased barking and trotted back to its own yard, satisfied that Dianne wasn't a burglar, after all.

Once they got to Astroworld and had the students safely deposited inside, everybody was on their own. Students were instructed to always stay with at least one other FHA member. They were given a specific time to report back to the gate to be checked out before getting back on the bus to leave.

Dianne and the other chaperones amused themselves by attending the shows, visiting souvenir shops, and going on some of the tamer rides. They were usually tired after lunch and tried to find a place to sit down and rest. If the weather was good, they opted for one of the many benches scattered around the park. One year Dianne and Peggy decided to sit under a tree so they would be out of the sun. They were relaxing and watching the crowd go by when Dianne suddenly felt something hit her left shoulder. She glanced at it and discovered she had been hit with bird poop.

"I can't believe a bird just messed up my clothes," she complained, as she picked the offending blob off her shoulder. "Thank goodness it was hard instead of runny."

"Just be glad it landed on your shirt and not in your hair," noted Peggy.

———

For a number of years, the club held an end-of-the-year Mother-Daughter Banquet. Club members could use any money left over after their trips to pay their banquet fees.

It was a semi-formal occasion during which awards were presented and officers for the following year were installed. The club used a variety of locations for the event, including Holiday Inn, Louisiana College, Piccadilly Cafeteria, and the Plantation Manor Restaurant. Eventually, it was discontinued due to decreasing membership.

In their final few years they held an end-of-the-year party instead. Some of their favorite outings included Chuck E. Cheese's, Red Lobster, Ryan's Steakhouse, and Taco Bell. Dianne rarely found a member who turned down a free meal. It was their last fling of the year.

———

Declining membership did have its advantages. Dianne got to know the FHA members a lot better and became quite close to some of them. Two girls, Debra Cazes and Vickie Roach, served as officers at both the local and parish levels for two years. Vickie, who was the Pineville FHA president during her senior year, was also elected their FHA Sweetheart that year. She entered the Golden Yam contest for several years and finally won at the local level her senior year. Although she didn't win the parish contest, her family nicknamed her "The Yam Queen," a title that became a standing joke between them and Dianne. The club also sponsored Vickie and Debra, along with Renee Scroggs, at the state FHA annual summer camp in Bunkie, Louisiana.

Other members Dianne would never forget included Patricia Garren, who participated in a number of STAR contests and eventually worked her way up to the office of club president. Christy Hughes, one of the most faithful FHA members who enrolled in every home economics course the school offered, was elected treasurer and then vice president. She also served as the parish secretary. Nicole Dunkley, who won the district Junior Job Interview contest, was another of the club's presidents and was elected FHA sweetheart during her senior year. The three Clayton sisters were some of the most active members. Lavonne won the Junior Job Interview contest at the parish level. Virginia and Angelia both served as club presidents. LaTonya Haynes, who served as the club president for two years, was another of the FHA sweethearts. She also won first place in the parish yam contest with her Yam Streusel Cheesecake. The only two Senior Job Interview contestants who won at the parish level were Robyn Jones and Delonda Woods. Robyn won the district contest and went to the state competition, the only Pineville member to achieve that status. Delonda, who failed to place at the district level, was elected club president during her senior year.

In 1982-83, the club gained its first male member, Michael Meeks, who was elected parliamentarian. The following year he also became the FHA Beau. His membership paved the way for other males to join the club. Some of the male members included Kevin Blade, Marcus Mallet, Benny Norwood, Tyrone Richardson, Demetrics Viree, and Freeman Young. Marcus, the only male who stayed in FHA for three years, received a special award of recognition on Awards Day during his senior year.

By 1999 the club had only a handful of members, all senior girls. The parish competition had also dwindled to just three schools—Pineville, Glenmora, and Rapides High. Dianne took it as a sign from above that it was time to dissolve the club. She called in the members, including Leanne Richardson, Jecole Roland, Natasha Williams, and Delonda Woods, and broke the news to them.

"Aw, Mrs. Lundy, I can't believe you're doing away with our club," exclaimed Delonda, the most outspoken member of the group.

"You're all seniors, and there's nobody left to pass the torch to. Besides that, the national organization is changing the name from FHA to FCCLA, and it's just not the same."

"FCCLA—what's that?" asked Jecole.

"It stands for Family, Community, and Career Leaders of America. Our organization is one of the oldest youth groups in the United States. We've been in existence over fifty years, and now they want to change the name. I don't agree with it, and it just doesn't seem right. The Pineville High club was started by Mrs. Frankie Skeeles in 1952. We've always been known as FHA, and that's how we will end our club. It's the right way to go out of the picture," Dianne explained.

The girls nodded in agreement. Dianne was somewhat saddened by the turn of events. She had a lot of good memories about the years she had worked with FHA. Under her leadership, the club had won the Award of Excellence, the top award for club achievement at the state level, four times. During the final parish meeting, Dianne and advisers Gerry Craft, Wanda Johnson, and Sandra Melder, were nominated as lifetime honorary FHA members.

It had been a long journey, but a worthwhile one. She had no regrets, just fond recollections about her years as the Pineville High FHA adviser.

Chapter 8

A number of students Dianne taught got themselves into trouble with the administration, some of them through their own doings, and some who were turned in by her. One day she stopped at the water fountain by the front office to get a drink of water just before sixth hour. As she was waiting in line behind several of the students, she overheard a conversation between two boys. They were planning to meet on the back parking lot to leave school and skip their sixth-hour class.

Dianne walked back to the office and reported the conversation to assistant principal Ralph Kees. He took down their names and told her he would take care of the problem.

The next day she saw him in the office.

"Did you find out anything about those two boys?" she inquired.

"They weren't in sixth hour, and they didn't check out, so they got caught for skipping class. They couldn't figure out how I knew about it," he reported.

"Sometimes it pays to keep your eyes and ears open," she said.

On another occasion the students in one of her Home Ec. I classes told her one of the girls was skipping class.

"She's been hiding in the restroom all day, Mrs. Lundy," they said.

Dianne reported the incident to Mr. Kees at lunch time.

"I'll check into it," he responded.

The next day she learned the girl had been caught when Mr. Kees called her father to confirm that she had not attended school all day.

"He wanted to know how I knew about it. I said one of her teachers turned her in, but I didn't mention your name," he told her.

"Let's just leave it a mystery," she responded.

Over the years, Dianne had pretty well learned how to predict when some students would be absent. Some never came on Mondays, and others never came on Fridays, giving themselves a three-day weekend. Still others could always be counted on to be absent whenever a test was scheduled. A few students were rarely absent, so whenever they were, she became concerned. Such was the case with Dean Greer, a ninth-grader who was one of her better students. After he had been absent for three days, she began to inquire if anybody knew what his problem was, but the other students had no answer. She thought maybe he had come down with the flu.

Dean returned to class the following week with an admit that listed five days as unexcused and the other three days as suspensions.

"What happened? I was worried about you. I thought you were sick," she told him.

"Naw, I got suspended," he replied.

"Suspended—whatever for?" Dianne inquired.

"Well, I decided to skip. I came to school every day, and then I caught the bus and went up to Natchitoches," he explained.

"What did you do in Natchitoches?" she asked.

"Oh, nothin' much. Just walked around."

"Didn't that get a little boring?" she continued to quiz him.

"Yeah, after a couple of days, but I just kept doing it, and then I got caught."

"Well, I certainly hope you learned your lesson," she said.

"I did, and I don't think I'll be skipping school anymore," he admitted.

A senior boy named Lionell Dorsey was also responsible for his own problems. Lionell was not one of Dianne's better students. He was barely passing, but he was usually in class and never caused any problems. Seniors were allowed to attend senior day at the local colleges to help them make their college selections. On the day Louisiana College sponsored their senior day, Lionell was absent. He returned to class the following day with one of their programs in hand.

"I went to college yesterday. I wasn't on the list to attend, so I brought back a program, and I had one of the speakers sign it to prove I was there," he told Dianne.

She looked at the program doubtfully, as he waved it under her nose.

"Okay, Lionell, if you say so," she responded.

Dianne complained to Denny Carlyon, one of the guidance counselors about the incident.

"Lionell Dorsey isn't even college material. Why was he attending senior day at Louisiana College?" she asked.

"Oh, he didn't really go. He just skipped school that day," Mrs. Carlyon replied.

"What about his signed program?"

"He had somebody else sign that program for him. It was a forgery."

Dianne wasn't too surprised when Lionell was suspended a couple of days later for skipping school. *When you lie, it usually catches up with you later,* she reasoned.

That wasn't the only time one of her students got in trouble for something they had forged. Dianne took up notebooks in all her classes every six weeks. When she was grading them, she often came upon some strange things students had written.

When she was grading Nathaniel Lemott's notebook she noticed he had been practicing writing assistant principal Ralph Kees' name on several pages. She mentioned this to Mr. Kees while she still had the notebook in her possession.

"He writes just like you do," she told him.

"Nobody can write like I do," Mr. Kees declared.

"I promise you, this boy does. He has your signature down perfectly."

"I'd like to see that. Bring his notebook down to me."

Dianne promptly fetched the notebook from her room and handed it to Mr. Kees, opening it to the pages with his signature.

He took a long, hard look before he said anything. "That's pretty good," he observed. "I think I'll just keep this notebook, and I'll be having a little talk with Nathaniel."

Dianne never found out what transpired between the two, but it was the last time she saw a principal's name written in Nathaniel's notebook.

Finding notes and even love letters in students' notebooks was nothing new. In fact, Dianne was used to it. Often they gave her insight about the students' way of thinking and their life outside the classroom. She had become pretty hardened to the callous language sometimes used, but one girl's writings stood out among the rest.

The notebook belonged to Tiffany Forrester, a cute girl who was very popular with the other students. In fact, she was elected class favorite for several years' running. Dianne was shocked when she found a set of notes filled with four-letter words and graphic descriptions of sexual acts in Tiffany's notebook. She carried the notebook to the office and showed it to Mr. Kees.

"I can hardly believe this. Did you know that girl's daddy is a preacher? I never thought she would be capable of anything like this," he exclaimed.

"Well, there it is, right in front of you," said Dianne.

"Let me keep this notebook, and I will have a conference with her," he decided.

Mother always said teachers' and preachers' children were the worst ones to teach, Dianne reflected, as she headed back to class.

———

Sometimes it was students' clothing or appearance that caused the problems. One year Jerrie Wilder, a girl with bleached blonde hair, decided to spray paint her hair orange for Halloween. She came to school the next day with the orange dye still in her hair. The day afterwards, she was absent.

"They put Jerrie out because of her hair color," reported one of her classmates.

Jerrie came back the following day. Her hair was still orange, but it was a lighter shade.

"The principals told me I have to get all of the orange dye out of my hair before I come back again," she told Dianne.

Several days later she returned with noticeable lighter hair, but it still had a slight orange streak. She brought a note from a beautician.

"This is to inform you that I have done all I can with Jerrie's hair. If I bleach it any more, it may break or fall out entirely," the note read.

"They still aren't satisfied," Jerrie lamented.

The following week she walked into Dianne's class with black hair.

"I see you've solved the problem," Dianne commented.

"Yes, and I hope this makes the principals happy," said Jerrie.

"Just don't dye it purple and green for Mardi Gras," Dianne warned her jokingly.

"The next time I think I'll just wear a wig," Jerrie replied.

———

The Rapides Parish School Board had established a dress code, and teachers at Pineville High were supposed to check students' apparel in their first hour classes every morning. Since Dianne did not have a first hour class for a number of years, she rarely had to worry about violations. Sometimes, students managed to skate by either wearing a jacket to cover up inappropriate tops or by rolling their skirt waistbands down for dress code check and then rolling them back up again after they left that teacher's class.

Occasionally, Dianne discovered a violation when a student walked into the room. One day in sixth hour sewing lab, she found a student who had made it through the entire day with a tee shirt that should have never left home.

The students had gotten their materials out of the cabinet and were busily engaged in sewing when one boy called out to Dianne from the back of the room.

"Mrs. Lundy, I can't concentrate with this tee shirt that Nancy Shelton is wearing," he complained.

"What's wrong with it?" Dianne asked.

"It's just bothering me," he replied.

Dianne decided she had better see for herself what all the fuss was about. She walked to the back of the room where Nancy was standing at one of the ironing boards. She had put her jacket on over the tee shirt.

"Let me see the tee shirt, Nancy," she instructed.

"No!" Nancy exclaimed, pulling the jacket tighter around her chest.

"You might as well let me see. If you don't I will have to send you to the office," Dianne told her, as she reached over and opened up the jacket.

For a moment she stood there, just soaking in what was before her eyes. The tee shirt contained cartoon sketches of bunnies having sex in various positions.

"What in the world would possess you to wear something like this to school? I can't believe your mother let you leave the house wearing that!" Dianne exclaimed.

The girl had nothing to say. She stood with downcast eyes, as her cheeks began to turn red.

"I told you it was bad," the boy insisted.

"Well, Nancy, I have no choice now but to send you to the office. You know you are not supposed to wear anything like that to school," Dianne informed her, shaking her head as she headed back to her desk to get out a form for dress code violations.

It was also a violation of the school's policy for students to sleep in class. Although Dianne usually woke them up, occasionally she let them sleep just to see what transpired. One day a boy named Roland Dugger fell asleep in her second hour class. He woke up when the next class came into the room.

After he left, Dianne made an announcement to the third hour class.

"The next time you see Roland sleeping, come in very quietly. Let's don't wake him up, and we'll see what happens," she told them.

A few days later, there was a repeat incident. This time, the third hour students tiptoed in and sat down. Dianne conducted class in the usual manner, and Roland continued sleeping. Suddenly, in the middle of third hour he woke up and looked around, completely bewildered.

"Boy, you in the wrong class. This is the middle of third hour," said the girl sitting behind him.

Roland jumped up and took off running, much to the amusement of the other students. Dianne reported the incident to the principal, Mrs. Evelyn Sisco.

"The next time he sleeps through the bell, send somebody down to get me," she told Dianne.

They didn't have to wait long. Less than a week later, the boy fell asleep again and didn't wake up. Dianne sent a note to Mrs. Sisco, who promptly appeared in the doorway just after the tardy bell rang.

Mrs. Sisco walked over to his desk and called his name. "Roland. Roland, get up and come with me."

The boy raised his head, and blood began dripping from his nose onto the desk top. At that point, Dianne was pretty sure he was on drugs and was probably snorting cocaine.

He never returned to class. Dianne later learned that his parents had sent him to a drug rehab facility in another state.

Well, maybe I did him a favor by turning him in, she reasoned.

———————

Other students were expelled as a result of Dianne turning them into the office. One day she had to walk down to the home ec. kitchen to get a sandwich bag of ice for a student who had been injured elsewhere in school. She warned her class to be quiet while she was gone.

"If I can identify your voice while I'm walking down the hall, I am going to write you up for disturbing class," she threatened.

She wasn't too surprised moments later when she heard someone yelling as she exited the kitchen, ice bag in hand. It was undoubtedly Monchondria Riley, a student whose voice she was quite familiar with, having been unsuccessful in getting the girl to stop talking during class for the entire year. She stepped back into the room just in time to hear the end of a heated discussion.

"I told you I didn't want to hear any yelling while I was out of the room. Monchondria, I distinctly heard your voice, and now I am going to have to send you to the office," she said, as she handed the icepack to the student office worker who had been sent to fetch it.

Monchondria had already been suspended three times, so she was subject to an automatic expulsion for her fourth offense. Dianne hadn't realized how much the girl had actually talked until she was gone. It was a peaceful end to the year in that class.

That wasn't the only time a student got expelled for yelling in Dianne's class. Another year she taught a boy named Aaron Stafford in Home Ec. I. He was not a very strong student, but Dianne had been working with him, trying to help him pass. Still, he couldn't seem to stay out of trouble. One day he stopped in front of one of the fans Dianne always kept sitting on one of the tables. The fan was running because it was hot that day. He began shouting into the fan at the top of his lungs.

Dianne had already warned him about such actions. "All right, Aaron. I have told you about yelling into the fan. Now I am going to have to write you up for disturbing class," she told him.

She learned the next day that Aaron was being expelled because he had already been suspended three times. She thought she had seen the last of him. Two years later she was surprised to see him walk through the door, back into another Home Ec. I class.

"I can't believe they sent you back to my class after you got expelled for yelling into one of the fans," she told him.

"That was a long time ago. Now I'm trying to pass so I can graduate," he told her.

"As long as you do your work, it shouldn't be a problem," she responded.

He managed to pass the second go-round and graduated with his classmates.

At least I know I won't be seeing him for a third year, Dianne reflected, as she recorded his final grade.

One student got into trouble for throwing ice in the cooking lab. Students had been complaining about being hit with ice cubes during lab, but Dianne had been unable to catch the culprit. She finally figured out which kitchen the ice had been coming from, so she came up with a plan. After the lab had started and all the students were busily working, she pretended to be tidying up the supply table in the middle of the lab. In reality, she was keeping an eye on the suspected kitchen, hoping to catch the guilty party in action. She didn't have to wait long.

From the corner of her eye, she managed to catch one of the

boys throwing ice. It was Demoris Newton, a boy who had been a constant source of trouble in both the classroom and during cooking labs. *Why am I not surprised?* she wondered.

"Okay, Demoris, I saw that!" she exclaimed.

"Saw what? I wasn't doin' nothin'," he protested.

"I definitely saw you throwing ice cubes. You know that is a violation of lab policy. It's also dangerous. You could injure somebody with an ice cube. I'm going to have to send you to the office," she informed him.

Demoris, it turned out, had already been suspended three times, so he, too, was expelled and sent to the Rapides Parish Redirection Academy. Students who attended the academy were required to wear military uniforms and perform marching drills each day.

"Boy, Mrs. Lundy, it was sure mean of you to get Demoris expelled," one student told her a few days later. "He's crying and saying he can't be doing all of that marching every day."

"Too bad. He should have thought of that before he acted up in class," Dianne replied, thinking that at least one student had met his just rewards.

<hr>

Once, Dianne took pity on a student and actually saved him from being expelled. Lonnie Sheppard, a senior male student, had signed up for two home economics classes. He was a pleasant student who made fairly decent grades, and Dianne enjoyed having him in her class. During the second semester, he got a job and had a hard time staying awake in class. Dianne endured it but had warned him that such actions would leave her no choice but to send him to the office.

About a week before graduation, he fell asleep for the second time in the same class period. Dianne woke him and handed him a discipline referral form.

"I'm sorry, Lonnie, but I have told you for the last time to stay up and awake during class," she said.

"Aw, Mrs. Lundy, do you have to send me to the office? I promise I'll stay awake from now on."

"It's too late. You've already been written up. Now you have to face the consequences," she replied.

A few minutes later, the class let out for lunch. Dianne heard a knock on her door. She opened it and was surprised to see Lonnie.

"Mrs. Lundy, you've got to help me. Mr. Prestridge said he's going to expel me because I've already been suspended three times. If I get expelled, I won't get to graduate with my class. He said for me to talk to you to see if you could give me a report for punish work so I won't have to be expelled," Lonnie pleaded.

"Okay, Lonnie, I'll assign you a report, but it has to be longer than five hundred words. You will have to write a seven-hundred-and-fifty-word report on "The Food Pyramid," she decided.

"Thank you so much, Mrs. Lundy. I'll have it for you the first thing tomorrow morning," he promised. "Now can you write a note to Mr. Prestridge letting him know that I can do a report?"

"All right, all right, here you go," said Dianne, as she hastily scribbled the requested note. "Now would you please get out of here so I can eat my lunch?"

In a school the size of Pineville High, fights were a common occurrence. Sometimes Dianne found herself right in the middle of them. One day when she was on hall duty in the middle of second wing, she heard a loud disturbance. Two girls were engaged in a shouting match. Dianne marched down the hall to confront them. By that time, the argument had escalated.

Just as she reached the pair, the two girls began swinging at one another. Dianne stepped between them to break up the fight. One of the girls managed to stab the other one with a ballpoint pen, drawing blood at the point of impact.

"Both of you go to the office," Dianne directed, as she followed them down the hall.

"I've got a fight," she announced, as they stepped into the office door. At that point, the girl who had been stabbed passed out and collapsed in the doorway.

It was then Dianne noticed her own clothing had been spattered with blood. She had worn a white blouse to have her picture made on picture day.

"You'd better go into the bathroom and get cleaned up. Then you can come back and fill out a report," said the principal, Mr. Homer Crouch.

"I guess you're right. There's no way I'll be getting my picture made today," she observed.

That wasn't the only time she stopped two girls from fighting. During a fifth-hour Home and Family class, two girls began shouting at each other. They sat on opposite sides of the room. Before Dianne could stop them, one girl jumped up and ran over to where the other girl sat. Both girls were soon standing nose to nose, shouting at the top of their lungs.

Dianne walked over and pushed them apart. "Cut it out right now," she said, standing between them as she spoke. Neither girl appeared willing to back down, so she continued holding them apart.

"Somebody go and get one of the principals," she instructed.

Several minutes later, Mr. Kees walked into the room, taking in the sight of Dianne still standing between the two girls, holding them off each other.

"Don't say another word. Both of you get your books and come with me right now down to my office," he told the girls.

Dianne never did find out what caused the fight, but it was the last time the two girls tangled during her class.

Another fight between two girls occurred in the middle of

one of the sewing labs. Laura McCobbie, one of Dianne's student teachers from Northwestern Louisiana State University, was actually in charge of the class at the time. Dianne had walked to the back of the room to help some students with their sewing projects. Suddenly, she became aware that something was not right in the front of the room. She spotted two females down on the floor, rolling around under the sewing machines. For a split second, she thought somebody had attacked her student teacher. Then she realized it was two of the students.

Before she could find out what the ruckus was about, Mrs. McLaurin, one of the teacher aides, stuck her head in the door.

"Mrs. Lundy, do you need some help?" she inquired.

"Looks like I've got a fight on my hands," Dianne replied.

"Well, I'm on my way to the office, and it sounds like you might need some help. I'll send one of the principals down here," said Mrs. McLaurin.

"Thanks, I would appreciate it," Dianne told her, as she headed towards the front of the room to break up the fight.

Together, she and Laura managed to pull the girls apart. They weren't hurt, but the sewing lab was a little worse for wear.

"I guess we won't be seeing you two for a few days," she informed the students.

———

What would probably go down as the most famous fight between girls in the history of Pineville High occurred one morning before school started. Dianne was unaware that anything unusual had happened until she walked into the front office. Lacresha Easley, one of her students, was sitting in Mrs. Allgood's alcove, holding an ice bag to her eye.

"What's going on, Lacresha?" Dianne inquired.

"Mrs. Lundy, I don't know what happened. I was just bending down to get something out of my locker. The next thing I knew, a girl was on top of my back," Lacresha replied.

"There was a big fight involving a bunch of girls down on fifth wing," Mrs. Allgood interjected.

"Oh, really? How many students were fighting?" Dianne asked.

"I think there was something like fifteen or sixteen. I don't know for sure, but it was a lot," answered Mrs. Allgood.

By the end of the day, Dianne realized just how many of her students had been involved. Almost every one of her classes was missing one or two girls. Her fifth hour Home and Family class was the worst hit, with almost half the class being suspended for a week.

Well, I guess that's a fight that won't ever be forgotten. That's probably the most girls in the history of the school who have even been suspended for just one fight, she reflected.

———

Sometimes the students weren't actually involved in fighting. All they did was threaten other students. Such was the case one year in a Home and Family class. Dianne always showed the movie "The Burning Bed" to the class after midterm exams. She felt it was a good way to demonstrate how violence could affect family life.

As the movie was playing, she had to walk down to the home ec. kitchen, once again, to get some ice for an injured student. The class was usually pretty well-behaved, so she felt leaving them for a few minutes would be a safe thing to do. When she walked back into the room, she was greeted with a complaint from Freeman Goody, one of the male students.

"Mrs. Lundy, some of those girls are threatening to set me on fire like that woman did to her husband in the movie," he said.

"Oh, don't be silly, Freeman, how are they going to set you on fire?" Dianne inquired.

"They said they have a lighter, and they are going to use it on me," he said.

"And just which girls would that be?" asked Dianne.

Freeman proceeded to name off the girls, citing two of the most reliable students in the class.

"Well, what about it, girls? Did you threaten to set Freeman on fire?" Dianne quizzed them.

"Oh, Mrs. Lundy, he's just making that up. You know we would never do anything like that," they responded, giggling as they spoke.

Dianne wasn't totally convinced, and the rest of the year Freeman referred to the group as "The Burning Bed Girls," still insisting they had threatened to set him on fire.

———

Fights didn't always have to be broken up by physical means. Sometimes just the presence of a teacher was enough to keep students from fighting. One of Dianne's Home Ec. I classes had two boys who positively despised one another. They never got along, and one day in the sewing lab they began having a shouting match just before bell time.

Dianne walked over to them and tried her usual technique of discouraging fights.

"Okay, guys, no fighting in class. Calm down," she told them.

The boys totally ignored her and continued shouting as they moved closer together. They were about to start exchanging blows.

Dianne could visualize the damage that might be done to the sewing machines should such a fight occur. In desperation, she tried one more thing.

She got right in their faces and yelled, "Hey!" at the top of her voice. It worked, because both boys looked at her, apparently surprised that she could actually produce such a volume of sound.

"Okay, I'm going to have to report both of you to the office when the bell rings," she informed them in a calmer voice.

She later learned that her "Hey" had been heard all the way down the hall by some students in another classroom.

"It didn't do my throat any good, but at least it stopped a fight," she noted to one of her fellow teachers.

———

A fight of a more serious nature also occurred in the sewing lab. The students had to walk from room ten into the sewing lab after roll check. Dianne was in the process of opening the lab door when a boy from another class walked by. He and Donavon Cooper, one of the students in Dianne's class, exchanged some words. She managed to get her class into the lab, and she thought the incident was over.

About that time, Donavon began arguing with Clemis Wright, another student in the class. Before Dianne could even move, the two boys began exchanging blows. Somehow, Dianne became trapped between the wall and a filing cabinet, right in the middle of the fight. Henry Bowers, another male student, managed to break up the battle just long enough for Dianne to escape. The boys continued brawling, traveling about the room, knocking over chairs and dislocating sewing machine cabinets in their wake.

By that time, Dianne realized she would not be able to stop them from fighting.

"Somebody go and get one of the principals," she instructed.

At that point, Donavon picked up a chair and began attacking Clemis, wildly swinging the chair in a circle. Dianne began to reach towards the chair every time it came by her, hoping to seize it before any real damage was done.

Some of the girls in the class began to scream, "Mrs. Lundy, watch out! Be careful!"

Determined to protect her other student, Dianne continued trying to grab the chair and finally managed to snag one of the legs as it swung by. Donavon dropped the chair, but continued to rain blows upon his opponent, who was matching him blow for blow.

"Mrs. Lundy, you could have been hurt," yelled Sherry Gentle.

"Yeah, Mrs. Lundy, we were scared for you," added Patsy Burns.

"Well, I couldn't let Donavon hit Clemis in the head with a chair," Dianne replied.

Just about that time assistant principal Roy Prestridge entered the room. "You guys stop fighting and come down to the office now," he told them.

He returned later to interview some of the students. Upon learning how the chair had been used, his decision was pretty well set.

"Using that chair as a weapon is an automatic expulsion. I don't think you will have to worry about Donavon for the rest of the year," he informed Dianne.

———

Of all the fights Dianne witnessed or broke up, one would always stand out among the rest in her memory. It occurred during one of her sixth hour Home Ec. I classes. The class had started out like any other day, with nothing apparently out of the ordinary. Then Adrian Tyson and Pete Shorter walked into the room, shouting at each other as they came through the door.

Pete walked to his desk, and Adrian followed him. It was almost time for the tardy bell, and other students were still entering the room. Dianne could see that something serious was about to develop.

"Okay, guys, let's break it up. We don't want to have a fight in the classroom," she said, as she approached the spot where they were standing.

Just as she got there, the two boys began swinging at each other. Dianne barely managed to jump back out of the way in time to avoid being hit. One of the other boys in class, Shaun Grimsley, who was a robust football player, tried to assist in breaking up the fight. He grabbed Adrian from behind and attempted to pull the boys apart. Pete kept swinging, and Shaun ended up with a bloody lip, causing him to release his hold on Adrian. By that time, Dianne realized that the fight was going to be bad.

"Somebody go and get one of the principals," she told the class. Two girls took off running down the hall. She was relieved to know help should soon be on the way.

By then, the rest of the class was in the room, and they were busy just trying to stay out of the way as the two boys worked their way across the room, regardless of what happened to be in their path. Desks were all askew, with some knocked completely over. One boy's head came in contact with one of the filing cabinets, leaving a dent in the side. Dianne had just gotten two new trash cans and a new chalkboard for the room. The two trash cans were completely flattened as the boys fell upon them. They got back up again and continued pushing and shoving each other across the room, making a long scratch across the face of the new chalkboard.

Dianne's briefcase, which contained her gradebook and some papers to be graded, was always kept on top of her desk. It was thrown completely across the room, with papers scattered everywhere in helter-skelter fashion. By that time, she was getting quite concerned one of the students would be seriously hurt. Help from the office seemed to be a long time coming, so she decided she needed to try an alternate course of action.

Her next-door neighbor was a male biology teacher named Greg Burns. As far as she knew, Greg wasn't afraid of anything, so he seemed the logical choice for someone to stop the fight.

She ran to his door and pounded on it frantically. Greg himself opened the door. He had apparently heard the fight, because he had a wild-eyed look that Dianne had never seen before.

"I've got a fight and I need some help," she told him.

He took off running, with Dianne following close behind. As they entered her room, she could see that the boys had fallen to the floor and rolled across the room, denting her metal magazine rack in the process. They were lodged up against the storage cabinet by her desk.

Greg got down on the floor, level with the students, following instructions in the teachers' handbook.

"I'm Mr. Burns, and I'm a teacher. Stop fighting now," he told them.

The boys ignored him and continued swinging at each other. He reached into the pile and began attempting to break them apart.

At that point, Dianne realized what danger he was in, and she began to pray silently, "Please, God, don't let anything happen to Mr. Burns."

Just about that time, the principal, Mr. Homer Crouch, and one of the assistant principals, Mr. Columbus Goodman, walked into the room. Between the three of them, they managed to separate the boys.

It took all three men to carry the boys out of the room and down to the office. Dianne and the other students began to straighten up the room and pick up the papers off the floor. The other assistant principal, Betty Tumminello, stepped into the room as Dianne was checking roll.

"I just came by to see if you were okay and if you needed any more help," said Betty.

"No, I think I've got it under control now," Dianne replied.

Later that afternoon, Dianne got an update from Irene Allgood.

"We could hear that fight all the way down in the office. We were scared for you," Irene told her. "It didn't actually stop after they got down here, either. Adrian jumped over Mr. Goodman's desk and grabbed his bolt cutters and tried to stab Pete in the throat with them."

"Well, I guess that means he'll be expelled," Dianne observed.

"No, I don't think they can expel him. He's an ADHD student, and they get special consideration. They have to let him back in," said Irene.

"Great, that means I'll be getting him back in class," Dianne lamented.

For once, luck was with her, and Adrian was assigned to another class. A few days later he and Pete got into another fight in the school cafeteria. Dianne never really knew what happened to them, but she heard through the grapevine Mr. Goodman loaded the boys into the back of his truck and hauled them home with instructions for them to stay there for the rest of the school year, which was only about a week away.

—~~~—

There were also times when students attacked Dianne, rather than fighting each other. One problem she encountered was girls who wanted to primp at the end of sewing labs. They were constantly dragging out compacts to apply makeup, as well as combing their hair and styling it with hairspray. Dianne had developed an allergy to perfumes and scented hairsprays, so she was constantly chastising students who used it in the classroom. One girl persisted in applying a peach-scented hairspray that caused Dianne to cough each time she inhaled it.

One day as the class was storing their materials in the supply cabinet, Dianne was standing in the front of the room, waiting to lock the cabinet. Before she knew what was happening, a boy ran up behind her and sprayed the back of her head with the offending peach-scented spray.

"What do you think you are doing?" she demanded to know, as she felt the back of her head and touched a wet spot. "I'm writing you up for an attack on a teacher. I'm allergic to that sort of stuff!"

She promptly pulled a disciplinary referral form out of her desk and proceeded to follow through with her threat. To her satisfaction, the boy was suspended for three days, but that didn't help her hair. It took her quite some time to get rid of the peach scent. Even with several shampooings, it was still there.

"Thank goodness it wasn't acid," she commented to one of her fellow teachers.

That wasn't the only time she was attacked in the sewing lab. In another class she had a student who had made it plain Dianne was not one of her favorite teachers. The girl had no patience for sewing and was always trying to hurry up and finish her projects. She was making a pair of shorts as her final project of the year. She brought them up to the front table for Dianne's inspection.

"The hem in these shorts is not right. You'll have to redo it," Dianne told her.

"Aw, do I have to? I don't care how they look. I just want to get through with them," the girl protested.

"If you're going to learn how to sew, you might as well learn the right way. It's not that much work. Just take out the hem and resew it," Dianne replied.

The girl snatched the shorts from Dianne's hand and swung them around, hitting Dianne in the back of the head in the process.

"You hit me in the head with those shorts! I'm going to write you up for that," Dianne exclaimed.

She filled out a discipline referral form and promptly sent the girl to the office. Soon afterwards, Roy Prestridge appeared at the door.

"I hear you've been attacked by a pair of shorts," he teased. "What happened?"

Dianne explained the situation to him. Roy told her he would have to check with several student witnesses. He was known as the Sherlock Holmes of the school because he regularly patrolled the halls with a pad and pen in his hand, taking notes whenever he investigated a disturbance.

"I always make sure I have all of the facts. That's why very few of our suspensions have been overturned by the school board," he once told Dianne.

The student witnesses supported Dianne's story, so the girl was suspended for three days, much to Dianne's satisfaction.

Another incident occurred in one of the Parenthood Ed. classes. Dianne was standing in front of the class just before bell time. She was about to make one final remark before the bell rang when she suddenly felt something wet and sticky on one side of her face. She looked up towards the ceiling, expecting to see something dripping down, but there was no sign of any kind of leak.

"Something just hit me in the face," she exclaimed, just as the bell rang.

She hurried down to the office where Mr. Columbus Goodman was standing and talking to one of the secretaries.

"Mr. G., you won't believe this, but some student just threw something and hit me in the face with it. I don't know what it is or who threw it, but it's starting to burn, and I think some if it got into my eye," she informed him.

Mr. George White, one of the civics teachers, was also in the office at the time.

"That's going to give you some grief later on today," he noted.

"I'll see what I can find out about it, but I'll need a list of students who were sitting near where you were when you got hit," Mr. Goodman said.

"I'll get it to you as soon as possible. Right now I have to go and try to wash this stuff off my face," Dianne told him.

Dianne furnished the list, and she waited anxiously to get the results of the investigation.

"You were hit with some of Kanisha Houston's baby's cough medicine. She brought it to school in a water gun. I'm suspending her for five days for an attack on a teacher," reported Mr. Goodman when Dianne saw him in the office after school was out.

"Well, thank heavens, it wasn't anything more deadly than that," Dianne observed.

———

The most serious attack occurred in one of the sixth hour Home Ec. I classes. The tardy bell had just rung, and Dianne was about to start class. One of the girls was standing beside her. Just as Dianne opened her mouth to say, "All right, students," she felt a sharp jab in her stomach.

"What are you doing? You just punched me in the stomach! I'm writing you up for that," she told the girl.

"Aw, I didn't really mean to hurt you. Please don't write me up," the girl said apologetically.

"It's too late. You have attacked a teacher in front of the entire class, so I have no choice," Dianne informed her, as she walked back to her desk for a discipline referral slip.

A short time later, as Dianne was checking roll, Betty Tumminello walked into the room.

"I need to speak to you outside for a minute," said Betty.

Dianne walked out into the hall.

"This is a very serious offense. Students who attack a teacher are now subject to expulsion," Betty told her.

"Well, I don't think the girl was really trying to hurt me," said Dianne.

"Do you have any witnesses who can confirm your story about being hit?" asked Betty.

"I don't know who saw it. Class hadn't really started, so most of them weren't looking up front," Dianne replied, as she scanned the room. "Maybe Cecil Hunter. He's sitting close enough to the front to possibly have seen something."

"Okay, let me talk to him, and then I'll have to see if there are any witnesses for the other side of the story. I'll get back to you on this later," Betty decided.

Betty's report showed that Cecil had supported Dianne's version of the incident. "Cecil Hunter states that Mrs. Lundy was struck in the stomach hard enough to lose her balance and lean forward," it read.

Thanks to Dianne's testimony that the girl was not really trying to hurt her, the punishment was a week's suspension, rather than an expulsion.

When the girl came back to class, she made a surprising admission. "I didn't mean to hurt you, Mrs. Lundy. I was just trying to get you to dance. I wanted to see you dance.

———

Not all the dangers Dianne encountered came from students. Sometimes it was the environment itself that caused the problems. The school was remodeled to improve energy conservation. Most of the windows were eliminated, and the upper-level windows were sealed off. During the process, the workers walking around on the roof loosened some of the ceiling tiles.

Bettye Watkins reported to Dianne that some of the ceiling tiles had fallen in her lecture room while she and her students were in the sewing lab. "We heard something that sounded like a bunch of people clapping. Then when I went back to my other room at lunch, the ceiling tiles had fallen all over the room. They had even hit the sink faucet and turned the water on."

"Wow, I guess it's a good thing you and the students weren't in there at the time," Dianne noted.

She had completely forgotten about the incident until later in the year. She always brought her lunch to school and stored it in one of the refrigerators in the home ec. kitchen. She usually sat at one of the supply tables in the middle of the kitchen to eat.

She was sitting there casually eating her lunch, when suddenly she heard a strange noise. It sounded like a bunch of people clapping. Bettye's story flashed into her mind, and she realized the ceiling was about to fall on her head. She jumped up and ran to the other side of the room just in time to see the tiles come crashing down on the very spot where she had been sitting.

Boy, that was a close call! I've been threatened by students and actually had some students attack me, but this is the first time I've ever been bombarded by a bunch of ceiling tiles. Now I feel like "Chicken Little," she thought, as she munched on the remainder of her sandwich.

———

Encounters with animals also provided some interesting experiences. The original Pineville High School building was opened in 1952. By the time Dianne arrived, some of the usual problems that plague older buildings had begun to emerge. Unbeknownst to the faculty and students, the baseboards of the older wings were invaded one year by termites during their mating season. When the eggs hatched, problems occurred. During one of Dianne's Home Ec. I classes, room ten was suddenly filled with live termites swarming everywhere. Some of the girls, including Lori Lollis, jumped up and began screaming and swatting, trying to fend off the offensive creatures.

Dianne reported the problem to the office. "I can't take my

students back in that room until the termites are gone," she told the principals. She solved the problem by moving her classes to one of the library's film rooms until her room could be treated.

Rats, mice, and roaches had also taken up residence in the building. One year a package of yeast was accidentally left in the home economics kitchen supply cabinet over the summer. When Dianne returned the following fall and opened the cabinet, what seemed like a thousand roaches ran out and scattered throughout the kitchen.

I didn't know yeast made such good roach food, she observed.

She tried several things to get rid of them. First, she put boric acid roach tablets in all the drawers. That didn't seem to do much good because every time a student opened a drawer during cooking lab, a roach jumped out. The students had to wash all the dishes and equipment they planned to use before each lab.

The next step was to fumigate the place, which she did one day after school, placing two fumigation cans in the lab just before she went home. The students weren't too happy when they learned afterwards they would have to wash every single piece of equipment in the lab, as well as washing down all of the cabinet shelves and drawers.

"Just be glad we're getting rid of the roaches and stop complaining," Dianne told them.

The situation did seem to improve after that, but the roaches still weren't completely gone. Dianne was almost out of options because the school-hired exterminator hadn't had much luck getting rid of them, either. Then she hit on a solution. She bought some Combat Roach Disks and put them in every kitchen. Almost like a miracle, the roaches were suddenly gone.

"You should write to the company about that. You might get on national TV," Rick commented.

Another year the roaches invaded the sewing lab. The school had flooded over the summer during heavy rains. The roaches had been forced to seek shelter in places they had never been seen before. Dianne's Advanced Clothing class always sewed in the fall so they could make lined jackets or blazers. They were the only class that used the lab during the fall months.

When they went down to the lab for the first time, they pulled out the machines and began to test stitch on them to see if they were working. As they pressed on the foot controls and accelerated the machines, roaches began to run out of the machine cabinets.

"Mrs. Lundy, you have roaches in your machines," yelled Sharon Norwood.

"What? You've got to be kidding! We've never had roaches in here before," Dianne exclaimed.

"Well, you've got 'em now," said one of the boys.

"Looks like I'll have to put out some Combat Roach Disks in this room, too," Dianne decided.

After that incident, she began to periodically place the disks in all the rooms of the home economics department, eliminating most of the roaches in the four rooms she was responsible for.

———

One very large rat had staked out fifth wing as his territory. He survived for years, successfully evading janitors in their attempts to catch or kill him. Anybody who left food in their room could expect it to be gone the next day, with candy wrappers and potato chip bags often dragged halfway across the room and gnawed open to access the food inside. When real food wasn't available, the rat made do with whatever was on hand. On one occasion, he ate a bottle of Wite-out, and apparently survived because signs of his visit were visible several days later when more food disappeared.

Although the rats and mice usually waited until nighttime to invade the school, they were sometimes seen during the day. One mouse that had taken up residence in the home economics kitchen ran out of a cabinet and across the floor during the middle of a cooking lab. The girls began to scream, and some of them jumped on top of counters and chairs as he scampered across the floor and disappeared behind a cabinet.

Dianne reported the incident to the janitors. They set out a trap, and the mouse was caught several days later.

On another occasion, the students made popcorn balls during cooking lab. They threw the leftover kernels that didn't pop into the kitchen garbage cans. After a janitor emptied the cans, a few kernels remained stuck to the bottoms.

The next day, Dianne went down to the kitchen before school to put her lunch in the refrigerator. She heard some strange scratching sounds coming from one of the garbage cans. When she walked over to the can, she was surprised to see three mice in the bottom, apparently trapped after they had jumped in to eat the corn. As she picked up the can, uncertain what to do, and the mice began jumping around. She was so startled she dropped the can, and they escaped, running into some of the cabinets.

She wrote a report describing the problem and her attempt to corner the mice. She stuck the paper into the mailbox of the head custodian, Mr. Curtis Simmons.

Later during the day she stopped by the office to see if anything was going to be done about the problem.

"We've been sitting here laughing at your note. Your description was so funny, we just couldn't help it," said secretary Irene Allgood.

"Never mind about that. My question is: when is somebody coming down to help me?" Dianne asked.

That afternoon after school, Mr. Simmons came down to the home economics department.

"Mr. Simmons, what are we going to do about the mice?" she inquired.

"Well, if we can't catch them, I guess you'll just have to name them," he told her.

During another year, Dianne did actually come up with a name for a small, fuzzy gray mouse that made itself at home in room ten. She became aware of its presence when it ran out into the middle of the room one day after she turned out the lights to show a filmstrip. Before she could do anything, the mouse disappeared just as quickly as it had appeared.

The next time she showed a filmstrip, the same thing happened. The mouse's visit didn't escape the students' notice.

"Mrs. Lundy, there's a mouse in here," some of the students observed.

"Oh, that's just Chester. He won't hurt you," Dianne replied.

The mouse continued his antics for the rest of the year. She never was able to catch Chester, but he apparently lived behind one of the storage cabinets in the room. He disappeared over the summer, and she never saw him again, but, for a time, she could say she had a pet mouse at school.

———

Some problems occurred with outside animals that invaded the building. One year the grass had grown especially tall before the janitors got around to mowing it.

Several snakes had been spotted in and around the building. Dianne sometimes opened her windows to let the rooms air out when the air conditioning wasn't turned on. There was a grassy area between wing one and wing two where her rooms were located. Although an occasional bug had flown through the windows, she had never encountered a serious problem until one fateful day.

She had finished checking roll in her third hour Home Ec. I class, and the students were getting ready to walk next door to the sewing lab. Dianne was still standing at her desk, putting some materials away when one of the girls walked over to the door to open it. The next thing she knew, the girl was screaming at the top of her lungs.

"What's wrong?" Dianne asked.

"There's a snake in the doorway," the girl exclaimed.

At that point, the other students spotted the snake and began running the other way, some of them shrieking loudly.

One of the boys, Jason Feazell, who was a stocky championship rodeo bull rider, rushed over to the spot where the snake lay waiting. He began stomping on the snake with his cowboy boots, crushing it to death.

Mrs. Sisco, who had heard the commotion all the way down to the principal's office, appeared on the scene.

"What's going on? she inquired.

"We have a snake in the room, but Jason killed it," Dianne replied, as she pointed to the now-dead snake that was lying in the doorway.

Mrs. Sisco walked over to Dianne's desk, picked up a manila folder and scooped up the snake. "I'll just take this outside. It's all over now, so everybody can calm down."

"Yes, I think it's all under control now," said Dianne. And I think I'll be a lot more careful about opening my windows after this, she thought.

———

Another year the school was invaded by a family of skunks. The saga began when people on first and second wings noticed a strange odor in the school every morning when they arrived. It was faint at first, but it grew stronger every day. Before long, everyone was certain it was coming from a skunk.

The exact location was determined to be near a corner of the building under the physics lab. Mr. Ronnie Nelson, the physics teacher, was well known for playing practical jokes on his fellow teachers, so some of them began to tease him about it.

"Are you sure this isn't just one of your famous experiments gone bad?" they inquired.

"No, I wish it was that easy. It's a real live skunk, maybe more than one. I haven't gotten close enough to count them," he said.

Exterminators were summoned. They tried several things but were unsuccessful in their attempts to get rid of the skunk. However, they did determine that it wasn't just one skunk—it was a mother skunk that had produced several offspring.

By that time, the entire student body had gotten into the act. The student council initiated a contest to name the skunk. Dianne didn't enter the contest, but she was thoroughly convinced that an appropriate name would be Pepe le Phew.

A few days later, an announcement of the winning title was made over the intercom.

"After much discussion, the votes are in. The winning name for our school skunk is 'Sisco's Kid,'" said the student council president.

Being nature lovers, the administration didn't want to kill the skunks, so one more effort was made to solve the problem. The exterminators managed to drive the critters out of their hole using smoke. The entrance was then sealed off, and the skunks had to move to the nearby woods.

"I hear your skunks are gone," Dianne commented to Mr. Nelson the next day.

"Yes, and I'm so glad. I can finally breathe again," he exclaimed.

Animals weren't the only source of problems in the aging building. For years the teachers and students had to cope with mold, mildew, leaky roofs, flooding, and air-conditioning problems. The most memorable incident occurred one year in the middle of the lunch hour.

Dianne had just finished eating her lunch and was heading down the hall towards the teachers' lounge when she heard an announcement over the intercom.

"Mr. Simmons, please report to the cafeteria. Mr. Simmons, please report to the cafeteria immediately."

I wonder what's going on now, she thought, as she continued moving down the hall.

Before she could reach the teachers' lounge, the fire alarm sounded. Following the fire drill procedures they had practiced on so many occasions, everybody began streaming out of the building towards the front parking lot.

"Is this just a fire drill, or is it the real thing?" Dianne asked one of her fellow teachers as they walked through the front doors.

"I don't know, but they don't usually have fire drills during lunch. It's either the real thing, or somebody just pulled the alarm as a joke," replied the other teacher.

"Well, I guess it's a good thing I have my purse and my keys with me," Dianne noted. "Since we're at lunch, I don't know how they are going to check to see if all the students are out of the building."

Just about that time, several fire trucks pulled up to the front parking lot. By then excitement was beginning to serge through the crowd of waiting students. Principal Evelyn Sisco appeared on the scene. Faculty members gathered around her to find out what was going on.

"We have a fire in the school cafeteria," she announced. "It doesn't look like we will be able to go back into the building anytime soon, so we are going to move all of the students down to the football stadium. I need your help in getting them all up there."

Everyone began the trek up the hill, traveling down Claiborne street towards the football field and Rebel stadium.

I guess I'm getting my exercise for the day, Dianne thought, as she marched along in the middle of the crowd.

Most of the students headed for the bleachers, while Dianne and the other faculty members took refuge from the sun under the stadium roof near the concession stand.

The students in the second lunch shift hadn't gotten to eat lunch, and some of them began to complain.

"We're going to have to try to feed them," Mrs. Sisco decided.

Food was brought in from some of the other area schools, and the cafeteria workers began dishing it out. Some of the students from the first lunch shift sneaked into the line and helped themselves to a second free lunch.

"There's no way we can keep up with who has already eaten, so we'll just feed some of them again," commented cafeteria manager Brenda Bonner.

"Why don't we just dismiss school early?" inquired one of the teachers.

"By the time I notify the bus drivers, it will be almost time for school to be out, so there's no use in trying to dismiss early," explained Mrs. Sisco. "I think what we will do is let the students who have cars leave early. The rest of them will have to stay until their busses get here."

By then it had grown quite warm, as the afternoon sun hit the bleachers full force. Some of the students got overheated, and a few began feeling dizzy. One of the cafeteria workers, an older lady fondly known to everyone as "Miss Daisy," fainted and had to be treated by EMTs who had arrived on the scene.

To everyone's relief, bell time finally rolled around, and the teachers and remaining students headed back to the front parking lot. Teachers only were allowed in the building to get their belongings, while students had to catch their busses.

The source of the problem turned out to be a bad breaker box located just outside the cafeteria. The problem was fixed, and school was able to resume the following day, much to the disappointment of the students and some of the faculty members.

Some of Dianne's problems occurred during after-school duty, rather than during regular school hours. Teachers were required to sell and take up tickets at both football and basketball games. During football duty, Dianne always hoped the weather would cooperate. If there was anything she didn't like, it was having to stand out in the rain or cold to take up tickets. She usually lucked out until the last few years of her tenure, when she found herself paired up with fellow teacher Alice North at the home gate.

For some reason, every time they had duty together, it poured down rain. One time it rained so hard Dianne had to take off her glasses because they had become so spotted she couldn't see. Holding an umbrella and punching season tickets at the same time was an almost impossible task. Getting wet usually gave her a cold, so she invested in a red hooded rain parka to try to ward off the moisture.

"Wearing that parka is a good idea. I see you went with the school colors," observed Alice.

The coincidence of rain during their duty slot had not escaped the notice of Roy Prestridge, who was responsible for the assignment. It became a running joke between him and Dianne.

"Well, we know it's going to rain for this game, because you and Mrs. North have duty together," he told her one year. "How many years does this make now that it's rained on you?"

"I don't remember. All I know is whenever Alice and I have duty together it rains, so maybe you should pair me up with somebody else next year," Dianne replied.

Duty for basketball games wasn't quite as traumatic. For starters, it was inside, so there was no danger of getting rained on. Also, teachers could sit down, rather than having to stand for the entire duty session.

For a number of years, Dianne was paired with a different teacher each year. One year she ended up with duty on Valentine's Day. Her co-worker for that game was Mr. John Maples, one of the special education teachers in the school.

"Happy Valentine's Day," she joked to him, as he arrived carrying the cash box and tickets.

"And Happy Valentine's Day to you," he said.

Dianne didn't think too much about the incident until she was paired with him again the next year, also on Valentine's Day.

"I guess they think we don't have anything else to do," Dianne observed.

The trend continued for several years until it became humorous.

"Are you ready for our annual Valentine's date tonight?" Dianne asked when she saw him in the teachers' lounge on duty day.

"I'll be there," he replied.

"Do you think our spouses are getting suspicious?" Dianne teased.

Since Dianne had the first duty shift, which began at 5:00 p.m., she opted not to go home after school. She ran into Roy out in the hall.

"Mr. Maples will be bringing the cash box and the tickets," he told her.

She headed back to her room to finish up the last preparations for the next day's work before reporting to her duty spot. She lost track of time and was almost late as she hurried down the hall towards the boys' gym.

At least I know Mr. Maples is always on time, so I'm sure he's probably already there taking up tickets, she thought.

To her surprise, when she entered the gym, Mr. Maples was nowhere in sight. It was almost game time, and she had no cash box and no tickets to sell. She let the people who had season tickets go in, but the others had to wait.

Just about that time, Roy walked into the gym lobby.

"Where's Mr. Maples? I have no cash box and no tickets," Dianne told him.

"Your duty partner has been run over in the front parking lot," Roy informed her.

"Oh, my God! Is he okay? What happened?" Dianne exclaimed.

"He saw some boys who were drinking on school property. He told them to leave. As they were speeding off in their car, they had one of the car doors open. It hit John and knocked him down. He was holding the cash box in his hand when it happened. I don't think he was hurt very badly, but he has to go down to the police station and identify the boys. The police already have them in custody."

"What about the cash box and the tickets?" she inquired.

"I have them here. Do you think you can manage by yourself for a few minutes?"

"I guess so. Gee, I can't believe Mr. Maples actually got run over. First Alice and I get drenched during football duty. Now my basketball duty partner is the victim of a hit-and-run. You'd better be careful who you pair me up with from now on," she joked.

Although Dianne managed to make it through her teaching career relying on a sense of humor to help her survive, she encountered a few tragedies along the way, some involving students and others involving teachers.

Two fellow teachers she would never forget were Nicey Brown and Linda Winn, who both became murder victims. Nicey was a beautiful black teacher who had a personality to match her looks. She taught business courses and was very popular with the students. She was the most elegantly dressed teacher on the faculty, wearing a different outfit, with shoes to match, every day. Dianne had taught her daughter, Natesha, in Home Ec. I and was looking forward to having her the following year in another home economics class. Over the summer, Dianne was stunned to hear a news bulletin announcing that Nicey and a male friend were found murdered mafia-style in Nicey's home. Police followed all leads, but the murder was never solved.

Linda Winn, a home economics major, taught biology briefly at Pineville High before getting a home economics job at another school. Dianne had actually met Linda several years earlier when she took a home decorating course through Sears with Linda as the instructor. Dianne was also shocked when she heard over the news that Linda had been stabbed to death one morning in her kitchen. That murder, likewise, remained unsolved.

Several of Dianne's students also met with tragic deaths. One boy, Wilbert Morgan, who was an outstanding track star, had given Dianne quite a few laughs during class. She had made a mobile illustrating the Basic Four Food Groups and kept it hanging in one of the back corners. During one of the foods tests, she discovered Wilbert was getting some of the answers for the test from the mobile, which she promptly removed. Although he had given her a few problems at the beginning of the year, he seemed to be settling down and doing better work in class. Then he got kicked off the track team, and things went downhill from there. Sadly, he was the victim of a drive-by shooting while he was standing on a street corner.

One of the girls Dianne taught also had an untimely death. Alicia LaCour was a very pretty and bright student who was also an FHA officer. During her senior year, Alicia became one of Dianne's lab assistants for a Home Ec. I class. Dianne was sure the girl would go far and be successful in life. Her predictions proved wrong when Alicia was accidentally shot and killed while a friend was teaching her how to use a gun.

Another girl, Kimberly Wright, met an even worse fate. Dianne taught Kimberly for two years. She was a talker, but during her sophomore year, she seemed to mature and had a much calmer nature. At the end of the school year she was hurrying to finish a pair of shorts she was making in Home Ec. II.

"I want to wear these during softball practice," she told Dianne.

"I didn't know you played ball," Dianne replied.

"I play on a team during the summer," said Kimberly.

While school was out for the summer, Dianne heard that Kimberly had been found dead in the room of a local motel. It wasn't until she got back to school in the fall she got the rest of the story.

Kimberly, it seemed, had become pregnant. One of her male friends told her he knew how to perform an abortion. When the abortion went wrong, he left Kimberly to bleed to death in the motel room.

———

Another male student, Floyd Nelson, determined his own fateful demise. Floyd had arrived at Pineville High School completely on the wild side. He was full of energy, jumpy, and had a hard time concentrating. Dianne, as well as his other teachers, had been working with him, and there was a vast improvement. She was in hopes he might be one of the students who could be saved and steered toward a better life.

Shortly before the Christmas holidays, Dianne walked into

school one morning to see Mrs. Sylvia Davis sitting on duty in the front lobby.

"Mrs. Lundy, did you hear about Floyd Nelson?" inquired Mrs. Davis.

"No, what happened to him?" asked Dianne.

"He was killed last night playing Russian roulette," Mrs. Davis replied. "He was playing board games with some of the other boys in the neighborhood. He took a gun along with him, and when the games were over, he just started waving it around. The other boys begged him to stop, but he kept on until he shot himself in the head."

"Oh, no! I can't believe it. He was improving so much!" Dianne exclaimed.

Dianne took up a collection in her third hour Home Ec. I class, the class he was in, and sent the money to the annual Doll and Toy Fund in his name. But things were never quite the same in third hour after that.

A ninth-grade male student Dianne had in homeroom was murdered one year shortly before school was out. He had walked over to Lake Bulow one afternoon to go fishing, as was often his custom. When he was returning home with his catch, he was met by several male acquaintances, one of whom he owed some money. It was a paltry sum of around two dollars. When he told them he didn't have the money, they killed him, leaving his body to be found sometime later.

Since he was one of her homeroom students, Dianne was responsible for closing out his records for the year. Closing out records for a deceased students was a problem she had never encountered, so she asked one of the administrators what she should do.

"Just mark him down as DOA," was the reply.

Astounded at such a response, she decided to seek advice elsewhere and received a more satisfactory answer from another administrator.

One of the most horrific crimes occurred near the end of her teaching career. By that time, the school had acquired TV sets for almost every room in the school through the Channel One system. Dianne never played her TV except during announcement time or when Channel One was on. Some of the other teachers periodically checked their local stations for news bulletins.

One day during lunch time Dianne was closing up her room when some of the students walked in to leave their books before going to the lunchroom.

"What happened to the man with the gun?" they inquired.

"What man? I don't know what you're talking about," Dianne replied.

"There's some man with a gun down at the Alexandria courthouse. A lot of the teachers have been watching it on their TV sets," they informed her.

Dianne put the incident out of her mind as she headed down the hall towards the teachers' lounge. She came upon Mrs. Phyllis Culbert, one of her fellow teachers who was on duty in the front lobby.

"Did you hear about the shooting?" asked Mrs. Culbert.

"No, what happened? Some of the students were trying to tell me about it."

"One of Mayor Fred Baden's daughters was shot and killed in the courthouse by her ex-husband."

"One of his daughters—do you mean Leah?"

"No, it was the younger one. I can't think of her name right now."

"Andrea. It was Andrea. I taught both girls. I had Andrea for two classes. I can't believe it."

"And that's not all of the story," added Mrs. Culbert. "They were trying to talk him into surrendering, but he shot himself in the head. The Channel 5 TV news crew was there, and they showed the whole thing while it happened."

"How horrible. I just can't believe it," Dianne repeated.

As a result of that incident, Rapides Parish teachers were forbidden to show any live telecasts to their students unless they had been previously approved by the school board. Dianne didn't have to be told twice. That was not something she would soon forget.

Several other students were killed in auto accidents. Sometimes it was their fault, and sometimes the fault of others. Hearing that one of her students had passed away was something Dianne never got used to. Dying young was always a tragedy in her eyes.

Dianne eventually took to reading the police blotter and Alexandria Marshal Byrd's "Most Wanted List" in the local paper, The Town Talk. Quite frequently she saw the names of some of her former students. Most of the offenses were for drug violations, but a few of them proved to be quite unusual.

One of her better students was arrested for terrorizing the patrons at a Wendy's when he carried a BB gun into the establishment. A female student was arrested for purse-snatching and then was arrested again several weeks later on her wedding day for unauthorized access of an ATM card. A male student was arrested for phoning in bomb threats to the Alexandria courthouse. Another male student was arrested for allegedly using an electric cattle prod to discipline his children.

Some of the more serious events involved murder or attempted murder. One boy, along with several companions, was arrested for beating an elderly Marksville man to death in his home when an attempted robbery went bad. Several other students were arrested for killing people during drive-by shootings. A group of males, including one of her former students, allegedly beat a young man to death, leaving his body in an abandoned house. Another student got into a fight at a pool hall and was arrested for attempted murder after he beat another patron with a cue stick.

Other students were arrested for burglary, forgery, passing bad checks, shoplifting, rape or attempted rape, lewd behavior, child pornography, child endangerment, and driving while intoxicated. The list seemed almost endless, and she wondered what they would think of next. All in all, she was glad that they were, for the most part, former students and she would not have to deal with them anymore.

"I used to joke and say I want to retire before I get shot or sued," she told Rick. "Now it's not much of a joke anymore. I guess I'd better stop saying that."

Chapter 9

*A*s Dianne progressed through her teaching career, events in her personal life also continued to evolve. After five years of marriage, she and Rick discovered they were about to become parents. She decided to keep working as long as she could and then take off the rest of the school year, using her accumulated sick days.

Fortunately, she was blessed with a healthy pregnancy and managed to make it through the entire first eight and one-half months without missing a single day of work. She wasn't plagued with any of the usual problems that tend to haunt most expectant mothers. There was no morning sickness, swollen ankles, or dizzy spells. She didn't even catch a cold. In fact, she seemed almost too healthy. The only problem she encountered was fatigue, and she learned to combat that by scheduling rest sessions in the afternoon when she got home from work.

She and Rick fixed up the spare bedroom for a nursery. Since they didn't know whether the baby would be a boy or girl, they opted for green and yellow as a color scheme for both bedding and clothing items. She didn't have to buy too many things because several groups sponsored baby showers for her. The ladies at her church gave her a shower, as did her teachers' sorority group, Kappa Kappa Iota.

She decided not to tell the students exactly when she was leaving school, figuring it would be easier to discipline them that way.

However, two groups did manage to surprise her with baby showers just before she was scheduled to leave.

Her sixth hour class, Parenthood Ed., which consisted of all girls, was the most excited about her pregnancy. They had found out when she accidentally let it slip during a lesson that she had visited an obstetrician. They even sent her a yellow rose on the school's annual Flower Day with a little poem that read, "You tried to fool us; Yes you did; But we found out; You're having a kid." Although she never really knew which student was responsible for the poem, she chalked it up to one of the most talkative girls in class, Linda LaFever. They managed to throw a surprise party, complete with cake, on the day before she left school.

What turned out to be the biggest shower was sponsored by the FHA club. She had no idea what was going on. On the Thursday of her last week, she had after-school duty in the back hall, so she headed down there, as usual. After her duty period, she was waylaid by Emily Needham, who had been instructed to keep her occupied until they had things set up for the party. When she finally walked back down the hall, she was met by Mrs. Wakefield and escorted into room nine. There sat most of the FHA members. They had brought a stack of presents, along with a large cake and a bowl of punch. The thing that caught her eye was their main present. They had all chipped in to buy her a blue and yellow stroller, and sitting in the stroller was a large fuzzy, yellow Teddy bear. She was astonished almost beyond belief.

"Wow, you really put one over on me this time," she exclaimed.

The baby proved to be quite active during the latter months of pregnancy. She was hoping for a girl, but Rick was positive it would be a boy.

"That baby's too strong to be a girl," he declared. "He's going to be a football player. I can just tell."

His remarks came after Dianne had endured several episodes of strong kicking by the baby. She was lying on the couch one night while they were watching the movie "King Kong" on TV. Every time the drums started playing in the movie, the baby kicked so hard it knocked her up in the air and almost threw her onto the floor.

Another time she attended a school assembly featuring a musical group from Northwestern Louisiana State College. As the music grew louder and louder during the performance, the baby became agitated and kicked so much she had to leave.

"Well, at least I know the baby's got good hearing," she commented to one of her fellow teachers, as she made her way out of the gym.

Her obstetrician, Dr. Martin Tanner, predicted the baby would be born sometime during the first week of May. Dianne decided to leave school after Easter vacation, giving herself several weeks to rest before the due date.

Her replacement for the remainder of the year was Ralph Kees's sister, Roslyn Nicewarner. She came to observe the classes one day shortly before Dianne was scheduled to leave. After lunch Mr. Kees stopped by Dianne's room with a message.

"Roslyn said to tell you that she's gone home because she has a headache."

"Really? I can't believe my classes would actually give anybody a headache," Dianne joked.

Dr. Tanner's predictions proved to be a little off, and the baby didn't arrive during the first week in May. By that time, Dianne was ready for it to be all over with, and so was Rick. People kept calling and asking if she'd had the baby.

"Not yet," she always replied.

Finally, one night it happened. Labor began in the early morning hours, and they made their way to Rapides General Hospital. Dianne had already pre-registered, so admission was a breeze, and she was wheeled right into one of the labor rooms. There was only one other woman in labor, and it was evident she was having a hard time. Dianne heard the whole conversation between the doctor and nurses as he decided to have the other woman transported to the operating room for a Caesarian delivery.

Gee, I hope that doesn't happen to me, she thought.

All in all, she made it pretty well through the labor process, but she started thinking about the story of Adam and Eve and how the pain of birth all came about after Eve listened to the serpent and ate the fruit from The Tree of Knowledge. The more she thought about it, the madder she became, placing the blame on Eve and the serpent for all the pain she was having to endure.

Finally, she sat up in bed and shouted, "All of this because of a stupid snake."

Just about that time a nurse came in and announced it was time to take her into the delivery room. A few minutes later, the baby was born. One of the nurses asked, "Do you want a boy or a girl?"

"A girl," Dianne replied.

"Well, you've got a boy," the nurse informed her.

Great, just great. All of that work and I end up with a boy. I don't know anything about boys, Dianne thought.

Her train of thought was interrupted by the baby's first cries as he received the traditional slap on the bottom from the doctor. Doctor Tanner was off duty that day, so the baby was delivered by Dr. Hyde.

"Do you know what day this is?" asked another nurse.

"Uh—Sunday," Dianne replied.

"It's Sunday, but it's also Mother's Day. You had your baby on Mother's Day," the nurse told her.

Rick was waiting outside as they moved her into the hall. "I've seen him, and he's cute," he exclaimed.

"Well, I guess you'd better let everybody know he's finally here," said Dianne.

"Yeah, I'll call our parents and Aunt Hazel. They'll want to know. I'll be up to your room later," he said as she was being wheeled into an elevator.

Dianne began getting acquainted with her new son when a nurse brought him into her room at feeding time. The first thing she did, as is typical of most new mothers, was to check and see if he had all of his fingers and toes.

Whew! At least I got that part right, even if it is a boy, she thought.

"You have an active baby," the nurse observed.

She couldn't quite see it. The baby always appeared drowsy and didn't drink much of his bottle. Although she had taught Parenthood Ed. and Child Development for years, her actual experiences with young babies was limited, so she felt quite awkward about the whole process.

Oh, well. I guess I'll get used to it eventually, she reasoned.

Rick decided to stay and feed the baby one night. He had to scrub down and don a surgical cap, gown and mask. Dianne almost laughed herself silly as he pranced around the room before the baby came in, referring to himself as "Dr. Lundy."

Several days later she was discharged. A nurse brought a wheelchair, while another one handed her the baby. Rick had gone downstairs to fetch the car and bring it to the front door.

As she was being wheeled through the lobby, the baby woke up and began to cry loudly. It got everyone's attention, and Dianne was quite embarrassed to see that people were staring at them and laughing. Nothing she did seemed to help. He cried all the way to the front door.

Well, we're off to a really great start. What happened to the happy picture of the mother and baby being wheeled out to the car? We haven't even made it out of the hospital, and he's beginning to cry. What's next? she wondered.

"Put him up over your shoulder," the nurse suggested.

Dianne followed her instructions, and the baby immediately ceased crying. He seemed pretty content on the way home, but he started crying again when they got into the house.

"I don't know what's wrong with him," Dianne worried. "Let's try giving him that bottle the hospital furnished us with."

They warmed up the bottle and fed it to him. That did the trick. He stopped crying and promptly went to sleep. Dianne laid him in the bassinette Mrs. Lundy had passed down to her. It was the one Rick and his brother had used when they were small.

"I guess he was just hungry," Dianne observed. "They just gave us one bottle, so we have to get the formula mixed and the bottles sterilized before he wakes up and wants another one."

Mrs. Lundy volunteered to stay with them for the first two days until Dianne got her strength back. The first night Dianne and Rick both woke up every time the baby cried, but they finally learned to sleep through it as long as someone else was there to watch him. Dolores came down and stayed for several days after that. Then Dianne felt she was ready to tackle the task of being a mother.

"I think I'm getting the hang of it," she informed everyone.

They had a hard time deciding on a name for the baby. They had been through the entire list of names in a name book. It was hard to find one they agreed on. Dianne liked the name "Scott," but it had just been taken by Rick's cousins, Buddy and Betty Tumminello. There were already too many Michaels and Christophers in the family, so those names were out. F. D. had positively forbidden anybody to ever name a child after him because he hated his first name. Mr. Lundy had already had a namesake. Finally, they settled on the only name they both liked—Jonathan.

"It's a Bible name, too," Dianne noted happily.

Once things got settled into a routine, Dianne was amazed she had such a good-natured baby. He rarely cried except when he was hungry, and finding ways to entertain him wasn't too hard, either.

"We're both Type 'B' personalities, so I guess he must be a double 'B,'" she joked to Rick.

They went through the usual stages of childhood, including watching him learn how to roll over and then sit up, seeing him take his first step in the middle of their living room one night, and listening to him learn how to talk. His first word, strangely enough, was not "ma-ma" or "da-da." Instead, he startled Dianne one day when he suddenly yelled, "Boo," right in the middle of a diaper change. She shouldn't have been too surprised because he had constantly heard her calling to her cat, Boo, who was still alive and kicking, although he was getting on in age.

Boo hadn't been too thrilled when she and Rick brought a baby home. He generally steered a wide path around Jon in order to avoid getting his tail pulled. One thing he did do, though, was assist Dianne in putting the baby to bed every night. He would follow them down the hall and wait until Dianne closed the bedroom door and headed back to the living room. She would then pick him up and give him a ride on her shoulder. It was a routine they continued until the last week of his life.

Until the baby's arrival, Boo had Dianne's undivided attention. He loved to chase a spool tied to a string. He also liked to wrestle, as well as play hide-and-seek and chase-and-tackle. He had the complete run of the house before the baby's arrival, except for the master bedroom. He could open any cabinet door and often did so, particularly in one of the bathrooms where he liked to climb inside a cabinet and nap. One day Dianne came home from school to find he had opened the cabinet where his food was kept. His box of dry cat food had been dragged out, and the food was scattered all over the floor. He had also taken out a box of Tender Vittles and opened every package.

"I guess he got hungry," Dianne commented to Rick later that night when she reported the incident to him.

Childproofing the house when the baby began to crawl put an end to Boo's antics. When they put latches on the cabinet doors, he could no longer open them. He was eventually relegated to napping on the couch and sitting on the living room window ledge for his afternoon sunning session where he was often visited by a neighbor's female cat named Calico.

Jonathan was a rather lonely child. He had few playmates during his early years because there weren't many children living in their neighborhood. He stayed with private babysitters for the first two years of his life. Then Dianne enrolled him in Peggy's Daycare Center, which was owned by Peggy O'Neal. When the time came for him to enter kindergarten at Pineville Elementary, she told him it would be fun and he would have lots of other children to play with.

She learned that was a mistake during his first week of school. While they were eating supper one night, he surprised them with an announcement.

"Teacher sent a note home today, but I don't have it anymore," he said.

"Where is the note now?" Dianne inquired.

"I tore it up," he confessed.

"I guess he takes after me. When I was five years old, I got a bag of switches for Christmas. I broke them all in half so I wouldn't get whipped with them," Dianne joked.

"Well, if the teacher sent a note home, it can't be good. You will just have to talk to her tomorrow to see what's wrong," Rick decided.

The next morning the teacher, Mrs. Davis, met them at the door as Dianne walked him to his classroom.

"Did you get the note I sent home yesterday?" Mrs. Davis inquired.

"No. Jonathan told me he got a note, but he tore it up before he got home," Dianne replied.

"The problem I'm having is that Jonathan won't stay in his assigned seat. He keeps getting up and running all over the room," Mrs. Davis explained.

"I'll tell his father, and we will have a talk with him tonight," Dianne promised.

That night Rick made it very clear to Jonathan what would be expected of him behavior-wise at school.

Several days later Dianne was met at the classroom door again by Mrs. Davis.

"I don't know what you said to him, but it's like the difference between day and night," she informed Dianne.

Although Dianne never received any more reports about Jonathan causing discipline problems in the classroom, it soon became evident attending school would never be one of his favorite activities. He frequently described to Dianne what the class had learned during their lessons. He would always end the narration with the same sentence, "But I already knew how to do that." His nursery school teacher, Miss Peggy, who was a certified kindergarten teacher, had apparently taught him too well.

Not only did Jonathan resist attending regular school, he didn't care for any kind of school. One summer Dianne decided to take him to their church's vacation Bible school. He didn't want to go and tried to kick the windows out of the car on the way over there. Determined not to be beaten by a child, for the four remaining days she doggedly dragged him out of bed and deposited him in the church auditorium.

On Friday night the church held a program to commemorate the end of their vacation Bible school. Parents were asked to bring a freezer of ice cream or some cookies. Dianne decided to make pineapple ice cream, just to be different. She talked Rick into attending by bribing him with the promise of free food.

When Dianne picked Jonathan up on the last day, his teacher, Cherry Holsomback, told her he would need a sheet to drape over himself as a robe for a skit their class was scheduled to perform.

"I don't want to be in the program, so I don't need a sheet," Jonathan informed her on the way home.

"Okay, son, whatever you say. Are you sure you don't want to be in the program?" Dianne quizzed him.

"Yep, I'm sure. I'm not gonna do it!" he declared.

After they got to the church that night he changed his mind.

"Mom, I've decided to be in the program, after all."

"Well, son, it's too late. You said you didn't want to do it, and I didn't bring a sheet," Dianne said.

Cherry overheard the conversation and came to their rescue.

"I have an extra sheet he can use," she said.

Dianne and Rick watched the program as the skit began to unfold. Jonathan was playing the part of a crippled man who was miraculously healed. He hobbled across the stage and knelt down in front of Jesus. After receiving the Master's touch, he stole the show by leaping off the stage, throwing his arms up in the air, and shouting, "Thank you, Jesus. I'm cured!"

Jonathan spent a large part of his childhood years trying to acquire just the right pet. What he really wanted was a dog. But Dianne and Rick, both having had experiences with dogs as they were growing up, said, "No way." So, he had to settle for some smaller pets.

First, they set up an aquarium in his room. He wasn't satisfied with that, so they bought a white albino hamster that he named Patton. They had a lot of fun with Patton, and for a while Dianne thought he might set a new record for the world's longest living hamster. When he finally passed away three years later, she and Jonathan were so depressed they went out and bought another hamster which was promptly named MacArthur. Unfortunately, MacArthur was not healthy and passed away after only a few days. Not to be outdone, they gave it one more try and picked out a third hamster which was bestowed with the name Eisenhower, shortened to Ikey. He was never as tame as Patton, and after he bit one of Dianne's fingers, she never picked him up again.

Disappointed in his replacement hamster, Jonathan wanted to try out a different kind of pet. With his usual ploy, he talked Dianne into buying him a bird.

"Mom, if you buy it for me I'll be the happiest little boy in the world."

They picked out a blue male parakeet Jonathan decided to name Billy. The bird learned quite a few tricks and turned out to be their most entertaining pet. He could whistle all sorts of ways, bob his head in greeting, and he always knew when it was time to hop onto his swing to go to bed.

Dianne felt they had quite enough pets to take care of with the aquarium, a hamster, and a bird. What she didn't know was they were about to acquire a fourth pet that would be with them for the next twelve years.

On the day after Halloween, Jonathan had gone up the street to visit Ryan Chadwick, one of his friends. It was getting dark, and he still hadn't come home. Dianne was beginning to get worried. She walked into the kitchen to start supper when Jonathan appeared at the back door. He had a small white kitten in his arms.

"What are you doing with that kitten?" Dianne exclaimed.

"I found it in the bushes," Jonathan replied. "Can I keep it?"

"Oh, son. I don't know. You know how your dad is about pets. Is it a boy or a girl?"

"I'm not sure. Can you tell?"

Dianne examined the kitten and determined it was a female. "We'll try keeping it on the carport," she decided. "But I have a feeling your dad won't like this at all."

Rick arrived home from work a few minutes later. "A kitten! Where did it come from?" he demanded to know.

"Jonathan says he found it in some bushes," Dianne explained.

"You should have just left it alone, and it would have gone home. I don't want any cats around here," he grumbled.

"Well, it's here now, so we might as well try taking care of it for a few days. I'll have to buy some cat food and cat litter. Look at the poor little thing. It's half-scared to death," Dianne said, as she held the trembling kitten in her arms.

Leaving the kitten outside proved to be unsatisfactory, because she started crawling under the hoods of the vehicles, getting grease all over herself.

"We'll have to bring her inside," Dianne decided.

They took her to the vet's office at Kees Park Animal Clinic. The vet, Dr. Tracey Benton, estimated the kitten was approximately three months old. She seemed to be in good health, so Dianne decided to have her vaccinated with all the usual shots. The vet bill totaled over one hundred dollars.

"Have you thought of a name for her yet?" Tracey inquired.

"How about Snowball?" Dianne asked.

"Yeah, that's a good name. That's what we'll call her," Jonathan agreed.

For the next few weeks they shut Snowball in the utility room whenever they left home. Dianne didn't think she was trained well enough to have the run of the house. Rick was not at all happy about having a new cat living with them, but he seemed to accept the fact the cat wasn't going anywhere.

Just about the time they had gotten used to having Snowball around, Jonathan surprised Dianne with an announcement.

"Mom, there's something I have to tell you about Snowball," he said.

"What is it, son?" Dianne inquired.

"You know how I said I found her in some bushes?"

"Yes."

"Well, that's not exactly true."

"Oh? How did you find her?"

"Remember when me and Ryan went trick-or-treating over in College Park?" he asked, referring to a neighborhood near where they lived.

"Yes, I remember that," Dianne replied.

"There was a lady in one of the houses there who had some kittens she was giving away. She told us if we came back the next day we could have one. We walked back over there and picked out the ones we wanted. Ryan got a white one with long hair, and I got Snowball. When we were bringing them home, Ryan's kitten jumped down and ran away, but I held on to mine real tight."

"That's quite a tale, son. Now you tell me after I've spent all of this money on the cat. I can't get over that! A lady who was giving away kittens for trick-or-treat. Now I've heard of everything. Okay, here's what we're going to do. You can never tell your dad how you got the cat. If he finds out, he will load her into his truck and carry her back to College Park. As far as he knows, you found the cat in the bushes."

"Okay. Does that mean I can still keep her?"

"I guess so, son. She's here to stay."

Although Jonathan never got over his yearning for a dog, he eventually learned to be content with Snowball as his pet for the rest of his childhood years.

⸻

In other areas of Dianne's life, times had not been so happy. Many of the relatives on both sides of their family were growing older, and some were not in good health. F. D., who had battled emphysema for years, finally passed away as a result of the disease. He had told Dolores, "If there is such a thing as reincarnation, I want to come back as one of your pets. You treat them so well."

Dolores's love of animals was well known. For her entire life she had always had a soft spot for any stray animal that was hurt or hungry. She often rescued them and brought them home as pets. There was rarely a time when she and F. D. were without a cat or dog, and they usually had several of them.

One of the last cats they had while F. D. was still alive was a black-and-white tuxedo cat Dolores had found as a kitten. She was headed back to Rocky Branch from West Monroe late one afternoon when she stopped at a dumpster to unload some trash. She spotted the kitten crouched beneath the dumpster. A storm was brewing with the sky growing darker and the wind starting to blow. She managed to coax the kitten out of her hiding place. Because the kitten had been abandoned by her former owner, Dolores appropriately named her Orphan Annie.

Their last dog was a white German shepherd F. D. had named Shasta. Sallie had rescued Shasta from an animal shelter and given her to Dolores when she was just a puppy. Shasta was a very smart and friendly dog and she seemed almost like another member of the family.

A few weeks after F. D. passed away, a new dog appeared on the scene. He was a large, black lab that just seemed to come out of nowhere. Dolores tried to run him off, but he wouldn't leave. She remembered F. D.'s vow to return as one of her pets. Even though she didn't believe in reincarnation, she half-believed he had somehow actually managed to succeed in fulfilling his promise.

She got down even with the big dog, took his head in her hands, and posed a question.

"Are you F. D.?" she asked.

The dog let out something that was a cross between a moan and a groan as he looked right into her eyes.

"I can't tell if you're saying, 'yes' or 'no,' so I guess I'll have to let you stay," she decided.

A few weeks later, Dianne, Rick, and Jonathan were visiting Dolores. Dianne was standing in the kitchen while they were preparing food for the noon meal. The two dogs were in the house, as Dolores frequently let them in and had even fixed beds for them to sleep in at night. It was the first time Dianne had seen the black lab.

"Well, I see you got another dog. What's his name?" she inquired.

"I decided to name him Sam," Dolores replied.

"There's something we need to tell you about Sam," Sallie added, almost hesitantly.

"What's that?" asked Dianne.

"We think he might be Daddy reincarnated," she said, and she proceeded to recount the story of exactly how Dolores had acquired another dog.

Dianne listened in amazement. She stared at the dog the entire time Sallie was talking. The dog stared back at her.

"You've got to be kidding. You don't really believe that—do you?" she exclaimed.

She then got down in the dog's face and proceeded to ask him the same question as Dolores.

"Daddy? Is it really you?"

The dog wagged his tail slowly, gazing into her eyes the whole time.

"If you notice, he has eyes like no other dog I've ever seen," Sallie commented.

"Gee, I don't know. Maybe he is Daddy," Dianne halfway joked. "I've got to tell Rick and Jonathan about this."

Later that day as they were eating lunch, Dolores added even more information to the puzzling story.

"The strange thing is, he has a lot of F. D.'s personality traits, too," she said.

Jonathan added more credibility to the story that afternoon. The rest of the family went outside to look at Dolores's fruit trees, leaving Jonathan alone in the house with Sam.

A few minutes later he came running out the back door, shouting as he ran.

"Mom, Mom, I have something to tell you."

"Slow down, son. What is it?" Dianne asked.

"Sam really is Pappy!" he exclaimed, referring to F. D. by the name he had always called him.

"And just how do you know that?" Dianne inquired.

"I asked him if he was Pappy. I told him to bark two times for 'no' and three times for 'yes.' He barked three times."

Sam's story became a running joke among family members and soon spread through the community. Sallie's boss, Mr. Wiley Hilburn, who was a renowned journalist, even wrote about it in one of his newspaper columns.

Sam, Shasta, and Annie, lived together peacefully for several years. Dolores was glad to have the pets to keep her company after F. D. had passed away. One night Dianne received a phone call from her. Dolores was almost crying as she spoke.

"Sam got killed last night. He was down by the cattle gap, and he got hit by a car. I found him when I went down to get the paper."

"I'm sorry. Did you bury him?" Dianne inquired.

"Yes, I buried him up by the barn in our pet cemetery. I don't know if he was F. D. or not, but I would always like to think he was."

Dianne didn't have the heart to tell her the final piece of the puzzle that had fallen into place, but she did tell Sallie a few days later.

"You're too young to remember this, but the place where Sam was killed was the same place a car hit Daddy. He was out feeding the cows, and he was real late coming home. When he finally did come back, one of his pants legs was torn, and the bucket was all smashed in. Mother asked him what had happened. He said a car had hit him and knocked him into the ditch. She never did believe he was actually hit by a car, but maybe he was. The thing has now come full circle. Perhaps Sam really was Daddy, and they were both hit by a car in the same exact spot. Maybe it was fate."

"Wow, I don't remember that," said Sallie.

"Let's don't tell Mother. It would just make her depressed," Dianne decided.

"You're right. We'll just have to keep it our secret. It makes me think more and more that Sam might have been Daddy, though," Sallie mused.

"I suppose we'll never really know," admitted Dianne.

Several of Dianne's other relatives met with tragic deaths. Not too long after F. D. passed away, his sister Corrie and her husband, Mina, were involved in a fatal accident just outside the Hollis's cattle gap. They had stopped to surprise Dolores with some may haws to be used in jelly making. As they were leaving the Hollis driveway, Corrie failed to see a huge log truck headed her way. She pulled out in front of it, and she and Mina were both seriously injured in the crash. Mina passed away a few days later, and Corrie soon followed, after remaining in a coma for several months.

Dolores, emotionally unable to deal with the situation, put the may haws into the freezer. She dragged them out several years later when Dianne was visiting.

"I've decided to make jelly out of Corrie's may haws. I can't let them go to waste since she gave her life getting them to me," she told Dianne.

"Yes, that's what she would have wanted. I don't know if I can eat any of the jelly, though," Dianne replied sadly.

One of Dolores's nephews, Albert Lloyd Bolen, also died tragically. Albert Lloyd was a teacher and talented baseball coach at Junction City High School, where F. D. had also taught for a number of years. He had been named the Arkansas State Baseball Coach of the Year several times and had led his team to quite a few championships. He was famous for a "squeeze play" he had invented to get an extra man out between bases. F. D., who didn't give many compliments, had described Albert as "the best I've ever seen working with a group of boys."

Albert was having heart problems and was scheduled for bypass surgery. It was time for the annual state playoff games, and he wanted to see his boys win one more time. They wouldn't let him be the head coach for the tournament because of his health problems, but he was allowed to coach third base. The game was in progress when he suddenly raised his hands and signaled for a time-out. He then collapsed behind the base, and everyone rushed over to see what had happened. Before they could do anything, he died from a heart attack in the middle of the baseball field. The game was called off and rescheduled for a later date.

Dianne, along with Sallie and Dolores, attended the funeral. She thought it was one of the saddest funerals she had ever seen. Albert Lloyd was dressed in his baseball uniform, including his cap that was lying on his chest. The entire baseball team acted as pallbearers. They buried him in a cemetery that was located by the baseball field. His grave was next to the fence that bordered the field.

As they were leaving, Sallie made an interesting observation. "Since he's buried by the baseball field, maybe somebody will hit a home run over the fence, and the ball might fall onto his grave."

"Yes, maybe it will. I think he'd like that," Dianne agreed.

A number of other relatives on both sides of the family passed away, although less dramatically. F. D.'s sisters Berdelle and Hazel, along with his brother, Donald, were the only ones left from his immediate family. Berdelle was in bad health and was not expected to live much longer. She and Hazel had not seen each other in years, so Dianne took it upon herself to arrange a visit. She chauffeured Hazel around north Louisiana to visit a number of aging relatives.

"I don't think Aunt Berd will be around much longer. I am

determined that she and Aunt Hazel will have one last visit," she told Sallie and Dolores.

True to her prediction, Berdelle passed away a short time later, making Dianne doubly glad she had made the extra effort to unite the two sisters.

While other people aged, Hazel seemed to flourish. She traveled extensively, visiting Europe twice, going on two Caribbean cruises, and making several bus tours to visit Canada and the western part of the United States. An avid amateur photographer, she always came back loaded with snapshots of the places she had visited. She could vividly describe each and every detail of the pictures to anyone she showed them to.

As time marched on, Hazel, too, began to feel the effects of aging. She began to depend more and more on Dianne, Rick, and Jonathan. Dianne made it a point to visit her frequently, even if it was just stopping by for a few minutes on the way home from school. Hazel had a bad habit of leaving her car lights on and running down the battery, so she often had to call Rick to come over and recharge it for her. She also had problems with her TV remote control, and either Jonathan or Dianne had to re-program it. Hazel was always sure the batteries in it had quit working, so Dianne frequently bought new batteries for the device. The pilot light on her hot water heater had a tendency to go out, and Dianne was the only one who could re-light it. No matter what went wrong, they were the first ones Hazel called whenever she had a problem.

Although Dianne felt her aunt Hazel was one of the most remarkable women she had ever known, she began to notice time was taking its toll. Hazel's memory was not what it used to be. She began to repeat herself during conversations, and she also lost things.

Hazel had worn dentures ever since Dianne could remember. One day, as happens with many older people, the dentures went missing. Hazel swore she hadn't thrown them away, but they were nowhere to be found. A few days later, Hazel's daughter Dhale and her husband, Charlie, came from Texas for a weekend visit. They searched the entire house and still didn't find the dentures.

"Dianne, we looked everywhere. We turned that house upside down. I just don't know where those teeth are. Mother had gotten a new recliner from Haverty's. She decided she didn't like it, and she sent it back to the store about the same time her teeth got lost. I'm totally convinced the teeth were somewhere in that chair," Dhale said.

"Well, I guess somebody will be in for a big surprise whenever they lean back in the recliner," Dianne joked.

Hazel's driving skills also began to diminish. She had been an excellent driver in her younger days, and she didn't believe in wasting any time whenever she was going anywhere. Dianne had learned from the start to never park beside her driveway after observing Hazel backing out one day.

"Always be sure to park your car out in the street, not by our driveway," her uncle R. V. had warned her. "Mama backs that car out of the driveway like a bat out of Hades. She and the neighbor lady across the street keep backing into each other. One time Mama saw they were about to hit. She got out of her car and tried to flag the other lady down, but the lady backed into her anyhow."

Hazel began to have accidents as she drove around town. Her car, a sturdily-built, pale yellow '77 Chevy Impala that she had bought shortly after R. V. had died, suffered only minor damages. She was never hurt, and the accidents were never her fault. Still, Dianne felt it was only a matter of time before some more serious problem might occur.

Her instincts proved right one day when Karen Burns, one of the school secretaries, knocked on her door during the middle of class.

"Do you have an elderly aunt who lives in Pineville?" Karen asked.

"Yes, I do. What's wrong?" Dianne inquired worriedly.

"She's been in an auto accident. She's not hurt, but there's a policeman on the phone who wants to talk to you. I'll keep your class while you go down to the office."

Dianne learned during the conversation Hazel had been involved in a hit-and-run accident at an apartment complex. She had been grocery shopping and decided she wanted some fried chicken. She mistakenly turned into the complex, thinking it was the parking lot of Kentucky Fried Chicken. Realizing her mistake, she turned around and attempted to exit the lot, accidentally backing into another vehicle in the process. Either not knowing she hit another car, or thinking it wasn't serious, she proceeded on her journey. Several witnesses managed to get her license plate number and a description of her vehicle. The officer had spotted her car parked at Kentucky Fried Chicken.

"Poor Aunt Hazel. Can you imagine a little old lady walking out of Kentucky Fried Chicken carrying her bag of food and getting nabbed by a policeman? I'm sure she was mortified," Dianne lamented to Rick later that day.

The policeman had made it clear that Hazel was no longer considered a safe driver. He had also instructed Dianne to pick up Hazel's car and keep the keys.

After school was dismissed, she attempted to phone Hazel's son, Hollis Fulton. His wife, Natalie, answered the phone. She informed Dianne that Hollis was on his way to Pineville to visit his mother.

Dianne waited until after supper to drive over to Hazel's house. She gave Hollis the bad news about the accident, along with the policeman's instructions that Hazel was not to drive anymore.

Hollis laid down the law to his mother and made it plain she would not drive from that day forward.

Things were never the same for Hazel after that. Losing her driving privileges meant loss of freedom. She was used to coming and going as she pleased. Her health began to decline. She eventually moved to a nursing home where she passed away several years later, just a few months short of her ninetieth birthday.

Dianne remembered Hazel had once told her, "I want to live to be one hundred, and then I want to go on 'The Tonight Show' with Johnny Carson."

She was saddened because Hazel had become almost like a second mother to her. The loss of her aunt meant she no longer had any relatives on her dad's side of the family living close by.

Chapter 10

Dolores had been the main guiding force in Dianne's life for as long as she could remember. No matter how big or small the problem, and no matter what went wrong, Dolores always seemed to have the solutions. Dolores had survived adversity, animosity, and more trials than one could possibly imagine. Through it all, her strength and her faith in God grew stronger. She was an inspiration to all who knew her.

After F. D. passed away, she continued to maintain the herd of cows they had owned since Dianne was a child. They stayed in the Hollises' ten-acre pasture that was across the road from the house. Dolores carted their feed and sometimes some hay in F. D.'s old '77 Chevy truck. No matter what the weather, the cows had to be fed and looked after. Dianne worried about Dolores possibly falling and breaking a leg during one of the ice storms that frequently hit during the winter months.

"Mother, you should get rid of those cows," she told Dolores, time after time.

"I need something to keep me busy. It gives me a reason to get out of the house," Dolores insisted.

"Can't you just get some chickens? Does it have to be cows?" Dianne asked in exasperation.

Several years later Dolores had a chance to sell the entire herd to a man in a nearby community who wanted to start a herd of his own. She hadn't had the heart to sell them at an auction where they would most likely be sent to a slaughterhouse. F. D. had treated them almost like pets.

"I always wondered why it took him so long to feed the cows. One day I went over to the pasture with him and watched while he hand-fed them individually out of a bucket. He had a name for every one of them, and he petted them like they were our dogs. Maybe they'll get to live a little while longer, since I didn't sell them at an auction," she told Dianne.

It wasn't as if Dolores had no other interests. She never missed a church service at the Rocky Branch Church of Christ. She was a member of the Union Parish Library Board, and she also worked as a Pink Lady at Union General Hospital in Farmerville. She had expanded her talents in art by enrolling in an art class taught by Mr. Laurence Holder, and she dabbled in ceramics. Besides that, she had started mowing almost half an acre of her five-acre yard. She was even asked to be a guest speaker at one of the graduation ceremonies at the Rocky Branch Elementary School, where she had served as a principal for over fifteen years.

She eventually found an additional activity to occupy her time. Since there was no garbage pickup in rural areas, the Union Parish Police Jury had provided dumpsters for the residents. Her favorite dumpsters were located about two miles from her house on a local road known as Chapman Road. One day when she was leaving her trash, she spotted two yellow-striped kittens that had apparently been abandoned. She tried to catch them but was unsuccessful in her efforts. Too soft-hearted to let them starve, she began to bring them food every day. She named them Ying and Yang.

"I would like to bring them home with me, but I can never catch both of them at the same time. I won't take one without the other," she told Dianne.

Dolores faithfully kept up her routine of feeding the two kittens late every afternoon. Other stray cats that hung out around the dumpster area soon became wise to the fact food was being provided.

They began to appear each afternoon, along with Ying and Yang. Dolores gradually increased her food supply as the cats' numbers grew. Word of her good deeds soon spread throughout the community, and she was nicknamed "The Cat Lady." People often blew their horns in greeting when they spotted her as they passed the dumpsters.

Dianne had heard about the cats for quite some time. One weekend when she was visiting Dolores, she decided to tag along at feeding time, just to see what was happening. She took a video camera to document the whole thing.

"Don't get out of the car. They won't come out of the woods for anybody but me," Dolores warned her.

So, Dianne sat in the car, camera in hand, and waited as Dolores made her way to a spot under a tree where she usually placed their food. She watched in amazement as cats emerged from their hiding places. There were cats of all ages and colors—black, white, yellow, gray, tabbies, and calicos, both long haired and short haired. She began counting them. There seemed to be around twenty-one cats, as best she could determine.

She managed to capture the whole scene on video tape.

"We could probably get a TV station to do a story about Mama and the cats," Sallie told Dianne.

But Dolores didn't want that. She was afraid too much publicity would cause someone to harm the cats, or maybe even kill them. In the end, they all decided it was best to just let things continue in the same manner, with Dolores feeding them at her leisure every afternoon, rain or shine.

When Dolores celebrated her eightieth birthday, she had reached a milestone. At that point, Dianne felt she might actually live to be one hundred. She was fiercely independent and still in relatively good health. She took great pride in her appearance and was driving fourteen miles to West Monroe every week to have her hair done by her favorite beautician, Linda, who was a sister to Charles Gates, one of Dianne's former classmates. She had started dying her hair when Dianne was a child.

"I'm never going to let my hair go gray. I intend to go to the grave with it dyed," she had once told Dianne.

One of the best-dressed women in her church, she believed in looking her best at all times. She started out every day by putting on make-up and combing her hair.

"You always feel better if you fix your face every morning," she told Dianne.

Dolores's face reflected her American Indian heritage. It was evident in her square jaw line and high cheekbones. Her great-grandmother had been a full-blooded Indian, a fact she was quite proud of.

Patriotic to the core, she believed in flying the flag on every American holiday, using the flagpole Dianne and Rick had erected on her front lawn. Her house contained many relics that symbolized her patriotic spirit, including an eagle plaque mounted above her living room door, an American bicentennial clock in her dining room, and an Avon replica of Betsy Ross stitching up the first American flag. She always looked forward to celebrating the Fourth of July with her family, even after F. D. passed away.

Instead of F. D.'s fried fish, they had barbeque, baked beans, and potato salad. Dianne usually furnished the dessert, typically some sort of cake or pie with a patriotic theme.

When Dolores retired from teaching, she made a pledge to try to visit as many people in the community as possible. She kept a record of everyone she had visited, and the list totaled over one hundred people.

"I'm going up and down the road, visiting as many people as I can," she told Dianne and Sallie.

Also, while both dogs were still alive, she took them for afternoon rides in F. D.'s old truck.

"They like to ride. They look forward to it every day," she informed Dianne.

But, as time progressed, Dianne and Sallie began to notice subtle changes in Dolores's personality. They didn't want to admit it, but their mother was showing signs of aging.

It was little things at first. She lost her car keys. She forgot how to cook meatballs and pasta, one of Dianne's favorite dishes. She also forgot her recipe for banana pudding, which she had made ever since Dianne was a child. Once, when Dianne was visiting for the weekend, she forgot where the dishes went in the cabinet.

"Mother, you really need to cook more. I believe you are forgetting how to cook," Dianne teased.

Dianne began to find little notes Dolores had written to herself. "My last dogs—Shasta and Sam." "Schools where I taught—Beech Grove, Antioch, Crossroads, Rocky Branch, Farmerville." "Colleges I attended—La Tech, University of Wyoming, Northeast." "My name is Calamity Jane."

Then one night Dianne received a call from her cousin Bessie Freeman, who also lived in Rocky Branch.

"Your mother has had an accident. She fell down and broke her wrist. The doctor won't keep her overnight in the hospital, so she needs somebody to come and stay with her," Bessie said.

Dianne tried to reach Sallie, who was attending an out-of-town convention, but she had no luck. She, Rick, and Jonathan made a flying trip to Rocky Branch, arriving at 10:00 p.m. Bessie and one of Dolores's neighbors had agreed to stay with Dolores until they arrived.

They walked into the living room to find Dolores sitting in a recliner with her arm propped up.

"What happened?" Dianne inquired.

"I was pulling up some old vines by the fence. My legs got tangled up in them while I was toting them to the trash pile. I felt myself falling, so I put my hands out to keep from falling on my face. I didn't want to break my nose again. I broke it when I was a little girl. I fell out of our wagon one day when Papa was driving the mules to town," Dolores explained.

"Well, you succeeded in that goal, but you broke your wrist instead," Dianne observed.

Dianne managed to contact Sallie the following day. They determined Dolores could not stay by herself, since it was her right wrist that was broken.

"She can't cook. She won't even be able to open the cans of cat and dog food," Dianne noted.

Sallie remembered the name of the lady who had stayed with Dolores after she had the problem with blood clots in her leg many years ago.

"We might be able to get Mrs. Nellouise Martin to stay with her. I know where she lives. I'll go down and try to contact her. If she's not there, I'll leave a note on the door," Sallie decided.

Mrs. Martin agreed to accept the job. Dianne and Sallie were greatly relieved, knowing their mother would be in good hands. Mrs. Martin stayed on until Dolores's wrist healed. Everyone was hopeful things would be back to normal after that.

But the brief respite did not last very long. Sallie began going to Rocky Branch every weekend to go to church with Dolores, eating lunch with her afterwards. Dolores was still cooking, but mostly on the weekends when Sallie came to visit. Sallie also began helping Dolores keep her bills straight, as she seemed to be getting confused about which accounts had and had not been paid. Dianne and Sallie decided there was a need for them to get approved with power of attorney in case of some emergency. They hired a lawyer who drew up the papers for that, as well as deeding over the Beech Grove property Dolores had inherited from her parents. They also had themselves approved for access to all her bank accounts. Slowly, but surely, they were taking over Dolores's business affairs. They wondered what would happen next. It was almost like waiting for the other shoe to drop.

And one day it did. Dianne received another call from Bessie Freeman.

"Your mother is in the hospital in Farmerville," Bessie informed her.

"What's wrong?" Dianne inquired.

"She was having back problems. She got these terrible pains

in her back and couldn't even sleep at night. She called me, and I convinced her to go to the doctor. Benny and I drove her up there, and they put her in the hospital," Bessie replied.

"Thanks for letting me know. I guess I had better come up there," Dianne decided. "What about the dog and cat? Is somebody feeding them?"

"Yes, Kelton Howard is taking care of them for her."

Dianne made arrangements for a substitute at school, packed her bags, and headed for Rocky Branch. Since she didn't know how long she would be there, she took along plenty of papers to grade. She stopped briefly at the Hollis house in Rocky Branch and then went on to the hospital.

Dolores was lying in bed with weights attached to her ankles.

"What happened this time?" Dianne inquired upon seeing the strange contraption.

"It's my back," Dolores replied, speaking weakly. "They're trying to stretch it out so the nerves won't be pinched."

"Well, that's the strangest get-up I've seen. I hope it works!" Dianne exclaimed.

Several days passed, with Dianne staying with Dolores during the daytime and sleeping at the Hollis house at night. Sallie drove over from Ruston and spent the one night with Dianne during the weekend.

Dolores didn't seem to be getting any better. In fact, her condition seemed to be worsening. They made the decision to have her transferred by ambulance to St. Frances Hospital in Monroe. She would be under the care of her primary physician, Dr. Hebert, who was a cardiologist.

Sallie picked up Dolores's cat, Annie, and boarded her at the vet's in West Monroe. Dianne planned to head back to Pineville, as she had to get back to work, and Sallie would go home that night to Ruston. Kelton could look after the dog again, they decided.

Dolores remained in the hospital for almost two weeks. She usually tried to be a good patient, but this time she was giving the nurses a hard time. She didn't want to stay in bed, and she had lost her favorite pair of shoes. They were nowhere to be found, and she had accused the nurses of stealing them. They kept asking her if she knew what day it was almost every time they came into the room. Disoriented and confused, she never knew.

Finally, Sallie was pretty much fed up with the whole situation. She told Dianne about it when she came back up on the weekend.

"I told them to quit asking Mama what day it is. She doesn't know! She didn't know what day it was when she was out of the hospital. How is she going to know it now?"

Dianne also heard the story about the missing shoes. While she was sitting in a chair talking to Dolores, she asked her what color the shoes were.

"They were the red ones that used to belong to Corrie," Dolores said.

"Well, I think I see a pair of red shoes under a chair," Dianne told her. "Is this them?" she asked, holding them up.

"Yes, that's the ones. Thank goodness you found them! I guess the nurses didn't take them, after all. Now I owe them an apology," Dolores admitted, almost shamefacedly.

Sallie had some more news for Dianne. They discussed Dolores's situation out in the hall.

"Dr. Hebert told me that he doesn't think Mama should stay by herself anymore. He says she's not taking her medicine correctly, and he thinks her mind is getting worse," Sallie said.

"Well, what are we going to do? Do you think we could get Mrs. Martin to come again to stay with her?" Dianne pondered.

"I don't know, but we can ask her. If she can't come, I don't know of anybody else. I'll try to call her tonight," Sallie decided.

Mrs. Martin agreed to become Dolores's caregiver. Dianne and Sallie didn't know what the future held in store for Dolores, but they knew she had to have somebody dependable and trustworthy to look after her. Mrs. Martin filled the bill on both accounts.

"Mrs. Martin understands she's in it for the duration, no matter how long it takes," Sallie informed Dianne.

Dolores, in the meantime, had grown even more restless. She

was just plain sick and tired of being in the hospital. She couldn't eat the food, and she missed her pets.

"I'm about ready to get my kitty cat and go home," she told her girls.

"That's what we're planning to do," Dianne said.

"Yes, we got Mrs. Martin to come back and stay with you," Sallie added.

"I don't know as I really need anybody to stay with me. I'll be okay by myself," Dolores protested.

"Well, we think it would be best if Mrs. Martin stays with you for a little while. Then we'll see what happens," said Dianne.

The next day, Dolores was discharged from the hospital. They managed to get her back home and settled in, with Annie and Shasta at her side. Mrs. Martin arrived a short time later. After completing the details of their arrangement, Dianne headed back to Pineville. Sallie was planning to stay overnight and then drive back to Ruston.

"We're going to have to let Mrs. Martin off on the weekends. I'll come over and let her off for the first couple of weeks. Then I'll let you know if I need you," Sallie told Dianne.

Several weeks later, Dianne received a call from Sallie.

"You said to let you know if I needed any help. Well, it's time," Sallie informed her. "I can't do it by myself. Can you come up next weekend and let Mrs. Martin off?"

"Let me check my calendar," Dianne replied, quickly flipping through the pages.

"Yes, I don't have anything for that date, so I can make it. Do you think I need to come on Friday night or Saturday morning?" she asked.

"Well, I've been going late on Friday afternoons. That way she has all day Saturday off," Sallie replied.

"Okay, I'll try it, but I don't know what time I'll get there."

Dianne packed her bags and loaded them into the car Friday morning so she could leave directly from school that afternoon. She didn't finish her work until almost 5:00 p.m., since she liked to have everything ready for the following week before she left on Fridays.

She always packed some crackers and a small Thermos bottle of water whenever she was traveling out of town. It was a habit she had picked up from F. D. He never had gone on a long trip without his water supply.

Well, I guess I can just eat some crackers to tide me over until I get to Rocky Branch. I don't have time to stop for food now. Mrs. Martin will wonder what happened to me, she reasoned as she headed out to her car.

Dianne couldn't see how to drive very well after dark, so she always tried to avoid nighttime driving. In this case, it was impossibility, as darkness was already beginning to descend. Besides that, it was starting to sprinkle. A few raindrops hit her windshield as she turned onto Highway 165 and headed out of town.

God, I just hope you will be with me on this journey and guide my way. I can't see too well, so I pray you will keep me out of harm's way was her silent prayer as she drove on.

The rain grew increasingly harder and the visibility decreased even more. Dianne was struggling to stay on the road as she approached Columbia. She even bypassed her favorite store where she usually stopped to buy gasoline and make a rest stop.

It's just raining too hard. I'm not going to stop. I'm already late, and I have enough gas to get to Rocky Branch, she decided.

She managed to make it to Monroe and drove on the interstate until she reached her exit. The rain still hadn't let up, and she knew she was about to head through a lonely stretch of road between West Monroe and Rocky Branch.

Gee, I hope I don't have any car trouble before I get home. It's going to be extra hard to see on this little country road. God, somehow, help me to get through this and to make it home safely, she again prayed, asking for help in a most trying predicament.

She was driving slowly, barely able to see the edges of the road as she passed through the swamp lands just outside of the West Monroe city limits. Then she spotted it. Somehow, out of nowhere, a large "semi" with bright taillights was suddenly driving in front of her. She had never seen such a large truck on that particular road at that time of night. She followed the "semi's" lights the rest of the way up the road to the Hollis's driveway. Then it was gone as quickly as it had appeared. She knew her prayers had been answered.

Mrs. Martin greeted her at the door.

"Where have you been? We've been worried about you."

"It took me a long time because it was raining. I could barely see where I was going. I don't think I'm going to drive up here at night anymore. I will just have to come on Saturday mornings," Dianne told her.

———

They soon settled into a routine, with Dianne and Sallie alternating weekends when they would travel to Rocky Branch to relieve Mrs. Martin. Dolores was still getting her hair done every Friday in West Monroe, with Mrs. Martin driving her to the beauty shop. Afterwards, they stopped at Dolores's favorite grocery store, Jowers Grocery and Meat Market, in West Monroe. Dolores had been shopping there for years.

Then Mrs. Martin informed the girls Dolores was unable to hold out walking long enough to get around the grocery store.

"We can pick up a few little things we need, but I think you girls had better do most of the grocery shopping from now on," she told them.

At that point, Dianne was still coming by herself, leaving Rick and Jon in Pineville to fend for themselves. She had developed a schedule where she could prepare enough food for them to heat in the microwave while she was gone.

When she arrived at Dolores's on Saturdays, she cleaned the house on Saturday afternoon and then cooked supper for her and Dolores. After that, she made out a grocery list that contained enough food for two weeks. On Sunday mornings she headed to town to buy the groceries and pick up any prescription medicines Dolores might need. After buying the groceries and returning to Rocky Branch to store them, she ate a lunch that usually consisted of a sandwich and some chips. Then she packed her bags and headed back to Pineville.

Her weekends in Pineville were spent in like manner. On Saturdays she cleaned the house and did the laundry. On Sundays she bought enough groceries for two weeks and cooked supper when she got home. At that point, she had pretty much given up going to church because it was all she could do to crawl out of the bed on the weekends. She was already tired from teaching five days a week and now had all of the extra work, to boot.

She never told Dolores about skipping church, but somehow Dolores knew. A mother always knows.

One day Dolores quizzed her about it. "Are you still going to church?"

"I go sometimes," Dianne replied, hedging around the question.

"I want you to go. I want us to all be together again after we pass away."

"Don't worry, Mother. I'll take care of it," Dianne assured her.

Sallie was still carrying Dolores to church on the weekends she was in Rocky Branch. Sometimes they went in the morning and sometimes they went at night. One morning after church they drove back up the Hollis driveway and spotted Shasta lying on the ground. She had died from an apparent heart attack. They buried her still-warm body in the pet cemetery beside the barn. That left Dolores with just one pet, Annie.

Dolores knew she wouldn't live forever, and she began to worry about what might happen to Annie, should the cat out-live her.

"I don't want her to be an orphan again. Would you take her?" she asked Dianne.

"Yes, Mother. Annie will be taken care of. She can go home with me," Dianne reassured her, thinking, *How long can the cat live?*

Dianne and Sallie had often debated on the cat's exact age. Dianne decided to find out one day when she and Dolores took Annie to the vet for her annual vaccinations.

"Do you know how old Annie is?" Dianne asked the vet.

"Well, according to our records, your mother has been bringing her here for fourteen years," he replied.

"I know she probably brought her in pretty soon after she found her, so she must be fourteen years old," Dianne decided.

———

Dianne and Sallie could only stand by and watch as their mother began a long spiral downward into a world of darkness and confusion. They learned from a home-health nurse that Dr. Hebert had classified Dolores as being in the early stages of Alzheimer's. Sallie had been outraged at first.

She came tearing into the house one day after speaking to the nurse, who was just getting out of her car. It was one weekend in the summer when both girls happened to be visiting Dolores.

"Do you know what that nurse just told me?" she asked Dianne. Not waiting for a reply, she continued. "She said that Mama has been classified as being in the early stages of Alzheimer's. How does Dr. Hebert know that? Is he qualified to make that kind of judgment?"

"I don't know. Maybe he was just going by what he has observed. You know Mother has been getting more confused and forgetful lately," Dianne replied. Both girls were talking in low tones, being careful not to let Dolores overhear the conversation.

"Maybe he's right. They say the family is always the last to know," Sallie admitted.

"I guess we'll just have to wait and see what happens. At least we have Mrs. Martin staying with her. That's all we can do for now," said Dianne.

After consulting with Dr. Hebert, they decided to try out a new drug that was supposed to help improve the memory of Alzheimer's patients. But it didn't seem to help much, so they discontinued it after a few months because it could cause damage to the liver.

Dolores had resisted Mrs. Martin's help at first, even arguing with her over who would do the cooking. But, as her mental faculties continued to decline, she eventually gave in and let Mrs. Martin do most of the work.

Her days were rather lonely, as she no longer had any outside interests. A few people from her church called periodically to check on her, including Mrs. Mittie Ann Laster, Mrs. Annis Smith, Nita Laster, and, of course, her close friend and neighbor, Jerry Howard, who, by that time, had become a widow. Corrie's son, Lanny Parker, sometimes dropped by for a visit. Her twin cousins, Joyce Watson and Jerrine Harrell, came to see her and even brought lunch. Aside from that, she really had nothing to occupy her time, since Dr. Hebert had forbidden her to do any more mowing.

"It's too bad nobody comes to visit Mother, especially since she made an effort to visit all those people after she retired," Dianne observed.

"I don't know what to say. I guess they just don't want to see her going downhill," Sallie responded.

"She wouldn't remember they came, but it would make her happy for a little while. I guess they don't realize that," said Dianne.

The girls did their best to brighten her days. They took her out to eat. Sallie took her to the movies. Dianne told her funny little stories about things that had happened at Pineville High School. But Dolores didn't always understand the stories. Dolores, who had always been the one with an amusing anecdote, had completely lost her sense of humor. About the only time she smiled was when she was playing with Annie.

She no longer read the paper, partly because she was losing her vision due to cataracts, but mostly because she could no longer comprehend the words. Slowly, but surely, she was losing her ability to read.

They began to encounter a series of events, some of which were amusing, some puzzling, and some downright scary. Dolores had always enjoyed providing food and water for the birds. She could watch them through the kitchen window and also through the patio door located behind her dining table. As soon as food was put into the feeder, the birds would immediately swoop down upon it.

One day Sallie noticed the feeder was full, but no birds were around. She went outside to check on it and found that Dolores had filled it with cat litter. It wasn't the first time she had done that.

"I'm thinking about writing a book one day about Mama's battle with Alzheimer's. I might call it something like 'Mama Put Cat Litter in the Bird Feeder Again,'" she jokingly told Dianne.

On another occasion, Sallie got up in the morning to discover Dolores had awakened during the night and had somehow managed to disassemble the entire central air-conditioning/heating unit. The pieces were lying on the dining table. She phoned Rick, who gave her enough instructions to patch the thing back together until he could come up and fix it. Dolores kept opening the door and removing the front of the unit, so Dianne had to purchase a doorknob that had a lock and key.

Mrs. Martin reported that Dolores had later tried to open the door several times, unsuccessfully, and had then given up.

"I guess she finally forgot about it," Dianne observed.

On another occasion Dianne came home to find that Dolores had taken the toilet plunger and rammed the handle into the drain of the toilet tank after removing its lid. She was barely able to get the handle out without cracking the porcelain fixture. Dolores was convinced something was wrong with the toilet, and she kept removing the tank lid and jiggling the handle.

"Mother, you are going to drop that toilet lid if you keep taking it off," Dianne warned her.

But Dolores stubbornly refused to listen. Dianne decided the only way to stop her was to fasten the toilet lid to the tank with duct tape. It wasn't a very attractive sight, but at least it did the trick. Dolores couldn't figure out how to get the lid off, once it was taped down.

"I had to do something. If she breaks that lid, we'll never find another one to match, since it's a pink toilet, and they don't make that particular color anymore," Dianne told Rick and Sallie.

Mrs. Martin reported several other problems that were occurring. Dolores's medicine had been kept in her bathroom, but she was getting into it and taking the wrong pills at the wrong time of day. They had to remove all the medicines and put them in the other bathroom in a cabinet where Dolores wouldn't see them. Dolores had also accidentally sprayed perfume into her eye, thinking it was her nightly eye drops for glaucoma. So, they had to remove all her Avon products she had enjoyed so much over the years.

"I don't think you should put any more of that solid air freshener in her bathroom," Mrs. Martin informed Dianne on one of her trips home. "I caught her pinching off some of it and trying to feed it to Annie."

"Did Annie eat it?" Dianne inquired.

"No, she had better sense than that," Mrs. Martin replied.

Sallie found Dolores drinking water out of a cat food can after she brushed her teeth.

"She told me she had always drunk out of a can like that," Sallie exclaimed, as she reported the incident to Dianne later.

Although Dolores could no longer cook, she still felt she should help out with washing dishes whenever Dianne or Sallie came home. She didn't always get the dishes clean, and she had forgotten all about modern inventions such as scouring pads.

"This pot doesn't want to come clean. I guess I need to take it outside and scrub it with some sand," she commented to Dianne one night.

Dolores had a bridge replacing several of her front teeth. She had gotten it when Dianne and Sallie were still children. That, too, began to cause problems. She was supposed to take it out at night before going to bed, and she began losing it. Once, Mrs. Martin found it wrapped in a piece of Kleenex. Another time it was in the medicine cabinet. One weekend when Dianne came home, Mrs. Martin had been unable to find it anywhere.

"If you find those teeth, we're going to have to store them somewhere else at night. Otherwise, she might end up flushing them down the toilet," Mrs. Martin told Dianne.

Dianne was reminded of the time her aunt Hazel lost her teeth and never found them. The teeth were finally located in one of the bathroom drawers, and they solved the problem by having her put the bridge in a glass of water and storing the glass in the other bathroom.

Up to that point, most of the incidents had been amusing, or, at the most, somewhat frustrating. Then one night, a more serious event occurred. Mrs. Martin had already told Dianne and Sallie that Dolores was getting up and wandering around at night.

"Sometimes I wake up and find her standing at the foot of my bed," she reported.

On that fateful night, Mrs. Martin had gone into her bedroom at her usual time. She liked to read or work word puzzles late at night before retiring. She walked back into the other part of the house and discovered Dolores was missing. She searched all the rooms, but Dolores was nowhere to be found. A trip around the outside perimeter of the house turned up nothing. Worried that Dolores might have wandered down the long driveway and walked out into the busy highway, she drove her car towards the road, calling Dolores's name over and over. There was still no response. Finally, as she drove back up the driveway and exited her car, she heard a faint cry coming from the far side of the yard.

"Help! Help! Somebody help me."

It was Dolores. She had managed to get clear across the immense yard and was trapped in some bushes out by an old wooden storage shed. She was scratched up and scared, but otherwise none the worse for wear.

Mrs. Martin concluded Dolores had opened the patio door, looking for Annie. Annie didn't come when she called, so Dolores went outside to hunt for her. She became disoriented and confused in the dark and took a wrong turn when trying to get back into the house. Annie, it turned out, had been inside the whole time.

When Mrs. Martin reported the incident to Dianne and Sallie, they decided they should purchase some sort of alarms to alert people whenever Dolores might open the door and try to go outside at night. Dianne found some alarms that could be hung over the doorknobs, and that seemed to solve the problem.

By that time, Rick had started accompanying Dianne on her trips to Union Parish. Dolores had been unable to keep a yard boy to mow the five-acre pasture with her Sears riding mower. It was an all-day job, not one that many people wanted to undertake. Rick decided he would come and mow the half-acre around the house every two weeks. They just had to let the rest of the pasture go. Dianne had hired someone to bush hog it once or twice, but it was too expensive and lasted only a few weeks before it was overgrown again.

The Hollis house, which was built by Mr. Truman Smith in 1966, was beginning to show signs of aging. Things were starting to wear out. The water pump to the deep well quit working, so they decided to hook into the Rocky Branch Community Water System. The water heater had to be replaced after it sprang a leak and flooded the hallway and master bedroom. The sewer system backed up and had to be replaced. The outside air-conditioning unit had been replaced, but the original inside unit was still working.

Then one weekend when Dianne and Rick were there, Dianne discovered a wet area in the carpet next to the air-conditioning closet. Rick investigated and found a leak in the drip pan under the unit. Since it was the weekend, they had to wait until Monday to call a repairman.

"It's probably not that big of a deal. Maybe he can just replace the drip pan," Rick commented.

But luck was not with them. The repairman informed them it was impossible to replace the drip pan because it was attached to the unit. The only way to solve the problem was to replace the entire inside unit, at considerable expense.

Dianne phoned Sallie and gave her the bad news.

"Well, I guess we have no choice. We can't live without air-conditioning. Mother has enough money in her checking account to pay for it, so I guess we'll go ahead and get a new one installed," Dianne decided.

She was pretty disappointed in the whole endeavor. The following day was their twenty-fifth wedding anniversary, an event she had been looking forward to for several years.

"There are two things I want for our twenty-fifth anniversary," she had told Rick. "I want to go out to eat at Tunk's Cypress Inn, and I want a heart-shaped diamond necklace."

As it turned out, she got neither. They spent most of the day sweltering while the repairman replaced the inside unit.

"This is the worst anniversary I've ever had," she complained to Rick. "Not only do we not get to eat out, but I have to cook, and I'm about to burn up in this heat."

"It'll all be over soon. The man is about through putting in the new unit. You'll be cooled off shortly," he replied.

"Yeah, but I still have to cook. And I'll tell you one more thing— that old unit had to be designed by a man. Only a man would design a unit with a drip pan that couldn't be replaced. If a woman had designed it, I guarantee you it would have had a replaceable drip pan."

———

The house wasn't the only thing going to pot. Dolores, who had taken so much pride in her appearance, simply let herself go. She no longer knew or cared what she looked like. When she got up in the mornings, she walked out into the kitchen with her hair all askew. Putting on make-up was a thing of the past. The only time she wore it was when Dianne or Sallie applied it before they took her out. She stopped going to West Monroe to have her hair done, and the gray began to grow out.

Mrs. Martin, who had been a beautician, began to cut and perm Dolores's hair. She also dyed it occasionally, whenever Dolores would let her. Still, the old Dolores was gone, and what remained was only a shell of her former self. She spent most of her time sleeping.

She also began to hallucinate. She thought she saw people in the yard, and she went around the house tapping on the windows, sometimes yelling at the imaginary people outside. She was positive that some girls who lived across the road were coming into her yard and stealing things. They had to keep the curtains closed most of the time to keep her away from the windows.

Mrs. Martin reported some other strange tales Dolores had concocted.

"She told me that she has some money buried somewhere out in the yard. She wanted to go out and dig it up."

"Maybe she's thinking about that twenty-dollar gold piece she found in an old truck from her mother's house. We don't know what she did with it," Dianne said.

"She also told me she had another child that was stillborn and was buried here in Rocky Branch. She said it was a boy."

"That's the first I've heard about that. I don't think it's true because she never told us anything about it. She's probably thinking about her half-brother, Otho, who died before she was born. He was only two years old," Dianne reasoned.

"I don't know. All I know is she keeps coming up with stories that are stranger and stranger," said Mrs. Martin.

Although Dolores's mind was getting worse, she still knew what was going on around her. When Dianne and Sallie were both there for one of the holidays, they were bustling around in the kitchen, getting all the food ready. Dolores had been assigned the task of setting the table on previous occasions, but she had become too confused to do it anymore. She was sitting on the couch, watching them work. Realizing she was no longer able to prepare the food for family holidays, she began to cry. Dianne and Sallie rushed over to reassure her it was okay and that they didn't mind.

"You took care of us all of those years we were growing up. Now it's our turn to take care of you," Dianne told her.

On another occasion, Dianne had bought Dolores a card for Mother's Day. Although she usually purchased cards with a humorous theme, the card that year was a sentimental one containing a poem about how special mothers are to their daughters. Since Dolores could no longer read, Dianne read it aloud. As she read, tears streamed down Dolores's face. Dianne shed a few tears herself and was barely able to finish the reading. Afterwards, she gave her mother a gentle hug. Somehow, she felt that Mother's Day might be Dolores's last.

Dianne knew that people with Alzheimer's eventually might not recognize their own family members. That was usually a sign things were getting pretty bad. But, so far, they had been lucky. Dolores always knew who they were. She had no concept of time and couldn't remember recent events. Then two incidents proved the disease was progressing even faster than they had thought.

One night Dianne and Rick were sitting at the table with Dolores as they ate their evening meal. Dolores leaned over to Dianne and whispered, "Who's that man sitting at the end of the table?"

"It's Rick, my husband," Dianne told her.

She reported the incident to Sallie.

"That's the first time she hasn't known one of us. I hope she doesn't forget us altogether," Dianne worried.

A few weeks later, Dianne and Sallie had both come home to celebrate Dolores's birthday. Sallie had arrived first and was bustling around the house doing a few chores when Dianne and Rick arrived. Dianne walked into the kitchen and greeted Dolores, who was sitting at the dining table finishing her lunch.

"Hi, we made it," Dianne told her.

"Who are you?" Dolores inquired hesitantly

"I'm Dianne, your oldest daughter," Dianne reminded her.

"Oh, yes. I know you now," Dolores said.

Dianne cornered Sallie in one of the bedrooms. "Mother didn't know who I was," she told her.

Sallie often theorized about Dolores's condition. "I think maybe you and I have blended into one person in her mind. She knows who we are when we come here separately, but whenever we're together she gets confused. She knew me because I was the first one here. Then you came in, and that completely baffled her."

"Maybe you're right. I suppose we'll never really know. It's a mystery," Dianne agreed, shaking her head.

———

It was approaching the four-year mark from the time Mrs. Martin had started staying with Dolores full-time. Dianne and Sallie's goal was to keep her at home as long as possible. They didn't want to put her into a nursing home unless it was absolutely necessary. But Mrs. Martin's health was beginning to decline, and they didn't know how much longer she would be able to hold out. Taking care of someone with Alzheimer's on a twenty-four-hour basis, day after day, was not an easy task.

Then one weekend in early July, Dianne and Rick came up to relieve Mrs. Martin, as usual. Everything seemed to be going along fine until late Saturday night. Dianne put Dolores to bed and went to take a shower in the bathroom located by the kitchen. She had been in there about ten minutes when she heard some heavy banging sounds coming from another part of the house.

Dolores sometimes wandered out into the hall near her bedroom and got lost. Dianne had tried putting nightlights in both the bedroom and hall, but Dolores kept pulling them out of the plugs, thinking they would catch the house on fire. She couldn't see in the dark hall and often banged on the walls or the door until Dianne or Rick came and turned on the light.

Boy, Mother sure is hitting the wall hard this time. She must be really lost, Dianne thought.

Just as she stepped out of the shower, Rick knocked on the door.

"Dianne, can you hear me? We've got a problem," he announced.

"What's wrong?" Dianne inquired anxiously.

"Your mother fell backwards into the bathtub in the other bathroom. I managed to get her out, but I think she's bruised up pretty bad."

Dianne threw on some clothes and rushed into her mother's bedroom

"Mother, are you okay? Did you break anything?" she asked.

"I don't know. I think I'm all right," Dolores replied.

An examination turned up some bruises on Dolores's leg and hip and a large bump on the back of her head. Dianne concluded she must have hit her head on the ceramic soap dish when she fell.

"Now what do we do?" she wondered.

"Why don't you call your sister and see what she says?" Rick suggested.

Sallie told them to call the home health office. The nurse on duty instructed Dianne to take Dolores to the emergency room.

Dolores protested and insisted she was okay. Dianne began to try to get her dressed. She simply would not cooperate and refused to put on any more clothes.

In the middle of the struggle, the home health nurse called back.

"Are you taking her to the emergency room?" she inquired.

"I'm trying, but she doesn't want to go," Dianne replied.

"Well, she really needs to go. Call me back if you can't get her there," the nurse said.

Dianne decided to just leave Dolores in her nightgown and a bathrobe. Between the two of them, she and Rick managed to get her mother out to Dianne's car.

"She'll have to ride in the front seat. She gets carsick when she's in the back," Dianne informed Rick.

Minutes later, they were on their way to West Monroe, having decided to use the emergency room at Glenwood Hospital. Dolores was still complaining about being hauled somewhere against her wishes.

"Don't want to go. Don't want to go," she kept repeating, as they drove down the road.

"Well, you're on your way now, so you might as well just sit back and enjoy the ride," Rick informed her.

"Yes, Mother, look at the pretty moon. Can you see it?" Dianne asked, hoping to distract her.

The tests and x-rays at the hospital showed she had no broken bones or fractures. After Dolores was discharged, they arrived back at the Hollis home at 3:00 a.m. Dianne put Dolores to bed. She phoned Sallie again, and then she and Rick fell into bed, totally exhausted from the traumatic experience.

The next morning, Dolores was stiff and sore from her fall. Her bruises had gotten worse. She couldn't get up and down by herself, and she could barely walk.

Dianne consulted with Sallie about the situation.

"I don't think Mrs. Martin is going to be able to take care of Mother until she gets better. Since she has back problems, she won't be able to help her up and down." Dianne said. "Rick and I will stay a few extra days. When can you come over to relieve us?"

"I can't come right now, but I'll be there as soon as I can," Sallie replied.

Between the two of them, they managed to work out a schedule so Mrs. Martin didn't have to deal with Dolores for a few days. Then, as if things weren't bad enough, even more bad luck befell them. They got a phone call from Mrs. Martin's daughter informing them Mrs. Martin had broken her wrist as a result of falling down her back steps.

"Now what are we going to do?" Dianne asked.

"Well, I know of one other lady who might be willing to come and stay with Mama. She called me once, asking if we needed any help," said Sallie.

"Who is it?" Dianne inquired.

"It's a woman named Marilyn Caraway. I think she lives on Albert Smith Road. I'll see if I can find her phone number, and I'll call her tonight."

"I sure hope she can come. Otherwise, I guess we'll just have to put Mother in a nursing home," said Dianne.

Marilyn agreed to take the job, telling them she could start working immediately.

Both girls were relieved, happy that Dolores would be able to stay at home a little longer. She perked up, having a new person to talk to and some new people visit with whenever Marilyn's family came by. Things were looking up, or so they thought.

But their good fortune only lasted a couple of months. Dolores began falling frequently, and she couldn't get up by herself. Rick was convinced the previous fall was embedded into her subconscious, even though she couldn't actually remember falling into the bathtub.

"She's scared she's going to fall again. That's why she keeps falling," he told Dianne and Sallie.

Marilyn was worried about Dolores falling during the night, so she began sleeping on the floor in Dolores's room. Dianne and Sallie realized that selfless act was above and beyond the call of duty. They were left with only two choices—either hire another person to come in at night to relieve Marilyn or put Dolores in a nursing home. Since there were few people available for "sitting" duties in a rural area, they felt a nursing home was their only option.

Sallie volunteered to check on the nursing homes in Ruston. That way she would be able to keep an eye on her mother. Dianne agreed, feeling Dolores wouldn't fare well if they moved her to the Alexandria/Pineville area. They finally settled on one that was not too far from Sallie's house.

They made the necessary arrangements and were ready to transfer Dolores to the facility about a month later. She wasn't getting any better and could still hardly walk as a result of her fall. They were in hopes she would receive physical therapy at the nursing home.

During the first week of August, Dianne made the trip to Rocky Branch to transport Dolores and her clothes to Ruston. She and Sallie had been undecided as to what they would tell their mother about the trip.

"We can't just tell her we are putting her in a nursing home. She won't get into the car. What can we say?" Sallie wondered.

"Why don't I tell her we are coming to visit you? Then after we get there, we'll tell her we're taking her someplace where they will help her leg get better. That's all I can come up with. It's sort of true. She never wanted us to lie, you know," Dianne suggested.

"That might work. I don't have any better idea," Sallie agreed.

Dianne worked diligently and stealthily during the afternoon while her mother sat in the living room, watching TV. She retrieved Dolores's suitcases from the closet and packed them, using the spare bedroom where Dolores wouldn't see them sitting on the bed. She had to blink back a few tears, knowing it would be her mother's last night at home.

After supper, Dolores sat in her favorite chair, watching TV, as Annie sat beside her. Dianne wished she had brought a camera to make their picture, but that would have only made Dolores suspicious. All she could do was memorize the way they looked, sitting there together for the last time.

Later that night, after Dolores was in bed, Dianne carried the suitcases out to the car and put them in the trunk. She was thankful she had managed to complete the task without Dolores even noticing.

The following morning they went through their usual routine, with Dianne arising first and eating and dressing before getting Dolores up. She awakened Dolores a little earlier than usual because they had to leave for Ruston. One of the home health nurses dropped by unexpectedly, so that caused them some delay.

"Have y'all decided what you're going to do about your mother?" she inquired, while Dolores was in the bathroom.

"We're putting her in a nursing home. I'm taking her this afternoon. Do I need to call the home health office?" Dianne responded.

"No, I'll tell them," the nurse replied.

The nurse, who had been a former beautician, gave Dolores extra attention that day. She styled her hair and applied makeup. Dolores looked more like her old self than she had in quite some time.

"Well, I have to go now. Goodbye, darlin'. I'll see you sometime," she told Dolores, placing a gentle kiss on her cheek.

Watching the whole procedure, Dianne blinked back more tears. She couldn't let on to her mother this day was anything out of the ordinary.

Sallie had called several times. She informed Dianne the people at the nursing home were going to meet them out front with a wheelchair for Dolores, so they needed to know when she would arrive.

"Call me just before you leave, and then I'll call them and let them know you're on the way," she told Dianne.

By 2:00 p.m. they were ready to go. Sallie called again just before they were leaving, and Dianne looked at the clock to check the time.

"It's two o'clock now, so we should be leaving no later than 2:15," she said.

Then she was faced with the task of getting Dolores into the car without incident.

"Mother, that was Sallie on the phone. She wants us to come over for a visit. It's nice weather, so I thought it would be a good day for us to go. Would you like that?" she inquired, hoping God would forgive her for telling a white lie.

"Yes, that would be good," Dolores replied.

Minutes later, they were on their way, with Dianne breathing a silent prayer of thanks she had been able to convince Dolores to make the trip. The next problem facing her would be getting Dolores out of the car and into the nursing home facilities. She mentally crossed her fingers, hoping she would be able to pull it off.

Sallie was watching for them, and she walked out to the car as soon as they pulled in her driveway.

"Hi, I'm glad you could make it," she said.

"Mother, Sallie and I have decided to take you to a place where they might be able to make your leg better," Dianne announced.

"Yes, I have already talked to them about it. The people are waiting for us," Sallie told her, as she climbed into the back seat.

They arrived at the nursing home a short time later. Some staff members met them and helped Dolores into a wheelchair, suggesting that Dianne and Sallie drive around to the back entrance to unload her belongings. Sallie had already prepared the room with a few of Dolores's personal items, including a TV set and some of her paintings. The nursing home staff had inquired about her interests. When they found out she enjoyed bird watching, they put up a birdfeeder just outside one of her windows. Someone had also bought a large stuffed cat and placed it on her bed.

They stored her belongings and then went to find her. She was in the administrator's office, sitting in the wheelchair.

"Why don't we wheel you around to look at the place?" Dianne suggested.

They wheeled her up and down the halls and then to her room.

"This is going to be your room, Mother. We are going to leave you here for a little while so the people can help your leg get well," Dianne told her.

"I 'spect I'd better not stay here. I'd better just go on home," Dolores protested.

"Now, Mama, we've gone to all the trouble to get you in here.

You need to at least try it out," Sallie responded. They were really hoping to be able to leave peacefully.

Just about that time, one of the staff members came in and inquired if they would like her to have some supper.

"Yes, I think that would be a good idea," said Dianne.

The food was brought, and Dianne fed it to her. She and Sallie sampled a couple of bites, just to see if it was edible.

"It's not too bad," Dianne decided.

After Dolores finished eating, the girls decided it was time to go.

"Mother, we're going to go on home now. It's time for us to eat supper. We'll be back to check on you before too long," Dianne told her.

"I hope we're doing the right thing," Sallie said, as they were exiting the building.

"Me, too," Dianne echoed the thought.

They walked out to their vehicles, making plans as they went. It would be best to get everything of real value out of the house as soon as possible, they decided. Dianne had brought some boxes for packing, and she would stop in Farmerville to see if any of the grocery stores had any more. Sallie would come over the following day.

Dianne knew it would be pretty lonely back at Dolores's house, so she wasn't in any hurry to get there. She made several stops in Farmerville and managed to get enough boxes to fill up her car. She then made the sixteen-mile journey home, reminiscing about the hundreds of trips she had made on that same road, oftentimes with her mother. F. D. had never liked Farmerville, but it was Dolores's "town." She preferred doing business in Union Parish whenever possible.

"I always feel safe whenever I get back into Union Parish," she had once told Dianne.

For some reason, a tune she hadn't thought of in years popped into her mind, and she began singing it as she drove. It was a song called "My Grandfather's Clock" that told the story about a large clock a man had acquired on the day he was born. The clock had served him faithfully during the ninety years of his life and then stopped working on the day he died.

Dianne reached the Hollis home a few minutes later and started unloading the boxes. She walked into the kitchen and glanced at the clock, wondering how long it had been since she left Ruston. To her surprise, the clock had stopped at 5:45.

That's really weird. Why did the clock pick today, of all times, to stop? I know it was working when we left because Sallie kept calling and asking me when we were leaving, she pondered.

Sallie came over the following day, and they began to go through Dolores's belongings, deciding what each of them wanted and what should be removed from the house immediately. First and foremost, they wanted Dolores's paintings. Those, more than anything, reflected Dolores's personality, and they were something she had created. They took turns picking out which ones they wanted and decided to give one of them to Jerry Howard and two to Mrs. Martin.

Dianne had forgotten about the clock incident until later in the day. She and Sallie were sitting in the floor of the living room going through some papers that were in a desk when she remembered.

"What time did we leave Mother at the nursing home yesterday?" she asked.

"I think it was about 5:45," Sallie replied.

"Well, you're not going to believe this, but when I got home, the kitchen clock had stopped at 5:45."

Sallie burst into tears. "Why did it do that?" she wondered.

"I don't know. Maybe God is trying to send us a message. Besides that, for some reason, I started singing "My Grandfather's Clock" on the way home."

"That's just too weird," Sallie declared.

———

They stayed at the Hollis house for two days, packing and sorting. Then Sallie headed back to Ruston, while Dianne made plans to leave the following day. She cleaned out the refrigerator and hauled the trash to the dumpster, setting out some food for the dumpster cats. Their numbers had greatly decreased after Dolores became unable to feed them anymore. But there were still a few cats hanging around, as other people put out food occasionally.

Back at the Hollis house, she loaded as much as she could into the car that night, leaving room for her suitcases and one more important item—Annie. The cat was beginning to get suspicious, as she knew something was amiss when Dolores wasn't there. Dianne was hoping she could catch her without getting scratched.

She managed to snag the cat the following day by tempting her with some food. Annie didn't like to travel, and she protested by squirming and yowling as Dianne picked her up and deposited her into a pet travel carrier. Annie let Dianne know she was displeased by continuing to meow loudly as Dianne made her final rounds in preparation for shutting up the house.

"I know, I know. I tricked your mama, and now I tricked you, but I can't help it. You are going to a new home now, and you'll have another cat to play with," Dianne informed her.

Dianne headed back to Pineville with a car so loaded she couldn't even see in the rearview mirror.

I'll just have to use the side mirrors. I hope I don't have a wreck or get stopped by a cop on the way home, she thought.

She stopped in Columbia to let her uncle Donald and aunt Euline know about Dolores being in a nursing home. Then she drove straight to Pineville with no further delays.

When she got home, the first thing she removed from the car was Annie. She walked into the kitchen, pet carrier in hand. Rick was none too happy about the situation.

"Just what we need around here—another cat!" he exclaimed.

"I promised Mother I would take care of her, and that's exactly what I plan to do. She will be with us as long as she lives," Dianne told him.

"And how long will that be?" he inquired, almost sarcastically.

"The cat is sixteen now. You do the math," Dianne retorted.

"Those two cats are not going to get along. What do you plan to do about it?" he asked, referring to their cat, Snowball, who had never learned her name, but simply went by Kitty.

"Let's put Annie in the living room and shut the folding doors. We can put her food and water and a litter box in there. Kitty will have to stay out here for a few days."

She toted the pet carrier into the living room and opened the cage door, hoping Annie wouldn't be too scared to come out. Annie slinked out and looked around. Then she took off running and promptly hid behind Rick's recliner.

"Well, she's out, at least. Let's just leave her there for a little while," Dianne decided.

Annie refused to come out of her hiding place until the next morning, when she finally emerged and promptly made herself at home on an old hassock Dianne had saved for Kitty's bed. She spent most of her time sleeping and refused to eat or drink anything.

Dianne was beginning to get worried.

"If we can't get her to eat or drink, she's going to get dehydrated. Maybe we should try to give her some water with a medicine dropper," she decided.

They managed to get some water down her, but she still wouldn't eat. One of their neighbors, Priscilla Wilson, who was an avid cat lover, was positive she had some food Annie would eat. She brought it over.

They walked into the living room where Annie was still sleeping. "Dianne, she's precious," Priscilla exclaimed. "I know she will eat some of this," she said, as she popped the top off the can.

They tried to tempt the cat, but it was no use. She simply was not interested in food.

"Why don't you leave it and I'll try again later to get her to eat," Dianne suggested.

"The cat's going to die if she doesn't eat," Rick observed.

Dianne decided to just put the food and water down on the floor by the litter box and wait. If Annie got hungry enough she would eat, she decided. That was all she could do.

True to her prediction, Annie finally woke up that night and began to eat and drink. She even used her litter box, a sure sign she was getting better.

"She's going to be okay," Dianne declared.

After keeping the cats apart for two days, they decided it was time for them to meet. Dianne was in hopes there wouldn't be a big fight resulting in injuries. She opened the living room doors and waited to see what would happen.

Both cats began hissing and spitting when they saw each other. They even swatted at each other, but neither one made contact. After settling down, they began walking a wide path around each other, neither one at complete ease. Kitty was especially unhappy because her bed had been taken over by a strange cat. She had made herself a new bed in a box top on some boxes Dianne had stacked in the hall. She jumped back onto the hassock, but Dianne shooed her off.

"You can't sleep there. That's Annie's bed now," she scolded.

Annie began following Dianne everywhere, not wanting to let her get out of sight. Whenever Dianne got dressed in the mornings, Annie sat in the hall by the bedroom door, waiting for Dianne to come out. Dianne called Sallie with a report on Annie's progress.

"I guess you have taken Mama's place in her mind," Sallie reasoned. "Y'all sort of look and sound alike. It's a good thing she already knew you. Otherwise, she'd be really traumatized."

By then it was time for school to start. Dianne made it through the first week and then decided to go and visit Dolores. She and Rick drove to Ruston on a Sunday morning. They walked into her room to find a plastic water glass on the floor with water spilled around it.

It was at that point Dianne fully realized how different things were for her mother. There was no telling how long she had sat there in her wheelchair, unable to get up, and no water to drink. She didn't even know if Dolores knew how to use the buzzer to call someone for help.

"Hi, we've come to visit," she had announced, as they entered the room.

"Who are you?" Dolores inquired, looking at them curiously.

"I'm Dianne, your daughter, and this is my husband, Rick."

"Oh, yes, I know who you are. I just didn't recognize you at first."

They stayed for about an hour. Dianne noticed her mother's knee looked swollen, and she reported it to the nurse on duty. The nurse promised to check it out.

"I certainly hope Mother's not getting a blood clot in her leg," Dianne worried, as she and Rick headed back to Pineville. "I really hate having to leave her there," she added.

"There's nothing more you can do. You and your sister both have to work, and you can't get people to stay with her around the clock," Rick noted.

"I guess you're right. I just worry about her having a stroke and lying there in bed helpless. I hope that doesn't happen to her. I really do."

Dianne went back to school the following week, but her mother was on her mind constantly. She offered silent prayers for God to look after Dolores. The thought of her mother possibly becoming a human vegetable was almost more than she could bear. Dolores had always trusted in God, and Dianne fully believed her fate was in His hands.

It was the second Friday of the school year, and school was about to let out for the Labor Day weekend. Dianne was looking forward to having a little time off. She had scheduled tests all day, as she typically did at that particular time. The day had gone off without a hitch when the bell rang to dismiss fourth hour. She walked towards her door after the students left the room. She was surprised to see the principal, Mr. Dewayne Lemoine, standing in the doorway.

"Mrs. Lundy, I need to see you in my office," he told her, with a very serious look on his face.

She followed him down the hall, wondering what she possibly could have done to get in trouble so early in the year. The only thing she could think of was maybe she had let too many people get a drink of water during class, as it was hot and her room was just around the corner from the water fountain. She began planning some sort of defense as they walked into the main office.

Then she spotted someone in his office. It was a woman, undoubtedly a parent.

Great, a parent. Now I'm really in trouble, and I don't even know what I did wrong. Why do these things have to happen to me? It's only the second week of school. If this is an indication of what the school year is going to be like, I'm going to have a hard year, she worried.

They walked into Mr. Lemoine's office, and he closed the door. Then Dianne noticed the woman wasn't a parent, after all. It was Liz Cross, one of the English teachers. The mystery deepened.

Mr. Lemoine spoke. "Mrs. Lundy, your sister is on the phone, and I have some bad news for you. Your mother has passed away."

Dianne sat in shock, unable to speak at first. "She's been sick for a long time," she finally managed to say.

"I'm going to leave you alone to talk to your sister now," he said, as he and Liz exited the room.

"Hello. Are you there?" Dianne inquired, speaking into the phone.

"Yes, I'm here at the hospital," Sallie replied.

"What happened?"

"From what I understand, they put Mama to bed for her afternoon nap. When they went back to check on her, she was gone. She just passed away in her sleep."

"I guess God was looking after her. My prayers have been answered. I was so worried she would have a stroke," Dianne commented.

"Yes, I do think God definitely had a hand in it. It's the best way she could have gone," Sallie agreed.

Dianne had to wipe away a few tears, but she didn't go into hysterics. She had known Dolores wouldn't live forever. She just didn't expect her to go so soon. She walked back out into the front office. Getting back to her unattended fifth hour class was foremost on her mind.

"You don't have to worry about your class. It's been taken care of. We called your husband, and he and your son will be here any minute," said Pam Burise, one of the school secretaries.

Just about that time, Rick and Jon walked through the door, looking totally bewildered.

"Grandma's gone, son, but y'all didn't really have to come. I'll be okay," Dianne assured them.

They left a few minutes later. Dianne stayed until almost 7:00 p.m., running off papers and making out lesson plans for the following week. She wasn't sure how long she would be gone, so she left enough materials for an entire week.

The following morning, she and Rick drove to Rocky Branch. Plans were for her and Sallie to meet at a funeral home in Farmerville later that afternoon. She had been in a state of nervous tension ever since Sallie's phone call. It was an uneasy and unsettling feeling in the pit of her stomach, and she couldn't seem to shake it.

As they headed out of West Monroe and crossed the Union Parish line, Dianne looked at the sign when they drove past it.

"Mother said she always felt safe when she was back in Union Parish," she reminded Rick, as a tear trickled down her cheek.

Then, almost as if by magic, she felt a strange sense of peace. She closed her eyes and leaned back in her seat, taking a deep breath. It was as if her mother's spirit had descended and enveloped her in a protective cloud.

She's here. I can feel it. She's watching over me now, Dianne thought.

She and Sallie met at the funeral home and made all the arrangements. Since it was the Labor Day weekend, the funeral had to be postponed until Tuesday. That gave them plenty of time to notify all the relatives and take care of any details they might have overlooked.

Dolores had actually written her own obituary. They found it in one of her dresser drawers. Although she hadn't written it as an obituary, it was the story of her life and her accomplishments. With a little rewording, it was perfect, just the thing they needed for the newspapers. Dolores had always believed in being prepared, and, once again, she had not let them down.

They decided to ask her favorite beautician, Linda, to do her hair and makeup.

Since Dolores had made it clear she didn't want to go to the grave with gray hair, they inquired about having it dyed.

"I've never dyed hair for a funeral, but I guess I could put some kind of temporary rinse on it," Linda decided.

"I hope the situation won't be too hard on you," Dianne told her.

The end results were beautiful. Dolores looked just like her old self, wearing makeup, with her hair dyed, curled, and styled. Since red roses were her favorite flower, they were the choice for the casket spray. Dianne also suggested that Dolores hold a single red rose in her hand.

The girls could not hold back their tears as they viewed the body privately. This was it. Their wonderful, sweet, and loving mother was finally gone, and they would never see her again.

"She was the best mother in the whole world," Dianne declared.

"Yes, she was," Sallie agreed.

Although the funeral service didn't go exactly as planned, it was still a beautiful service, with Jerry Lee and Kenneth Brantley officiating. Both of them had plenty of stories about Dolores.

The burial site was the Antioch cemetery in the Spearsville community, close to where Dolores and F. D. had grown up. It was a hot and sultry day, as there had been an extreme heat wave during the summer, with temperatures reaching one hundred and eight degrees. Dianne was concerned about people becoming overheated, especially the men who were wearing suits.

Just as everyone gathered around the grave and Jerry began speaking, a breeze sprang up out of nowhere. It was just enough air to keep the crowd cool. The breeze continued until the end of the ceremony, and then it died away. It was as if Dolores's spirit had descended one final time to watch over her loved ones.

Dianne knew it was the end of an era. Their parents, who had resided in Rocky Branch for over fifty years, had both taught at the Rocky Branch School, and both had also served as its principal. Dianne and Sallie had attended that school while they were growing up, and they had known almost everyone in the community. Most of those people had either died or grown up and moved away. All they had left from their childhood years was the Hollis property, their own little piece of Nip 'n' Tuck.

There was no point in keeping the property, as they no longer had any blood relatives in Rocky Branch. The girls had established themselves as members of other communities, Dianne, in Pineville, and Sallie, in Ruston. Neither of them had any plans to ever live in Rocky Branch again.

Marilyn's husband, Charles, volunteered to keep an eye on the property for them until it could be sold. He refused to take any pay for his services.

"All that we ask is that you pass the favor along to someone else," Marilyn told them.

Several days after the funeral, Dianne drove back to Pineville in a somber mood.

They had already removed everything of real value from the house. Without Dolores's paintings and little homey touches, the house had lost all its personality. Aside from her sister, the only living thing now connecting her to Dolores was her cat, Annie. As long as Annie was alive, it was like a little piece of Dolores was still with her. Every time she petted Annie, she thought of Dolores. The cat would be well cared for, she resolved. Dolores would have wanted it that way.

Chapter 11

olores's death brought Dianne to the realization that her life was about to change drastically. Not only had she lost her mother, but she had entered the final year of her teaching career, a time span that had occupied the last thirty-two years of her life. During that time, she had seen many changes.

Although the faculty composition at Pineville High had remained fairly constant for the first few years she was there, some of the familiar faces were replaced with new ones. She was amazed to be teaching with several of her former students, some from Ruby-Wise, and some from Pineville High. Jackie Sharbano Belgard joined the faculty in the special education department. Linda Stucklik, one of her former rally students, taught in the English department. Janice Williams, one of her homeroom students, became a science teacher. Donna Kirkland Reed, a former Ruby-Wise student, replaced Emily Needham as the school's chemistry teacher when she retired. Aleta Savoie Johnson, who had been a bride in one of Dianne's mock wedding receptions, became a teacher's aide.

Her two co-workers, Peggy Wakefield and Bettye Watkins, both retired, and no replacements were hired, leaving Dianne with the responsibility of managing the entire home economics program. Peggy had left when she completed the thirty years she needed for retirement. Bettye, however, had been forced into early retirement due to health problems.

Dianne had received a call from Bettye's daughter, Tracy, one Sunday afternoon shortly after midterm. Tracy informed Dianne that Bettye had suffered an apparent heart attack, and she had the instructions for lesson plans for the substitute.

"Mama was calling out stuff to me as they were wheeling her out the door to the ambulance. She said for you to call Mr. Kees and tell him to get a substitute for her," Tracy told Dianne.

After almost a month of searching for a replacement teacher certified in home economics, the principal, Mr. Homer Crouch, gave Dianne some bad news.

"I'm not having any luck in finding a certified home ec. teacher. It looks like we're going to have to hire somebody who's uncertified," he said.

Dianne had been giving the matter some thought. She was in one of her best years of teaching. Bettye had all of the lower-level classes—three classes of Home Ec. I and two classes of Home Ec. II. Some of Bettye's students were not the best quality, and she also had the special ed. students in her fifth hour Home Ec. I class. Dianne, on the other hand, had been sailing through the year with the upper-level classes and very few discipline problems.

Bettye's classes were scheduled to sew for the entire second semester. That meant they needed a teacher who knew what she was doing. An uncertified teacher in that situation was sure to run into a lot of problems, not to mention the fact that the students would probably be taught incorrect sewing techniques. With these two factors in mind, Dianne made her decision. A few days later, she walked into Mr. Crouch's office to tell him about it.

"I think I have a solution to your home ec. teacher problem," she told him.

"What's that?" he asked.

"I am volunteering to switch classes with the substitute. I will take over Bettye's classes and teach sewing, and the substitute can teach my classes."

"Well, I really appreciate that. You may have just saved the home ec. department," he told her. "I'll see who I can find, and we will try to get the switch made whenever you are ready."

Mrs. Elaine Tellifero had been covering for Bettye ever since she had been taken ill. Although Dianne had seen Elaine around the school for several years, she didn't know her very well. Elaine was an attractive lady who dressed extremely well. One of the things she was best known for was a fur-covered purse she carried. It had caught the attention of all the students, and they often referred to her as "the purse lady." Aside from that, Dianne's knowledge Elaine was sketchy, at best.

Mr. Crouch's decision was to have Elaine take over Dianne's classes when Dianne moved into the sewing lab with Bettye's classes. Dianne met with Elaine to discuss the situation, and she decided the best thing to do was to give Elaine all of her lesson plans, worksheets, and tests for the classes Elaine would be teaching. That way, the students would still cover the same materials, no matter who their teacher might be.

What Dianne didn't know was she was about to make a lifelong friend. As the year progressed, she and Elaine got to know each other very well. They often met after school to talk over the day's problems, and they usually had some funny stories to exchange. It was a tradition that continued on past that year and lasted until Dianne retired.

After that year, Elaine continued to "sub" at Pineville High on a regular basis. She was a favorite among both teachers and students, and Dianne always requested her for a substitute whenever she was absent. The students, always looking for a shortcut, nicknamed her "Mrs. T.," and the name stuck. Elaine's dedication and dependability were rewarded one year when she was recognized as a "Super Sub" during the school's Awards Day.

Changes had also taken place in other areas of Dianne's life. Her sister, Sallie, had gotten married, much to everyone's surprise. Sallie had been engaged several times and had even picked out her wedding dress on one occasion. But she had always broken it off. As a career woman, a college professor, and a widely published journalist, she enjoyed her independence. She began dating a man of mid-eastern descent, a professional artist named Hooshang Khorasani. They had met at a party sponsored by one of her friends.

The family didn't know what to make of it. They had never associated with anyone from that background, and they didn't know where the relationship was headed.

Dianne had never met Hooshang, but she had heard about him through Dolores. Then one night she received a call from Sallie.

"I have some news for you. You'll never guess what it is," Sallie told her.

"You got married," Dianne exclaimed.

"You guessed! How is everybody guessing before I even tell them?" Sallie lamented.

"I don't know. Instinct, I suppose," Dianne replied. "So, give me all the details."

"Well, we eloped. We went to New Mexico and got married. I borrowed a wedding dress from one of my friends. We had been talking about it, and we just decided to do it. I always was cut from a different cloth, you know."

"Congratulations! I can't believe it. I'm a sister-in-law. When am I going to meet the groom?"

"Soon. We'll have to meet at Mama's house one weekend."

The meeting took place several weeks later. Dianne found her new brother-in-law to be a handsome man with a kind and gentle spirit. She felt her sister had made a good choice. As the years passed, she also grew to appreciate his talents as an artist, especially after he opened his own business, Hooshang Studio, at their home in Ruston.

"I hope to be famous someday," he told Dianne. "Unfortunately, many artists don't become famous until after they die. It won't do me any good then because I won't get any money from that."

"Keep plugging away at it, Hooshang. Maybe you'll become famous a little at a time," Dianne advised.

———

Likewise, changes had occurred in Dianne's immediate family. Jonathan had made it through his childhood years with the usual problems most children encounter. Dianne had survived his bouts with the chicken pox and poison ivy, both of which had caused him to miss the end of school. She had assisted him with numerous projects and stayed on his case about completing homework and studying for tests. When he was in the seventh grade, he decided to take band, with the trumpet being his instrument of choice. It was at that point he began to make friends who, it turned out, would stick with him throughout his teenage years and beyond.

In the ninth grade, he became a freshman at Pineville High, a new situation for Dianne. She was used to working at her own tempo after school. Suddenly, there was her son, waiting for a ride home after band practice. She tried to pace herself to be finished when he was, but on some occasions, she had to take him home and go back to school to complete her work or to buy groceries for cooking labs. She was glad when the time came for him to take Driver's Education during the summer after his freshman year.

Although Dolores had taught Jonathan how to drive using F. D.'s old truck when he was visiting her during the summers, he still needed practice. Dianne and Rick took turns taking him out to drive around empty parking lots. He successfully completed the Driver's Ed. class and got his driver's license.

Then Dianne decided it was time for him to have his own vehicle. He wanted a truck. They searched through ads in the local paper and even went for test drives in several vehicles, but none of them seemed right. Finally, one day, Dianne spotted an ad for an '82 Chevy truck that sounded like just what they had been looking for. They went to check it out and decided it was definitely the one. They made arrangements to pay for it, and they picked it up the next day.

Dianne and Jonathan were both ecstatic—he, because he had his own truck, and she, because she had her car back. Rick had refused to get involved in the situation.

"You two do what you want. You can pick out a vehicle without me," he had told them.

What Dianne didn't know was Jonathan would develop a lifelong love for that old truck. He began working on it during his spare time, every chance he got. He repaired or changed out almost every part, even replacing the entire engine one summer with assistance from his friends Brock Beall and Mike Filasek.

"I'm never selling my truck," he told Dianne and Rick.

The truck had been repainted in a dark brown metallic color. Rick and Dianne referred to it as "The Brown Bomb," but Jonathan's friends had another name for it. They had dubbed it "The Turd," because of its color.

Jonathan successfully completed his four years at Pineville High and was offered scholarships to both Northeast and LSUA colleges. Dianne was totally shocked when he also won the John Phillip Sousa Band Award. She was expecting it to go to one of his friends, Nathan Randall, who was the most talented band member.

Jonathan's graduation brought Dianne to the realization that her boy was no longer a boy, but a young man. He had completed an important milestone in his life.

The next challenge that lay ahead was his college career.

Her original plan had been to retire the same year he graduated.

"We'll be graduating together," she joked to everyone.

Then she began to investigate the state's incentive program for keeping experienced teachers in the classroom longer. It was a deferred retirement option program known as DROP. It allowed teachers to continue working and collect extra money for up to three years after their retirement. Since it seemed like too good an opportunity to pass up, she elected to remain at Pineville High for three more years, which would bring her career total to thirty-three years.

During her tenure at Pineville High School, Dianne had not escaped the extra duties of sewing projects for other departments. She had been called on to repair football jerseys, alter band uniforms, repair shop lab aprons, shorten ping pong nets, and she had even repaired a pair of pants for one of the assistant principals when an emergency occurred in the middle of a school day. Her most memorable sewing feats, however, involved making costumes for the school's dance line.

One year they decided to go to the competition dressed as crawfish. Bettye designed the costumes, and Dianne assisted some of the mothers while they were using the home economics sewing lab to make the costumes one Saturday morning.

Another year, they came up with the idea of dressing up as lollipops and dancing to the old song "Lollipop." They would then shed those costumes and transform into Tootsie Rolls, dancing to the song "Tootsie Roll."

Bettye was an expert pattern designer. Although she had retired, she agreed to design the costumes. She made the patterns for three different-sized costumes. Dianne made two sample costumes from the patterns and carried them over the gym, where the dance line was practicing after school.

The girls thought the costumes were perfect, and so did their sponsor, Mrs. Sylvia Davis. Dianne volunteered to make enough patterns for the entire dance line, along with instruction sheets.

A few weeks later, some girls seemed to be having problems finding anybody to make their costumes. Dianne volunteered to help out by making costumes for those girls for twenty dollars each. Before she knew it, she was in charge of making all of the costumes, a total of forty. It was a formidable task, but she felt she could do it.

She put in a lot of late nights and weekends working on the costumes, and she managed to finish them just before the girls left for a national competition in Florida. She anxiously awaited their return, wondering what the results might be.

She got the report from Mrs. Davis and Mrs. Sandy Yates, one of the school secretaries who was also a co-sponsor.

"Mrs. Lundy, we won fourth place. Can you believe it? Fourth place in the nation, and we couldn't have done it without your costumes," Mrs. Davis told her.

"Those costumes made quite an impression on everybody," added Mrs. Yates. "Ordinarily, people don't clap for anybody but their own group. But our girls were out on the floor dancing, and when they tore off the red lollipop outfits and turned into Tootsie Rolls, they got a standing ovation. Everybody in the whole place was clapping."

"Wow! I wish I could have seen that," Dianne exclaimed.

"If you ever want a job making dance line costumes, just let me know," said Mrs. Yates.

"I'll second that," added Mrs. Davis.

Dianne had hoped to breeze through her final year of teaching. But her plans went awry due to two unforeseen circumstances. First, the faculty had voted to change from the traditional six-period day to a semi-block schedule. It consisted of five periods, with the two middle classes being ninety minutes long. That meant she had to re-do her lesson plans, worksheets, and tests for just one year of teaching. She was not too happy about that, but there was nothing she could do about it. During her twenty-five years at Pineville High, her mottos had become "Swing with the punches," and "Go with the flow."

Second, the school had been approved for a bond issue which allowed them to build a new facility. It had been the brainchild of two women, Principal Evelyn Sisco and their school board member, Sylvia Pearson. The old building had been deemed unsuitable for renovation, so building a new one was the only option.

Dianne had been hearing about the new school for several years. In fact, she, as well as the rest of the faculty, had been in on the planning since its inception. She had no objections to the new school, but she had hoped the actual move would not occur until after her retirement.

Luck was not with her when it was announced the new building would be finished by midterm of her final year, rather than the following summer, as originally planned. That meant she was going to have to clean out the entire home economics department, pack up the materials to be moved, and unpack them in the new school building.

"Let the students do it," everyone told her.

What they didn't understand was it wasn't a task for students. The department storage cabinets were stuffed full of things that had to be sorted, with her deciding which ones to keep and which ones to throw away. Some of the materials dated back to the 1950's, when the school was first built.

She had actually started working on cleaning out the department during the spring semester of the previous year, reasoning it would be too much to tackle in just one semester. Her instincts proved right, and she ended up requesting that some barrels be placed outside the sewing lab because there was too much stuff to put in the wastebaskets.

She had made friends with Roderick Sices, the janitor who swept her room, and he managed to get the barrels for her. She was usually still working in her room when Roderick came in to sweep, and she often entertained him with some stories about the day's events.

"You know, you should write a book, Mrs. Lundy. You've got some really good stories," he told her.

"I've been thinking about it, Roderick," she replied. "I'm always joking with my students and telling them I'm going to write about them."

"Well, if you write a book, I'll be sure to buy a copy. And I want mine autographed, too," he said.

―――――――

Dianne rearranged her lesson plans so the classes would be

through with their cooking and sewing labs by the end of November. That way, she would have the whole month of December to finish sorting through the materials and then packing them to be moved to the new building. After getting rid of the outdated papers and teaching materials, the next logical place to tackle was the home economics kitchen.

She had been collecting boxes for moving since the previous spring, nabbing any sturdy-looking empty box she spotted in the halls around the school. She had stored them in the unused home economics living room, and it was crammed full with just about all the boxes it could hold. Roderick told her of a room where the janitors had also been hoarding empty boxes in anticipation of the move just in case she needed more.

Each kitchen unit in the department had been assigned a color, and each piece of equipment had been painted with a dot of color to show which kitchen it belonged in.

She decided to pack the equipment by kitchens, rather than by type, labeling each box as to its contents and the kitchen color.

Rick volunteered to help her, so he began coming in after school several days a week. They worked quite late, even past their mealtime. Dianne had planned ahead and brought meals from home to reheat in the microwave ovens. The janitors informed her that the smells from the warming food were drifting down the hall.

"Boy, you and Mr. Lundy must be eating really good. That food smells so good it makes us all hungry," Roderick told her.

After working diligently for several weeks, they managed to get everything packed and ready to move. The janitors began moving teachers' boxes and some equipment to the new building shortly before the Christmas holidays. She and Rick wheeled the microwave ovens, AV carts, books, and some other materials down the halls and into the new building. Then, on the last day before school let out for Christmas vacation, the students were sent to a two-hour Christmas program. While they were in the assembly, the boys in the athletic department were assigned to assist teachers with moving their furniture to the new school.

Dianne had to direct them on where to place the sewing machines, as well as the tables and chairs from the kitchen. She had already decided in advance just how she wanted the furniture arranged. Her new department consisted of two main rooms—the sewing lab, which would also serve as her classroom, and a kitchen. An enclosed corridor between the rooms contained storage cabinets and a place for the department's washer and dryer. There was a walk-in pantry for the kitchen, and it was large enough to hold the department's four older refrigerators and a freezer. It also had shelves for storage of food and other items.

The new building had a lot of features that had been lacking in the older facility. For starters, it contained a central climate control system, with each room having its own thermostat which teachers could adjust to suit their own particular needs. There was a phone in each room, so teachers had instant communication with the office, and they could also be connected with any other teacher in the school through the office secretary. One thing all the teachers had requested was plenty of storage space, and the architects had met that requirement adequately.

Dianne had made sure her department was located downstairs. She had no intention of having to cart groceries upstairs for cooking labs. She also had her own private entrances from the outside to both labs, and they could be opened with an electronic keypad which only she, the principal, and the head custodian had access to.

The thing Dianne was most proud of was the department's showcase, complete with its own lighting and electrical plugs. She felt it would be the perfect way to show off student projects and get publicity for the department. She had always enjoyed arranging displays and creating bulletin boards, and putting the showcase to use was something she was looking forward to.

After the assembly, students had to report to homeroom. They had to clean out their lockers and gather up all their books. Plans were for their homeroom teachers to direct them on how to get to their homerooms in the new building. They would be assigned lockers in the new building. After that, they would go through a mini-schedule so they would know where their classes met when they returned from the holidays.

Dianne had run off maps of the new building for her students. She also showed them on a transparency where the new home economics department was located and described exactly how to get there. Then the bell rang to dismiss homeroom, and all bedlam broke loose.

True to form, Dianne's students got lost, with only a few of them making it to their assigned destination. They were instructed to follow her down the hall, but some of them made the wrong turn once they got in the new building. They finally showed up in homeroom, looking totally bewildered.

"Where have you been?" Dianne asked. "You were supposed to follow me."

"Somehow, we got lost and ended up on the second floor," they responded.

"Just remind me not to follow any of you during a fire drill," she told them.

Even more confusion followed during the mini-schedule, but most of the students eventually managed to find their right rooms. Dianne was glad when the whole thing was over and the final bell rang to dismiss students for the holidays. She was looking forward to getting some rest after spending the last month packing and moving.

But she didn't get as much rest as she had hoped for. There were still a lot of things in the home economics department that needed to be moved. She and Rick went back out to school several days and used his truck to transport items from the old building to the new facilities. By that time, the old building was looking pretty bare. In a way, she was sad to be leaving it because she had spent the last twenty-five years of her life working there. *But you can't stop progress, and it will be good to be in a new facility. Besides, there's no choice in the matter,* she reasoned.

She soon learned the new building wasn't without problems. For starters, the plugs for the stoves and the dryer didn't match the outlets. None of them could be used until electricians installed new plugs on those appliances. That meant she had to rearrange her lesson plans for the second semester to delay the cooking labs until the stoves were ready. Also, one of the sink drains was totally stopped up with some plaster the workers had poured down it. The school janitors were unable to unstop it, so she had to wait until a plumber could come to repair the damage.

The delays had their advantages. She had time to unpack all of the kitchen equipment, decide exactly where to place it in each kitchen, and label each cabinet and drawer as to its contents. She discovered there were no provisions for storing students' aprons, so she had the janitors move the apron cabinet out of the old building into the kitchen. She also needed more locking cabinets for the AV materials, so she had her AV cabinets moved into the sewing lab. Rick repainted all three cabinets to match the department's color scheme.

By the time they were able to start having cooking and sewing labs, Dianne had everything under control. She found students behaved much the same way in lab, no matter what their facilities might be. The new kitchens each had an under-the-counter refrigerator, which helped to prevent the sly ones from stealing other students' Kool-Aid. Due to the design of the floor plan, it was also easier to keep an eye on all of the students during cooking labs.

She hadn't been too happy about losing her lecture room because she had experienced the trials of conducting class in a sewing lab in other schools. But the students adjusted, once they found out she meant business, and class went on as usual.

Separating students during tests was a problem she solved by assigning them alternate seats during tests. Each student knew where their spot was, and they automatically went there during testing time without protest.

Her department was located in the back of the school, not too far from the railroad tracks. They could hear every train that passed, and the windows often vibrated in unison with the rotating train wheels.

"Don't worry, Mrs. Lundy. If a train derails, I've got your back. I won't let anything happen to you," said Jared Bayles, one of her senior students.

"Thanks, Jared, that's nice to know," she responded, with her usual quirky smile.

———

Moving to another facility wasn't the only new thing Dianne experienced that year. Instead of entering grades on grade sheets, teachers were required to record them by computer at the end of each grading period. Although Dianne had taken a course in computer science years ago, her computer skills were, at best, rusty. Most of the time, she managed to enter at least one student's grade incorrectly, and then she had trouble correcting it. Her worst mistake, however, was the time she managed to completely shut down the system. A message came onto the screen stating that someone in authority would have to call the school board to get the system up and running again.

She wasn't the only teacher using the computer lab to enter grades at the time. All the teachers who were off that period were entering their grades. Suddenly, everybody's screens went blank.

"What happened?" they wondered.

"It was me. I think I goofed," she announced.

She headed down to the guidance office to inform Mrs. Faye Hood, the guidance secretary, about the problem.

"Don't worry about it. You're not the first one it's happened to," Faye told her.

"Maybe not, but it's still embarrassing," Dianne lamented. "Leave me around a computer long enough and I'll figure out some way to mess it up."

Besides that, she lost the secret password teachers needed to get into the system. She thought she had dropped it somewhere in the hall, but, thankfully, she found it later in the day, wedged in between some of her other papers.

Boy, if a student had gotten hold of that, there's no telling what might have happened. Suddenly, everybody would have ended up with straight "A's" on their report cards, she thought.

~~~~~~~

As if she didn't have enough problems, it was also her turn to be evaluated that year. Tenured teachers were evaluated by their principals on a rotating basis once every four years. There was no way to get out of it.

"You're retiring, and they're evaluating you?" asked her co-worker Greg Burns incredulously.

"Yes, I'm afraid so."

"Why?"

"Beats me. It's a waste of time for me and the principal."

"Maybe they think you're coming back next year."

"No way. I've been looking forward to retirement too long. I have no intention of ever teaching again," she told him.

She had developed a secret system that let her know exactly how many days of teaching she had left. She called it DTG, or "Days to Go." On any given day, she could quote the exact number to anyone who asked. It became a running joke between her and Sandy Yates. She also liked to tease Sylvia Davis about it every chance she got.

"You need to stop tormenting those other teachers about how many days you have left," Rick told her. "They're going to get mad at you."

"Oh, they know I'm only joking. Besides, their day will come, too, before they know it," Dianne replied.

At least one fellow teacher was in her corner. Mr. David Cox, one of the English teachers, had the same greeting for her every time he met her in the hall or the teachers' lounge.

"Happy, happy, happy," he would say, and Dianne would just smile.

~~~~~~~

Although Dianne had sometimes wondered how she would ever make it through the year, the final few weeks of her teaching career suddenly lay before her, bringing her to the realization that it was almost over. She really didn't want a retirement reception, one of the traditions at Pineville High, and she tried her best to get out of it.

"Oh, no, you're not leaving without a reception," said Mrs. Pam Burise, one of the school secretaries.

She managed to come up with a list of people to invite, and she was delighted to learn she wouldn't be the only retiree. Mr. Curtis Simmons, the head custodian, would also be retiring.

"Thank goodness, there's at least one other person retiring. I didn't want to be in the spotlight all by myself," she told Rick.

After consulting the school calendar, she and Mrs. Sissy Beaubouef, the chairman of the retirement committee, decided on a date. It would be during the last week of school, just before final exams.

A few days before the reception, the school board was, once again, in the news. They had approved a substantial raise for all the principals in the parish. That had ruffled the feathers of the lower-paid employees, particularly the cafeteria workers, some of whom qualified for food stamps. With assistance from the media, more and more people became involved in the situation, showing their support for the lower-paid employees. Some of the workers began to picket the school board office. It all came to a head when they planned a walkout on the day of Dianne's scheduled reception.

By that time, some teachers had gotten involved, threatening to join the other workers on the picket lines. The situation was getting serious.

"Great, just great. Why did they have to pick the day of my reception to walk out? That's just the kind of luck I have," Dianne lamented.

"I can't change the date of the reception," she told Sissy. "It's too late to notify everyone, and my sister is coming from out of town."

"Don't worry. We're still having the reception, no matter what happens," Sissy reassured her.

A faculty meeting was held the day before the walkout was to occur. A phone committee would contact each employee to confirm whether or not they would be at school the following day, it was announced.

That night, Dianne waited by the phone, fully expecting a call, but she had heard from no one by 10:00 p.m.

"They have a lot of people to call. Maybe I'll hear from them in a little while," she told Rick.

She carried the portable phone around with her as she prepared to get ready for bed, even taking it into the bathroom. The phone was still silent. She waited and waited, but there were no incoming calls. Finally, about 1:00 a.m., she gave it up.

"I guess they're not going to call. They said they were calling everybody, but somebody forgot about me," she decided.

When she saw Jackie LaBorde the next day, she mentioned the oversight to her.

"Nobody ever called me," she complained.

"Well, Dianne, we *knew* you were going to be here," Jackie told her.

She had reported to school, as usual. But it was not a usual day. She was going to be in the spotlight, so she wanted to look her best. She had spent quite a bit of time looking for the right outfit for the occasion. She had given up wearing dresses to school long ago because her hose always got caught on something. She finally found just what she needed, a tailored navy pantsuit with white accent stitching and mother-of-pearl buttons. That, together with some comfortable navy shoes, would allow her to make it through the day and still look presentable.

She had finally acquired the heart-shaped diamond necklace she had wanted for her twenty-fifth wedding anniversary. Rick had given it to her for Christmas the following year. Paired with some diamond stud earrings, it would be the perfect complement to the outfit. There was just one more thing she planned to wear—an antique starburst rhinestone pin that had belonged to Dolores. That way, a little part of Dolores would be with her at the reception. Dolores had always been proud of her daughters and their accomplishments. She knew Dolores would be looking down on her during her moment of triumph.

Since news of the walkout had been widely publicized, the

majority of the students had elected to stay home that day. The principal, Mr. Dewayne Lemoine, had scheduled an assembly as soon as the bell rang for school to take in. All teachers and students present that day were required to attend.

He decided to divide the students up among the teachers and have them study for their final exams, which would begin the next day. Dianne ended up with a group of students she had never seen before. She had been planning on having small classes, giving them seatwork, and using the day to grade papers and get her gradebook in order. This was throwing a monkey wrench into her plans.

Can my luck get any worse? she wondered.

She escorted the students back to the home economics department and told them to study or work quietly. A few students wanted to leave and go to other classes where their friends were. Relieved to be rid of as many people as possible, she agreed, once she had phoned the other teachers to make sure it was okay. In the end, she was left with about ten people to supervise for the rest of the day.

She did manage to get quite a few papers graded, but she was in a state of nervous tension most of the day, having to deal with students she had never seen before. Things were so hectic the retirement committee forgot to send someone to watch her students during the last class period so she could report to the reception ahead of time, a courtesy they had traditionally provided for all retirees. She eventually realized she was stuck in her room until the final bell rang.

Just before bell time, Sallie and Hooshang knocked on the door, much to her surprise.

"Who are these people? Are they your students?" Sallie inquired.

"No, I've never seen them before. I've been babysitting all day," Dianne replied.

"Why are all of the people walking around outside with signs?" Hooshang asked.

"Yes, what's going on?" Sallie wondered.

"They're picketing in protest of the principals getting big raises, while the lower-paid employees didn't get one," Dianne explained.

"Oh, a picket line. I wondered why some of them were giving

us dirty looks when we walked into the building. Hooshang, you're seeing democracy in action," Sallie exclaimed.

"Yes, and they had to pick the day of my reception to do it. This has been one of the worst days of my entire teaching career. Thank goodness, it's almost over," said Dianne.

"Well, I guess we had better head over the reception. Where do we go?" Sallie asked.

Dianne explained to them how to get to the school's temporary library, which was located in the old ROTC building, telling them she would be over there shortly after the bell rang.

Minutes later she found herself in the library, which had been decked out for the reception. There was a table with flowers and a bowl of yellow punch. Two cakes had been provided, one for her and one for Mr. Simmons. Several people had brought gifts, and they were stacked on another small table. Facing her were rows of chairs, some filled with her former co-workers and principals.

This is it—the moment I've been waiting for. I can't believe it's really here. Will I have to make a speech? she wondered.

Principal Lemoine began the ceremony by introducing Dianne and Mr. Simmons. He then asked Dianne to introduce her guests. She started around the room, hoping she wouldn't leave out anyone. Two of her former principals were there—Mr. Eugene Millet and Mr. Aubrey Sanders. Quite a few of the former secretaries and teachers were in attendance, as well as her cousin Jerrine Harrell. She had personally called one of her former students and issued an invitation to her. LaTonya Haynes Harris, who had once been a headache to teach, had grown very close to Dianne and told everyone she was her "adopted daughter." Representing the school board was Dianne's supervisor, Ms. Carolyn Pecanty. Despite the fact that some people were missing because of the employee walkout, all in all, it was a nice-sized crowd.

Mrs. Donna Reed presided over the ceremony. She started by informing the crowd that she had been one of Dianne's former students at Ruby-Wise. She named off all the things Dianne had done while working there, including sponsoring the boosters and cheerleaders and giving them an end-of-the-year party at her apartment.

"But one of my friends, Kim Allen, who was also one of Mrs. Lundy's students told me that there's one thing she will always remember about her. Mrs. Lundy taught her how to make perfect fried chicken. She said she follows Mrs. Lundy's recipe, and it comes out perfect every time," Donna told them.

Several other people spoke, and then LaTonya stood up.

"I just have to tell you about my experiences with Mrs. Lundy," she said. "I was in her class in the ninth grade, and she sent me to the office every day. Every day. I went to see one of the assistant principals, and I told her, 'Me and this lady are just not getting along. You've got to get me out of her class.' She told me to give it another try, so I went back and stuck it out. Then I signed up for Home Ec. II, and I stayed with the program. Now I think the world of Mrs. Lundy. She's my example, my ideal, and my role model."

The next person to speak was Roderick Sices. "I want to tell you that Mrs. Lundy is one of the hardest working people I ever met. She stays up here working late, and a lot of times she was in her room working when I came by to sweep. She talked to me while I was sweeping. She was steady working, but she was talking at the same time. I got to know her pretty well, and I just want to say, that if LaTonya is her adopted daughter, I want to be her adopted son."

Everyone, including Dianne, had to laugh about that. After a few more speeches, Mr. Lemoine presented Dianne and Mr. Simmons with the gifts for the faculty. They then cut their cakes and refreshments were served. People began to leave soon afterwards, as it had been a long day for everyone.

Dianne didn't open her gifts until she got home. The faculty gift turned out to be a cut crystal biscuit barrel. She found out the next day it had been selected by Betty Tumminello Smith when Betty dropped by her room.

"I just wanted to see if you liked your gift, since I was the one who picked it out," Betty told her.

"Yes, it's beautiful. Thank you so much," Dianne replied.

There had been one important person who was missing at the retirement reception—Gary Nugent, the president of the Rapides Federation of Teachers. Dianne had been a member of that group almost since it was first formed. She knew that retiring teachers were traditionally presented with a plaque from the organization. However, she wasn't too surprised that Gary didn't put in an appearance because she knew he was probably tied up in negotiations regarding the employee walkout.

Oh, well, I guess I'll be getting the plaque some other time. Maybe he will come over and give it to me on the last day of school, she reasoned.

There were only a few remaining days left in the school year, and Dianne was totally occupied with trying to finish up students' grades, as well as closing up the department. She made a complete inventory of the department, thinking there should be some sort of record of all the equipment and teaching materials with a new teacher taking over the reins.

Several people were interested in the job, she learned, including one of her former student teachers, Dianne White. She met Dianne one afternoon after school and showed her through the department. She felt Dianne would be the ideal choice for the job, but the decision was not up to her. It was the decision of the principal, Mr. Lemoine, and the parish personnel director. She was disappointed when she learned the job would go to someone else.

"Don't worry about it," Rick told her. "It won't be your problem anymore after this year."

The last day of school, a teachers' workday, finally rolled around. Everyone bustled about, trying to get through so they could go home for the summer. About 2:00 p.m. an announcement was made over the intercom for all faculty members to report to the library for their last faculty meeting of the year.

It was at that meeting that the principals always made their farewell speeches to the faculty, and paychecks were also handed out. Assistant Principal Roy Prestridge liked to try to add a little humor to the situation by giving out award certificates for unusual things teachers had done during the school year.

Dianne had looked around for Gary Nugent, but he wasn't there. She was sitting at one of the tables talking to another teacher when she heard her name called. She barely snapped back to attention in time to hear what she was being rewarded for.

"Now the award for being the best-dressed teacher goes to Mrs. Dianne Lundy. She told us she was going to wear a different outfit every day during the last month of school, and she did it," he informed the faculty.

Dianne went up to get her certificate, laughing the whole time. "It was a joke," she told him.

Well, at least I went out on top. I had a retirement reception. I got an award for being the best-dressed teacher, and somebody also nominated me for "Teacher of the Year." Thank heavens, I didn't win that award. I didn't even vote for myself on that one. She had to chuckle again, this time to herself.

Plus, I got nominated several times during my career for Who's Who Among America's Teachers, something I never expected to happen.

One nomination, she had learned, came from one of her former FHA members, Nicole Dunkley, who had been one of her favorite students. Several years earlier, she had been totally surprised when she was notified that she had been nominated by a former student named Lashunda Freeman, one of her rally contestants.

"I didn't know I made that much of an impression on the girl. They can nominate only one teacher they had from kindergarten through college years," she had told Rick.

"Teachers don't always know how much they influence students," Rick had responded.

After the faculty meeting, Dianne headed back to her room to finish up the final details of closing down the department. It was a routine she had practiced for the twenty-six years she had been at Pineville High. The only difference was this time it was in a new school building.

She was always the last one to leave since there were so many things to be done. Rick had helped her haul some of her belongings home earlier in the week. She looked around to see if she had forgotten anything, but everything seemed to be in order. The only thing left was to turn her keys in to the office. She walked down the hall to the office, leaving her classroom door open so she could walk back through it and exit to her car.

She handed in the keys and said her "goodbyes" to everyone. It was a happy, but also a sad occasion to know she would never walk the halls as a Pineville High faculty member again. She had been telling people about the book she planned to write.

"Now be sure to let us know whenever you get your book written," said Mrs. Pam Burise.

"Don't worry. I'll keep you posted," Dianne replied.

She walked back to her department and picked up her few remaining belongings as she headed out to her car, which was parked behind the department. She climbed into the car and started the engine. She had brought a camera with her, and she snapped a picture of the department's exterior before she left.

Then she put the car into gear and eased around the corner of the school building.

Several of the janitors were standing beside a truck, talking among themselves. She waved to them as she exited the school's parking lot.

Well, I guess that will make the perfect ending to my book. I exit the parking lot, waving to the janitors, and drive off into the sunset. It can't get any better than this, she thought.

Chapter 12

Dianne had plans for her retirement years. Big plans. For starters, she and Sallie still had to sell Dolores's house in Rocky Branch, along with the ten-acre pasture that sat across the road from the house. They had been unable to sell it during the school year, partly because of the time it took to get the succession papers completed, and also because they had both decided it was too much work to tackle while working full time. Waiting until school was out was the best way to go, they had concluded.

So, she had that chore ahead of her—she and Sallie had to go through the rest of Dolores's belongings and sort them out for an estate sale before putting the house on the market. Then she and Rick wanted to remodel their house. Besides that, she had her book to write. She had also thought about taking keyboard lessons. She had taken piano lessons for several years while in elementary school, and she wanted to brush up on those skills. There was also the matter of volunteer work. She was interested in getting involved in Partners for Literacy, a program to teach adults how to read. It would be something worthwhile, she felt, especially after dealing with so many students who had been poor readers. Plus, there were plenty more volunteer organizations. The list of things to do seemed almost endless. She was eager to get started.

As soon as school let out for the summer, Dianne and Rick

headed to Rocky Branch to begin sorting out things for the estate sale. Sallie planned to join them as soon as she could get off from work at Louisiana Tech. There were still some things they wanted to keep, either for themselves or for Jonathan to use whenever he got out on his own in an apartment. It would take at least a week to go through Dolores's belongings, they estimated.

Dianne and Rick drove up the driveway of the house they had not visited in several months. The yard had grown up from lack of mowing, and the whole place had a deserted look about it. Rick was planning to mow and weed-eat the yard in preparation for the sale.

Dolores had owned two lawnmowers, a self-propelled mower for the yard around the house, and a Sears riding mower for the larger part of the yard. The self-propelled mower was in sad condition, and Rick had barely been able to keep it going. They had promised to give it to Charles Caraway in return for checking up on the house for them. That mower, along with an old weed eater that leaked gasoline badly, had been left on Dolores's carport, as there was no other place to store them.

When they drove up to the carport, Rick exclaimed, "Where's my lawnmower? Where's my weed eater? Did somebody steal them?"

"I don't know. Maybe Charles borrowed them," Dianne replied.

"Well, call him and see. I need them to mow the yard," Rick instructed, all out of sorts about the situation.

A call to Charles confirmed that he had checked the house the day before and both the lawnmower and the weed eater had been in their usual places on the carport.

"No, I didn't borrow them," he informed Dianne. "I can't believe they just disappeared overnight."

"Well, they're gone, that's for sure. Do you have a small push mower we can borrow for Rick to mow around the edges of the yard?" she inquired.

Charles, it turned out, did have a mower they could borrow, and the riding mower was still safely stored away in the barn.

"Well, whoever stole them didn't get much," observed Rick. "The pulling mechanism in the self-propelled mower didn't work anymore, and I was going to throw away the old weed eater when we finished using it because it leaked so much gasoline."

"Maybe the weed eater will catch on fire with whoever stole it. It would serve them right!" Dianne declared.

Later that evening while they were eating supper, Rick spotted a vehicle coming up the driveway.

"Here comes somebody," he announced.

"I wonder who it is," said Dianne.

Before either of them could get up from the dining table, the vehicle, a small blue truck with a Styrofoam ice chest in the back, turned around and made a hasty exit down the driveway.

"I'll guarantee you, that is probably who stole the lawn mower and weed eater, coming back to see what else they could find. They saw our car in the carport and got scared," Rick noted.

"Well, it's just too bad I didn't have time to get their license plate number," Dianne lamented.

"I don't think they'll be coming back," said Rick.

"Let's hope not," she replied.

———

Part of the preparation for the estate sale included cleaning out the attic, a chore Dianne dreaded. She had attempted to assist her parents in cleaning out the attic on at least one other occasion. After crawling up into the attic and throwing down a number of items, only to have Dolores declare, "That's still good. We can't get rid of it," she had pretty much given up. She had just toted the stuff back upstairs and stashed it away for a future generation to deal with. Now she and Sallie had become that future generation.

Growing up as a child of the Great Depression era, Dolores believed in saving everything, "just in case" she might need it. The attic had provided the perfect spot for hoarding her "stash" of goods. F. D. and Sallie had floored the entire space above the carport with one-by-six boards. It was a sturdy and clean storage space for all shapes and sorts of items, some of which Dianne and Sallie couldn't even identify.

Dianne had to chuckle, remembering the time Dolores had insisted on "saving" a flocked Christmas tree they had bought one year in West Monroe. Dolores had wrapped the tree in brown paper, tied string around it, and handed it up to Dianne, who had strongly advised against storing such a flammable item in the attic.

"Mother, you're going to catch the house on fire with this tree," she had warned.

The tree had remained up there for several years until Dolores finally admitted it couldn't be used again and hauled it off to the dump.

The only way to work in the attic during the summer months was to get up early in the morning before the sun heated the roof. After Sallie arrived the following day, Dianne climbed into the attic while Sallie remained in the carport below. The plan was for Dianne to hand or toss items down to Sallie, and they would then decide what to keep and what to discard.

Dolores had stored all their dolls up there. The girls were totally amazed the dolls had not melted over the years in the intense attic heat.

"Here's one of my last dolls, Theresa Dolores. I recognize her hair," Dianne exclaimed. "And here is my favorite doll, Sarah, but she's in pretty bad shape."

Sarah, a large baby doll and one of Dianne's first dolls, had a cloth body with vinyl arms and legs. Her head, which was wooden, had been damaged and was eventually wrapped up with adhesive tape. One of her fingers was also missing, having been bitten off one Sunday afternoon by Preston Johnson, one of their preachers' sons. Despite surviving all of those hazards, Sarah, it appeared, had finally come to the end of the line. Both her eyes were missing.

"Well, I guess Sarah will have to go. She doesn't have any eyes," Dianne observed rather sadly.

"What about my dolls? Do you see any of them?" inquired the real Sallie.

"Yes, there are several of them up here in my little doll bed," Dianne replied.

"Do you see Penny?" Sallie asked anxiously, referring to one of her favorite dolls that had long blonde hair.

"Yes, here she is," said Dianne.

"How does she look?"

"She looks pretty good. I think she's okay," Dianne informed her, picking up the doll.

As she lifted the doll out of the bed, both her arms fell off.

"Uh, she's not quite okay. Now she has no arms!" Dianne exclaimed.

"Well, hand her down, anyhow. Maybe we can patch her up some way," said Sallie.

The girls continued rummaging through the attic, finding things they didn't even know existed. There were two boxes of novels that had apparently been collected back in the 1940's when Dolores was a member of a book club. There was also a box of *Hit Parade* magazines and some sheet music, including Shirley Temple's "On the Good Ship Lollipop" and Harry James's "When You're a Long, Long Way from Home." Tucked away in the box with the sheet music was an autographed photo of Harry James and another photo of his *Chesterfield Music Makers* band.

"I wonder if any of these things might be worth something on e-Bay," said Sallie.

Dianne found a box of homemade patterns she had created for some doll clothes, along with some commercial patterns for Barbie doll clothes.

"Wow, I had forgotten all about these. I used to make clothes for all our dolls. guess I was just destined to become a home ec. teacher," she noted.

The pile of items to discard had grown quite large when their eighty-eight-year-old cousin, Josh Hollis, drove up in his red pick-up truck.

"I came by to see how you two girls are progressing and when you might be ready to sell the house," he told them.

"Well, we're trying to get it cleaned out this week, and I guess we will be ready to sell shortly afterwards," Dianne replied.

"Just let me know, and I can still sell it for you," he said.

After a brief visit, Josh took his leave. "I guess I had better let you girls get back to work. I've got a lunch date with three women, so I have to get going."

Dianne and Sallie exchanged glances as they waved goodbye to their departing cousin.

"A date with three women... I wonder which one will win out," Sallie mused.

After spending the entire week sorting, discarding, and labeling items to be sold, they felt they were ready for the estate sale. It was a sad occasion, but one they had to face. They placed an advertisement in *The News-Star*, the Monroe paper, and put up a poster in the local grocery store. All they had left to do was wait to see if anybody showed up for the sale.

Dianne had devised an organized plan to move people in and out of the house. She and Sallie would take turns handling the cash box. Rick, along with Jonathan and Hooshang, both of whom drove in for the occasion, would manage the items located outside and on the carport.

They were not disappointed in the turnout. People came from all around. Some people they knew, but many they didn't. Some of those attending included a few of Dolores's former students she had taught at Rocky Branch Elementary. They bought some of Dolores's costume jewelry pins, stating they "just wanted something to remember her by."

All in all, the sale was a success, with most of the smaller items being sold, along with a good bit of the furniture. Even the refrigerator and freezer were gone. Most of what was left would be donated to charity, they decided, as they all sat down to rest from their long and exhausting day.

Dianne and Sallie gave the house a thorough cleaning after the estate sale, preparing to put it on the market. They had carted off everything else they intended to keep, and almost all of the furniture was gone. They decided to leave a bed, along with some chairs for Rick and Dianne to use because they would still have to come up and mow the yard through the summer months until the house was sold.

The house attracted interest almost immediately because it was still one of the most appealing home sites in the Rocky Branch community. Although the landscaping needed some work, it was still a desirable place to live with a lot of almost five acres, including a meadow and pond in front and a barn in one of the back corners. Their old home place still held lots of possibilities for its future owners.

Within three months, Dianne received a phone call from her cousin Josh telling her he had found a buyer for the house. Relieved it had sold so quickly, she and Sallie made arrangements to meet the prospective buyers at a bank in Monroe to sign the sale papers. The buyers turned out to be a nice young couple who said they were finally getting their "dream home." Dianne and Sallie felt they were a good choice. After all, they wanted the Hollis house to go to somebody who would love and appreciate it. F. D. and Dolores would have been satisfied, they agreed, as they signed over the deed to the new owners.

With the sale of the Hollis house out of the way, Dianne was free to concentrate on matters back at home. She and Rick wanted to get started on their remodeling plans as soon as possible. They had been discussing what they wanted to do for several years but had decided to postpone everything until after Dianne retired. That time had now come.

They wanted to enlarge the patio and put a cover over it. In order to do that, some trees close to the house would have to be cut. Getting rid of the trees would be their first step, they decided.

Their lot had been covered with pine trees and a few oak trees when the house was new. Over the years, they had lost two large pines due to pine bark beetles, and other trees had been cut to thin out the thicket, and also to make their house safer. Finding a reliable arborist with reasonable prices was not an easy task, but they finally settled on one they felt would do a good job. On the day the tree-cutting crew arrived, they watched the process from a safe distance. Dianne was a little sad to see the trees go, and the yard looked somewhat bare afterwards. But Rick reminded her that things would look a lot better, once they added their new patio to the rear of the house.

Another thing they needed to do before starting the remodeling process was to have the house's foundation leveled. Over the years, the foundation had settled, and a few cracks had formed. They consulted some people who had gotten similar work done, and they finally found a man they trusted.

He inspected the place and gave them an estimate and a complete description of exactly what needed to be done. They agreed on a price, and he and his crew showed up a few days later to begin the process. It was quite a mess, as they had to dig down under the foundation to put in the stabilizers, but, all in all, Rick and Dianne were quite satisfied with the results.

By that time the holiday season was approaching, so they decided to postpone any more remodeling plans until after New Year's. They had waited this long, so there was no big rush. When the holidays were over, they began to call people to come over and give them estimates. Many remodelers never returned their phone calls, and those who showed up were too expensive. Disheartened with the results, they decided to postpone their plans for a few more months.

In the meantime, Dianne had another project to get out of the way. Ever since Dolores had been moved to the nursing home, their house was crammed full of boxes Dianne had brought back from Rocky Branch. She hadn't had time to go through the stuff while she was working, and then they had been busy with selling the Hollis house. But Rick insisted that the stuff was getting in his way, and she had to do something about it.

So, she bought some plastic storage boxes to replace the various assortment of cardboard boxes which, by that time, were beginning to fall apart. She planned to go through each and every box, sorting out the items. They would then be placed in the plastic storage boxes where they would be less susceptible to the elements.

It took several weeks for her to complete the task, but once it was done, they rented a storage bin close to their house and moved all the boxes over there. Dianne wasn't too happy about having to put her "treasures" in an un-air-conditioned climate, but Rick was elated to have the boxes out of his way.

"Now I can finally move around again," he exclaimed.

The summer season was approaching, and they still hadn't found anybody suitable to do the remodeling. Dianne was also starting to have some back pains, but she brushed it off as being a result of spending so much time sitting hunched over the boxes when she was sorting out her stuff.

"It's just part of getting older," Rick told her.

I'm sure he's right. Everybody gets back pains sometime during their life. A little rest and I'll be fine. It's really nothing to worry about, nothing at all, she told herself.

Chapter 13

The summer months brought about two sad occasions. Dianne saw a notice in the paper stating that Peggy's husband, Robert "Fly" Wakefield, had passed away. She phoned Bettye and asked her if she wanted to go in on paying for a flower arrangement for the funeral. Bettye agreed, telling Dianne to just notify her about how much half of the bill would be. Little did Dianne know that would be the last time she would talk to her friend.

A few weeks later, Dianne heard their doorbell ring. Rick answered the door and walked out into the carport. She peered out the carport door, wondering who the visitor might be. She was surprised to see Bettye's daughter, Tracy, and her daughter.

Dianne walked outside and began to talk with Tracy.

"Wow, this is a surprise. How are you doing?" she asked. Then, looking at Tracy's face, she knew something was wrong, very wrong.

"It's Bettye, isn't it? Something's happened to her," Dianne spoke softly.

Tracy nodded, unable to speak.

"She died, didn't she?" Dianne asked somberly.

Tracy nodded again, and Dianne reached over to hug her neck.

"I'm so sorry. What happened?" she asked.

Tracy proceeded to give Dianne a complete description of Bettye's demise, stating that she had died from a heart attack several days before.

"The announcement is coming out in the paper tomorrow. I said I had to go and tell Mrs. Lundy. I couldn't let you find out about it that way," Tracy told her.

"I appreciate you coming by to tell me," Dianne responded.

The funeral, Dianne learned, was to be held in the Colfax Civic Center. Because Bettye had known so many people and touched so many lives, that would be the only place big enough to hold the crowd of people who wanted to pay tribute to her.

Dianne called a florist and ordered flowers. She had attempted to notify Peggy, but had been unable to reach her, so she plunged ahead with the project on her own.

"I want red flowers with a silver ribbon," she told the florist, because red and gray were the Pineville High colors, and she felt Bettye would have liked that.

On the day of the funeral, she arose bright and early, dressed, and drove the seventeen miles to Colfax. She thought she was arriving in time to get a good parking place and a good seat, but she had underestimated Bettye's influence on the community. She barely managed to find a parking spot in the field across from the civic center, and when she entered the building, she couldn't even see an empty seat.

After looking around for several minutes, she finally spotted an empty chair at the end of an aisle near the center of the floor. When she found out the seat was not taken, she settled into it with a sigh of relief.

She had been there only a few minutes when she was approached by an attractive black lady who looked somewhat familiar.

"You don't remember me, do you?" the lady inquired.

"I'm thinking. I know you," Dianne responded.

"It's Laura," the lady told her, "I was your student teacher at Pineville."

"Oh, Laura McCobbie, of course, I know you. I just haven't seen you in so long. How have you been?" Dianne exclaimed.

Laura informed Dianne that her name was now Laura Willis, as she had re-married. She sat down and took Dianne under her wing during the service, explaining exactly what was happening. It was Dianne's first time attending a black person's funeral. She was one of only five white people in attendance. She was somewhat surprised that more of Bettye's former co-workers had not shown up.

It was one of the most touching and beautiful funerals Dianne had ever been to. She looked around for her flowers and spotted the arrangement sitting at the head of the coffin. It was the only arrangement of red flowers with a silver ribbon, so she knew it had to be hers.

I'm sure they put it there because of the colors, not because it was mine, she reasoned. But I think Bettye would have been glad, anyhow.

The funeral proceeded, with several speakers paying tribute to Bettye. One of the speakers was Tracy, who spoke of Bettye's many talents and described all the good food she had prepared for them over the years.

"All that talk about pork chops, turnip greens, cornbread, and chocolate pudding is making me hungry," Dianne whispered to Laura.

"Me, too!" Laura agreed.

Tracy did a good job. Bettye trained her well, and she would have been proud, Dianne thought, as the narration proceeded.

A large choir made up of choir members from several area churches provided the music. Dianne thoroughly enjoyed listening to the old-time gospel hymns, as it brought back memories of her days at the Rocky Branch Church of Christ.

At the end of the service, people lined up to pay their respects to the family before they filed out of the building, passing by the coffin as they exited. Dianne went down the line and spoke to the family members, shaking hands with Bettye's son, Ray, and his son, Poo. She hugged Tracy and Bettye's sister, Bernice.

Then she came to Bettye's husband, Otho. "She was a good friend," Dianne whispered as she hugged his neck.

"I know she was," he replied.

Dianne could barely bring herself to look into the coffin as she passed by. Bettye was beautiful, resting in a white coffin, dressed in a white dress that was complemented with a white hat.

"She looks good, really good," Dianne told Laura, as she blinked back a few tears.

Laura walked Dianne back out to her car, and they exchanged phone numbers, vowing to keep in touch.

As Dianne drove back to Pineville, she burst out singing "I'll Fly Away," one of the hymns that had been used at the funeral.

Well, I can truly say that's the first time I've ever driven home from a funeral singing. If Bettye didn't make it to heaven, nobody else will, either, she thought.

———

As the summer months progressed, Dianne continued her usual activities of taking care of the shrubs and flowers in her yard. She liked to grow things. She supposed it was in her blood. F. D. had always liked watching his garden grow, and Dolores had possessed a green thumb, being able to start a new plant from any cutting she happened to obtain. She had passed on to Dianne a pink rose bush she had gotten from the old Gunter place and also two red rose bushes grown from cuttings taken off the roses in front of the old Rocky Branch school.

Dianne continued experiencing back pains, so she had to cut back on the yard work. But the pains came and went, so she really thought nothing of it.

"You must have done something to your back," Rick told her.

She insisted that she had done nothing wrong, and she had no idea why she was having back problems.

The pains began to increase in intensity and strength, so she decided to pay a visit to her regular family physician, Dr. Alejandro Perez, to see if he could diagnose the problem. He thought she might be developing bursitis because, by that time, one of her hips was also starting to hurt. He gave her a cortisone injection and also gave her instructions for some stretching exercises.

She followed the procedures outlined in the pamphlet he gave her, but the exercises didn't seem to help much. The pains were also getting worse, so she made another appointment. At that point, the doctor was puzzled as to what might be causing the problems. He gave her a prescription for a pain killer and told her if the problems continued, she would need to get an MRI.

Dianne went home somewhat depressed. She had always been in fairly good health, and she wasn't used to being hampered by some sort of pain that interfered with her everyday activities. She had pretty much given up on doing any more yard work. Her back problems were taking priority over all of her activities.

Several nights later, she was awakened by a severe cramp in one of her legs. Since she rarely got leg cramps, she was surprised. The cramp seemed worse than any she had previously experienced. It was located in her thigh, rather than the calf of her leg, and it took a long time to go away. She lost quite a bit of sleep waiting until the pain from the cramp subsided.

Little did she know it was the beginning of the battle of a lifetime, one involving perils she had never faced before. For the next few nights, she was up and down, as the cramps in her legs and back worsened. Finally, she realized that lying down seemed to bring on the spasms, so she completely gave up going to bed at night, remaining in her recliner or on the couch in the living room.

"There's no use of both of us losing sleep," she told Rick, who wholeheartedly agreed, as he had been awakened every time she got up.

The cats, Kitty and Annie, slept in the living room area, so their routine was upset. Every time Dianne got up to walk around whenever she got a cramp, they thought it was time to eat.

Dianne had devised nicknames for both cats. Kitty was sometimes referred to as "Kits," "Skitter," or "Kit Kat." Annie became "Anna Banana" or "Anns." They didn't really care what she called them, as long as they were fed. Having somebody stay in the living room all night was just fine with both of them.

She invented a game, just to keep them guessing. Whenever they would get up from their beds and follow her into the kitchen, she would look at them in total amazement.

"Hungry?" she would ask, almost incredulously, awaiting their response.

One or both cats would respond with a loud meow.

"Again?" she would continue to quiz them until they meowed a second time.

"All right, all right, just a bite," she would say, as she spooned a small bit of food into their two bowls. "You two can't keep eating around the clock, or you'll get too fat."

That was about her only source of entertainment except for television programs. She had tried reading, but the attacks of pain interfered too much with that, so she had given it up. The pains became more severe, sometimes lasting as long as thirty or forty-five minutes. She had called the doctor and requested stronger pain medication on two occasions, resulting in a warning from the drugstore that taking all the medications at the same time could result in psychosis, coma, or even death.

"As if I didn't have sense enough to know that," she told Rick.

"Well, they have to make sure you know. It's just a precaution," he responded.

Dianne was tough. She had to be, growing up in the country. There weren't many things that could make her cry, and she could withstand a lot of pain without complaining, but these pains were different from anything she had ever experienced. She couldn't help letting out a moan or having an occasional cry whenever the pain struck.

"This is worse than having a baby," she complained to Rick. "At least with labor pains you get a break. This goes on and on and never seems to stop."

"Why don't you try a chiropractor?" Rick suggested. "Remember that time I hurt my back? I came home and couldn't even sit down to eat supper. The chiropractor sure helped me."

"Which one should I go to?" Dianne wondered.

"Well, I used Dr. Rabalais, and he's right down the road from us. Why don't you try him?"

Dianne took Rick up on the suggestion and called for an appointment the next day. She had used a chiropractor on one other occasion, and it didn't help, so she was rather leery about trying one again.

Dr. Rabalais turned out to be very nice, as did his receptionist, who was his wife. He made an x-ray of Dianne's spine, just to see if there were any indications of what might be causing the problems. It was the third x-ray Dianne had gotten over the last few months, two of them under other doctors.

"I don't see anything unusual in the x-ray," he told her.

That was the same report she had received from the other doctors. According to all the x-rays, she should be fine.

So why am I having all this pain? she wondered.

He recommended several procedures, and Dianne's back did seem to feel better afterwards, so she scheduled another appointment for the following week.

"I like Dr. Rabalais," she told Rick. "He even wanted my recipe for cornbread dressing."

"Did you give it to him?" Rick inquired.

"No, I told him I would have to bring it the next time, because I couldn't remember all the ingredients," she said.

But the relief from the chiropractor's treatments was short-lived. The pains returned two days later, so Dianne called Dr. Perez's office for another appointment. He was out of town on vacation, the receptionist informed her, but she could schedule an appointment for Dianne as soon as he returned.

Frustrated at not getting any help, Dianne agreed to the earliest appointment available.

I can't believe this! There are something like sixty thousand people in the Alexandria-Pineville area, and I can't find one person who can help me. I don't know how much more of this I can take, she moaned silently.

Dianne was still staying up most of the night. Try as she might, she couldn't help moaning and sometimes crying from the pain. One night Rick exited the bedroom and came out to check on her.

"You're keeping me awake with all that noise," he complained. "If you don't hush, I'm going to load you into the car and take you over to the emergency room."

"I can't help it. I'll try to moan a little more softly," she told him, as he tucked a pillow behind her back.

Somehow, he found just the right position for the pillow because the pain stopped, and she was able to get a couple hours of sleep.

The following night was turning out to be a repeat performance. It was then Dianne made the decision to go to the emergency room at Cabrini Hospital.

"I can't stand much more of this pain, and the pain killers aren't working. Maybe they can do something to help me," she told Rick.

Luck was with them, as there were few people ahead of them. After a quick evaluation by the nurse in admitting, Dianne was sent down the hall to the "Minor Care Facility." She followed a nurse down the hall, barely able to keep up, as she hobbled along.

When she finally saw one of the doctors, she took out her pill collection and lined it up on the counter, explaining what medications she had been taking and describing her symptoms.

"It looks like you have just about every pain medication that can be prescribed, so we are going to try something a little different," he decided.

He gave her a shot in the hip that had been bothering her and told her to be sure to keep her appointment with Dr. Perez the following week.

Dianne rode home in an elated state. "The pain is gone! I can't believe it. I'm actually going to be able to get a good night's sleep," she exclaimed.

She went right to bed as soon as they got home. Then she awoke two hours later, jolted out of a sound sleep by another bout of pain. She got up, totally disgusted, and began to pace the floor again.

"Well, the shot wore off, so I guess I will head back out to the living room," she told Rick.

Two days later, her legs and feet began to swell. It was a Saturday afternoon, and she was looking forward to watching the LSU football game on TV that night. She had gotten interested in their team several years ago, and she never missed a game, be it on television or the radio.

She sat with her legs propped up, trying to relieve the pressure. They also tried applying icepacks to her legs, but it did little good. Rick tried to get her to go to the emergency room, but she refused.

"I'm not going until the LSU game is over," she declared. "They didn't help me much the other time, so I can't see much use of rushing over there. Besides, if we wait until later, the crowd should be cleared out."

The game proved to be an exciting one, with LSU winning in the final few seconds. Dianne felt it was worth the wait.

"See, if we had left earlier, I would have missed out on that fantastic finish," she told him.

When she got to the emergency room, the attending physician sent her to get a sonogram on her left leg to check for blood clots. The procedure was very painful and left a bruise on her leg, but no blood clots were found. The doctor advised her to buy some elastic stockings and sent her home with instructions to be sure to see her regular doctor on Monday.

"Well, that was a complete waste of time," she told Rick on the way home.

"And a complete waste of money," Rick added.

"Now I'm really glad I stayed home long enough to watch the game!" she exclaimed.

On Monday she reported to her 10:15 a. m. doctor's appointment.

By that time, both her feet had swollen too much to even wear shoes. She had to wear her bedroom slippers, and the only way she could walk was with the aid of an old cane she had found in one of their bedroom closets. Besides that, the lack of sleep was beginning to catch up with her. It had been weeks since she had gotten through an entire night without waking due to the pain.

She was called back to the exam rooms, and a nurse came in for a pre-conference. Dianne explained the problems to her, ending with the tale about her lack of sleep.

"I'm like a walking zombie," she told the nurse. "I have had only about four hours sleep in the last two days. Besides that, I have gained ten pounds in three days from all this fluid I'm accumulating. Something has to be done. I can't go on like this!"

Dr. Perez scheduled her for an MRI the following day and a bone density test on Wednesday. He told her he would also have papers filled out for her to be admitted to the hospital.

The MRI was scheduled for 4:45 p.m. Dianne and Rick realized that the doctor's office would be closed by the time the procedure was over, so she sent Rick to pick up the admission papers, just in case she couldn't make it through the MRI.

They reported to the MRI center on time, and Dianne informed the attendant she wasn't sure she would be able to lie still long enough to complete the procedure.

"I'll give it a try, but I have severe pains whenever I lie on my back," she told him.

About ten minutes into the procedure, she got the bad news.

"I'm not going to be able to complete your MRI," he said. "You keep moving, and you have to be completely still for it to work."

"I tried, but it just hurts too much," she lamented.

She and Rick decided the only thing left for them to do was to go on to the hospital. She had packed a bag and overnight case of items for the hospital, and they had the admission papers with them.

Rick let her out near the emergency room entrance because the admission office was closed at that time of day. She managed to hobble in, only to find a room full of people waiting to be attended.

She didn't know how long it was going to take, but she filled out the admission form and wrote "Admit to hospital—Doctor's Orders." Those were the magic words because she got called up right away and got an I. D. armband. They said her room was ready, but she had to wait because, technically, the last person using it had not checked out.

It was a short wait, and Dianne was admitted in about ten minutes, which she found out later from friends must have been some kind of hospital record. An attendant wheeled her to room 631. It was a nice large room with a bed and two couches. The only problem was the bed had a really terrible mattress. It was lopsided, and whenever the bed was let up or down, it made a terrible noise. The slanted mattress gave her even more pains in her back and legs. Even the attendants complained about the bed because it didn't steer correctly, and they had a terrible time wheeling her up and down the halls later for tests.

Finally, an aide named Brenda managed to secure a new bed for her. Dianne was up for a trip to the bathroom when Brenda came into the room.

"Don't get back into bed yet because I'm going to change your bed," Brenda told her.

Dianne sat down on one of the couches and watched in amazement as Brenda wheeled her old bed out and brought another bed into the room.

"I thought you were going to change the sheets when you said, 'change your bed.' I didn't know you meant change out the whole bed!" Dianne exclaimed.

"No, when I said, 'change the bed,' I *meant* change the whole bed," Brenda explained.

"Well, I really appreciate that. It was really sweet of you to do that for me, but what are you going to do with the old bed?" Dianne inquired.

"I'm going to take it to the basement and hope they don't give it to anybody else," Brenda declared.

It was like the difference between day and night. For the first time in days, Dianne was finally comfortable, and her back didn't hurt as much. *The staff is a wonderful group,* Dianne concluded. As soon as she rang the buzzer, someone was there to see about her. She tried to memorize everybody's names, but there were just too many people to remember. Brenda was her favorite, but several of the nurses were especially good. Two of the nurses she really liked were named Pam and Bessie. Then she learned another nurse had been her former student at Pineville High.

"You probably don't remember me, but my name was Dewanda Wilkins," the nurse told her.

"Yes, I do remember you. I taught you and your sister, too," Dianne exclaimed.

"I'm so proud of Dewanda," she commented to Rick later. "She's a very good little nurse."

Doctors were still puzzled as to what was causing Dianne's problems. The only way to find out, they told her, was through running tests. Finally, she was scheduled for a CT scan, and the nurses instructed her not to eat or drink anything after midnight. The following morning, a nurse came in with a bottle of white liquid for Dianne to drink.

"You're supposed to drink this before they wheel you downstairs for the CT scan," she said, as she poured the nasty-looking solution into a plastic glass.

Dianne eyed the concoction doubtfully. "I don't know if I can drink it or not," she replied.

"Well, you have to try. It contains a radioactive substance they need in order to read the test results," the nurse told her.

Dianne picked up the glass and began to swallow the stuff, grimacing as she forced it down. She was feeling pretty proud of herself when the glass was finally empty.

Then the nurse came back in and filled the glass again.

"You didn't finish it yet. This is the rest of the bottle," the nurse informed her.

"I don't know how much more I can swallow. I'll give it a try," said Dianne. But she could drink only a few more sips.

"That's all I can drink," she decided.

"You're supposed to finish the whole bottle," the nurse told her.

"I can't help it. That's all I can swallow. If I drink any more, it will all come back up," said Dianne.

A few minutes later, she was wheeled down to radiology. She was somewhat surprised to see Dr. Perez but was glad he was there.

"Hello, how are you?" he inquired, taking her hand.

"I'm not sure. I'm still having pains in my back and legs. I hope you doctors can figure out what's wrong with me," she replied.

Getting from her bed to the CT table was a slow, painful process, but she finally managed. Lying on the hard surface was almost more than she could bear, and she couldn't help letting out a few moans as she was turned from one position to another. It was a new experience for her, and not one she particularly relished. She was elated when it was all over and she could get back to her room.

She was just about to enjoy her breakfast when a nurse came running into the room and told her not to eat anything. Dianne paused with a forkful of scrambled eggs halfway to her mouth. She hadn't even eaten one bite of the food.

"All you can have is clear liquids because you are scheduled for some more tests," she informed Dianne, as she hastily removed the tray. "I'm so sorry. I'll bring you some apple juice."

Then before Dianne could drink any of the juice the nurse brought her, she had a call from Dr. Leo Lowentritt, a urologist who had been assigned to her case because she had begun to experience urinary problems.

"Don't eat or drink anything today," he told her. "You have a blockage to your kidneys, and we are going to have to perform surgery to put in some urinary stents this afternoon."

So, she had to make it through the rest of the day without food or liquids. It wasn't an easy task because the saline solution fed to her constantly through an IV was making her mouth extremely dry. Her mouth felt like the Sahara Desert, and she couldn't remember when she had ever been so thirsty.

It was a relief to finally be wheeled into surgery, a completely new experience for Dianne, who had been healthy most of her life. Having surgery had been something she had always dreaded because she didn't know how she would respond to being put under anesthesia. The thought of being completely unconscious was a scary thing to her, but there was no way around it. She simply had no choice in the matter.

After asking her all kinds of questions, they told her they were giving her a shot to "help her relax." The next thing she knew, she heard her name being called and she awoke to find herself in the recovery room. After the prescribed length of time there, she was, once again, wheeled back to her own room.

The nurses made their rounds later that day and brought her the usual number of pills. She swallowed them on an empty stomach.

"I'm about to starve. When am I going to get something to eat?" she asked one of the nurses.

"It's about suppertime, so they should be bringing your food around shortly," the nurse replied.

Dianne was really happy when she finally got some food. She began to eat it, and then it felt like she had to burp. Instead of burping, all the food came back out, as she forcefully spewed it across the floor, along with the burp. Suddenly, she lost her appetite. She slowly made her way back across the room to the buzzer and called the nurses' station.

"I need some help down here," she told the attending nurse.

"What's wrong?" the nurse inquired.

"Just get me some help," she pleaded, as she crawled back into the bed. All interest in food had disappeared. All she wanted to do was lie down.

She continued to gain weight as the fluid build-up continued, and her feet and legs continued to swell. Her stomach also began swelling to the point where she looked pregnant. She had been walking around her room periodically, trying to prevent blood clots from forming in her legs. But the increased swelling made it an almost impossible task. One night when she got up to brush her teeth, she barely made it back to bed. After that, she decided she should not try to get up by herself, or else she might end up falling.

"Have they figured out what's wrong with me yet?" she asked one of the nurses who came around to check her "vitals."

"They think you have a tumor in your abdomen," the nurse replied.

Dianne sat in total shock. A tumor. How could this be happening to me? I have had checkups every year, and besides that, I had three x-rays in the last few months. How could I have a tumor and nobody not even know anything about it?

A little while later, a lady walked quietly into her room and introduced herself as being with the Cabrini Cancer Center. I'll just leave you a card, she said, placing the card on the nightstand beside the bed.

Why is somebody from the cancer center coming to visit me? Do I have cancer? Surely not! This just can't be happening to me. Not me, of all people. Not me who had my physical exam every year. This whole thing is totally crazy, Dianne tried to reason with herself.

Rick came by later that afternoon, making one of his daily visits.

"Somebody from the cancer center came by and left a card," she told him.

"The cancer center! Do they think you have cancer?" he asked incredulously.

"I don't know. One of the nurses said I may have a tumor in my abdomen."

Before they could continue the conversation, they were interrupted by a knock on the door. When they called out for the person to come in, a tall, lanky doctor walked into the room.

"Hello, I'm Dr. Hafez Halawani," he told them, speaking with an obvious accent.

"You talk like Dianne's brother-in-law. What country are you from?" Rick asked curiously.

"I'm from Jordan," he replied.

"What kind of doctor are you?" Dianne inquired.

"I'm an oncologist, a cancer doctor. You have a tumor, and we think it is cancer, but we won't know if it's malignant until we do a biopsy. We are going to be transferring you to the oncology ward on the fourth floor just as soon as a room is available."

"Do I have to move?" Dianne inquired. "Everybody on this wing is so nice. I hate to leave."

"The nurses on the oncology ward are specially trained to deal with cancer patients, so it will be better for you to be there," he responded.

———

Dianne was moved to the oncology ward later that day. She said her goodbyes to the nurses and aides who were on hand, hoping she would get some who were just as good in the new ward.

She quickly learned that getting help on the oncology ward wasn't as easy as it had been on the sixth floor. There were only two nurses on duty, and they had no regular aides. So, whenever she pushed the buzzer, she had to be prepared for what sometimes seemed like a long wait.

She tried to get some rest, but the nurses looked in on patients every two hours, and vital signs were checked every four hours. Besides that, technicians always came to draw blood at 4:30 a. m. So, getting a good night's sleep was next to impossible.

Also, she had been having strange dreams, almost hallucinations, about her mother and other family members. She dreamed her mother was still alive, and they were riding around town in Dolores's little '87 Dodge sedan. Sometimes it was just her and Dolores, and sometimes her sister, Sallie, was with them. Why they were driving around, Dianne didn't know, but they were on some kind of mission, trying to gather supplies before a disaster occurred. It was almost as if her mother were in the same room with her. When she awoke, it was an odd feeling.

More tests soon followed. It almost seemed as if every day brought about some new kind of test. By that time, Dianne had become completely bedridden, so she was at the mercy of the medical staff and had to go wherever they chose to wheel her and her bed. She had several more CT scans and also a bone scan to determine if there had been any deterioration of her spine. The Thanksgiving holiday season was approaching, and a lot of the staff members were taking off for the holidays. Dr. Halawani was anxious to have a biopsy done in order to determine the extent of the cancer. She needed to have a sample of bone marrow taken from her hip, he informed her. Since the doctor who usually performed the procedure was off until Monday, he decided to try to do it himself with Dianne still in her own room.

Dianne had heard all sorts of things about the horrors of bone marrow samples and how painful they could be, so she was pretty nervous. The doctor and an assistant came into the room, along with a nurse from the oncology ward. They injected some pain killer into her IV, and the procedure began. Dianne was so scared she was literally shaking, something she had never done before in her entire life. The nurse from the oncology ward stood by and held her hand through the entire procedure. She could feel the needle going in, and then, excruciating pain. They gave her some more pain killers, but they didn't help much, either. After making several attempts, the doctor announced he was unable to obtain a sample and they would just have to wait until Monday when the regular doctor was on duty.

She didn't get much sleep that night, worrying about the upcoming bone marrow test. The following day, it was all she could think about until the aides finally came to fetch her that afternoon.

When she got down to the lab, one of the nurses turned out to be another one of her former students. The doctor promised to give her plenty of pain killers, and they shot her up with one that almost put her to sleep. She was thankful because on that test she felt only a little prick. However, she was left with two holes in her lower back from where the needles had gone in to obtain the samples.

By that time, Dianne had been in the hospital for almost two weeks, and it looked like she wasn't going to make it home for Thanksgiving. The doctor came in for a conference with her and Rick and informed them of the test results.

"You do have cancer. You have what is known as non-Hodgkin's lymphoma," he told them. "It consists of a large tumor in the abdominal area, and that has crowded all of your internal organs. It has not invaded any of your organs, so what we have to do is shrink the tumor. We will use chemotherapy and then maybe some radiation. We need to begin the chemotherapy treatments as soon as possible."

"How big is the tumor? Is it as big as my fist?" Rick asked.

"Oh, much bigger. That thing is humongous," said Dr. Halawani.

Dianne had just two questions. She wasn't worried about whether or not she would be cured. The first question reflected the concern of most patients who learn they will be receiving chemo.

"Will it make me sick?" she worried.

"No, we will give you some anti-nausea medicine before each treatment, so you shouldn't feel sick," the doctor replied.

The second question was one every woman asks before chemo. "Will all my hair fall out?" she asked.

"No, you may lose some of your hair, but you will not lose it all," he reassured her.

The doctor then went on to explain exactly how the procedure worked and told Dianne he would send some literature for her to read before the treatments were started.

She also had to watch a video explaining the procedure, he said. He wanted her to have the first round of chemo before she left the hospital.

Dianne received her first chemo treatment on Thanksgiving

Day. It consisted of two bags of solutions that had to be administered through her IVs. She didn't get nauseated, but she chalked it up as the worst Thanksgiving she had ever experienced.

The only thing that saved the day was some home cooked food sent to her by her twin cousins, Joyce Watson and Jerrine Harrell. Jerrine's son, Jimmy, and his wife and son delivered the food. It was a welcome treat, even though the hospital had provided a Thanksgiving meal for the patients. Dianne couldn't eat all of the food, but Rick came over and ate some of it and took the rest home.

Her cousins were among the few visitors Dianne had during her hospital stay. She had talked to quite a few people on the phone, but not a lot of them came to see her. One of the first visitors was her former co-worker, Peggy Wakefield. Her neighbor and friend, Priscilla Wilson, also came several times, and Priscilla's daughter, Brandi, accompanied her mother during the Thanksgiving holidays. Rick's cousin Jean Rambo, who was a nurse at Cabrini, looked in on her. Sallie drove down from Ruston and brought flowers and some chocolate candy. Rick came every day, and Jonathan dropped by several times. But the strangest visitor was one Dianne did not know at all.

It was a Sunday afternoon, and Dianne was about to doze off while watching TV when she heard a knock on her door. She called out for the visitor to come in and a man she had never seen before entered the room. It was a black man who was shabbily dressed. He walked with a cane and carried his hat in his hand. He told Dianne his name was Joe. He then asked for her name, and she told him. Then, almost before she knew what was happening, he began to pray over her. As quickly as he had come, he was gone, leaving Dianne to wonder if he was a man or some kind of angel. She never saw him again.

Dianne was very much in need of an angel, any kind of angel. She had gone through the phases that most cancer patients go through when learning they have the disease. First, there was denial. She just couldn't believe she actually had cancer, especially since she had been getting her checkups every year and had just had three x-rays done by three different doctors, none of whom could find anything wrong with her.

Then there was anger. She couldn't understand why this was happening to her. God, why are you doing this to me? Why me, of all people? All I have done my entire life is try to help people, and this, THIS is my reward! Is this all I have to show for it? There are all kinds of criminals walking around out there in perfect health, but I have to be stricken with cancer. It isn't fair! It just isn't fair! Then she thought about Dolores. Dolores, who was supposed to be in heaven, watching over her now. Mother, why have you let me down? You are supposed to be my guardian angel now. Where are you when I need you? All of these thoughts raced through her mind as she lay in the hospital bed, contemplating her situation.

Finally, there was acceptance. She realized she had cancer, and her only choice was to fight it. She had never lost a fight in her life, and she wasn't about to start now. She was going to lick this thing if it took every ounce of strength she had! Let them bring on their chemotherapy and their radiation treatments! She was ready!

———

She received treatments for two more days, and then she was visited by Dr. Ule, one of Dr. Halawani's associates. Dr. Ule informed her that she still had one more treatment to go, and it was the most strenuous one.

"We can't decide whether or not to give it to you at this point. This particular phase of the treatment is hard on the kidneys, and we don't know if your kidneys can take it," said Dr. Ule.

In the end, Dianne was given the final treatment the next day. It was the one that would destroy most of her immune system, and she had to be closely monitored as the drug was being administered because some people had an adverse reaction to it. A nurse named Lynn stayed in the room with her and recorded her vital signs.

Dianne didn't feel any different, but from that point on she was treated differently, which was a little disconcerting. All the nurses and aides who entered the room wore masks and latex gloves. She received special instructions on what to do about disinfecting herself and her surroundings whenever she got to go home.

It was about that time she noticed her hair was beginning to fall out. There were clumps of it lying on the floor, and whenever she brushed it, a lot of it ended up in the brush.

Well, I wonder if Dr. Halawani really knew what he was talking about. I am losing my hair, and at the rate it's falling out, I may just go bald, after all, was her foremost thought.

She didn't have much time to dwell on the hair situation because they had started talking about letting her go home. After being bedridden for almost two weeks, she had to learn how to walk again. She began physical therapy treatments and had to practice walking with a walker, as she didn't have enough strength to stand on her own. After two more days, she received the good news that she was being released from the hospital.

It was a cold and rainy day when she finally got to sign all the release papers. Rick gathered up all her belongings, and she dressed to go home. The only clothes she could get into were a tee shirt, a sweater and some sweat pants. Her feet were still swollen and she couldn't even get her slippers on, so she had to wear some socks and paper booties. By the time they left the hospital it was 6:00 p. m.

Her cousin Jerrine Harrell had loaned them a walker and also a shower seat. When they pulled up under the carport, Rick fetched the walker and then she had to wade through some puddles of water to get to the back door. By that time, she was starting to feel the effects of the chemotherapy, and she barely had the strength to make it inside.

Both cats were scared of her when she first came through the door. Their eyes were as big as saucers.

"Hey, Kitty. Hey, Annie. Don't you know me? It's your mama. I'm home again," she announced.

The cats continued to eye her suspiciously, backing away as she approached them.

"I guess they're afraid of the walker," she lamented, as she made her way to the couch and collapsed from exhaustion.

"I'd better get out of these wet socks and booties and clean my feet off. You know what they said about germs," she told Rick. He brought her a clean, damp washcloth and towel, along with some clean socks.

The original plan had been for her to stay in the bedroom, but when she finally managed to make it down the hall to check it out, she decided the room was too cold and the bed was too hard. She maneuvered her way back to the living room, where she settled down on the couch.

Yes, the couch is definitely the best place to be. This will be my headquarters for the next few weeks until I get my strength back. I'm home, and I've never been so glad to be here. I thought God had deserted me, but I know He's still with me. I'm sorry I ever doubted Him. With His help, I will fight this thing and win. God has never let me down before, and I know He won't let me down now.

Chapter 14

Dianne didn't sleep very well her first night at home. She had been given sleeping pills while in the hospital, plus she was used to being awakened every few hours by the nurses. As a result, she awoke at 5:00 a. m. the first morning and entertained herself by watching "Gunsmoke" on TV.

By that time she was feeling hungry because she couldn't eat much food at one time, so she had to yell for Rick. He finally heard her and came into the living room to see what troubling her. She told him she was hungry, and he inquired what she wanted for breakfast.

She had been eating cereal and milk before going to the hospital, but the thought of those two foods was nauseating, so she decided on eggs and toast. Because Rick didn't know how to cook an egg in the microwave oven, she had to call out the directions to him. The egg was a little tough because she forgot to tell him to add milk. The next day she had him add a teaspoon of milk, and the egg came out perfectly. After that, he fixed breakfast for her every morning with egg, toast, and coffee, just like a restaurant.

Since neither Rick nor Jonathan could cook, they ate soup and sandwiches for lunch and TV dinners for supper for the first few days. Rick went to Wendy's one night and got some food, but Dianne could eat only half of her sandwich, so she saved the rest of it for the next day.

Finally, he felt confident enough to prepare a meal using canned and convenience foods. Following Dianne's instructions, he cooked Dinty Moore beef stew, instant rice, green peas, and breadsticks. He and Jonathan both learned how to make tea, although Jonathan's first pot turned out to be too strong and had to be diluted to half-strength.

Dianne had bought a lot of lemons before she got sick, and they were about to ruin. She had planned to make a lemon icebox pie. Rick was leery of making it by himself, but Jonathan wanted to try. She had them bring her some of her cookbooks, and she found a recipe similar to one she had used when growing up. She called out the directions to them as she sat in the living room on the couch. The pie turned out good, except for the crust being too hard because they cooked it too long.

Rick was supposed to make another meal that night, but he said making the pie had worn him out, so they had to settle for another TV dinner. The next night he prepared a meal consisting of Chef Boyardee ravioli, Beefaroni, green beans, and French bread. Dianne ate all of hers because she was so glad to get something other than a TV dinner.

By that time the cats had grown accustomed to the walker. They were happy to have someone staying in the living room twenty-four/seven because it meant they could be fed around the clock. Dianne would often awake to find one or both cats sitting in front of her, meowing or watching her expectantly, waiting to be fed.

What they couldn't understand was why she couldn't pet them. Because of her compromised immune system, she wasn't supposed to touch any animals, so she had to shoo them away whenever they got too close. Rick was assigned the chore of cleaning out their litter boxes, a task that he absolutely despised, but he tolerated it since Dianne couldn't be exposed to germs.

She was still having trouble getting around. She barely had enough strength to make it up and down the hall on the trips to the bathroom. Whenever she walked, her left hip hurt from where the bone marrow samples had been taken, so she had to lie down on the couch for ten to fifteen minutes to wait for the pain to subside every time she walked anywhere. The pain gradually diminished to the point where she felt it for only about five minutes after each trek.

Because everyone had been so nice to her while she was in the hospital for fifteen days, she decided to send two fruit baskets as thank-you gifts—one to the nurses and staff on the sixth floor and one to the oncology ward. She ordered the baskets and also phoned in an order for a Christmas dinner from the Piccadilly Cafeteria because Sallie and Hooshang were coming down to visit on Christmas Day.

The swelling in her right leg had diminished somewhat, but her left leg was still swollen to twice its size. Once she had gotten over the shock of being diagnosed with cancer, her sense of humor had returned, and she began to joke about it. One night she and Rick were watching a show about the Crocodile Hunter on TV, and she said, "I think I am going to just call myself 'Crocodile Lundy,' because that's what my leg reminds me of—a big old crocodile. Whenever I walk, it's like dragging a crocodile around."

She had been home only a week when her left leg began to turn red at the ankle, and it felt hot to the touch. They had been warned to watch for blood clots, but she didn't feel any pain, so she didn't think it was a blood clot. Once again, they tried applying ice packs, but it didn't seem to help. As much as she hated to admit it, she needed to go back to the emergency room for the third time.

After spending an entire day trying to get the leg to respond, they decided to go to the hospital the following morning. Since they didn't know how long they would have to wait, they ate breakfast first. Rick, once again, let her out at the entrance to the emergency room and went to park the car. She could barely walk, and her progress was so slow that he caught up with her before she got inside.

There was only one other person ahead of them, so Dianne thought it would be a breeze to get admitted. She was wrong. It seemed to take forever for the man to be interviewed, and she began to feel weak and thirsty, so Rick had to buy her a bottle of water. When she was finally called, she told them she was a chemo patient, and they put her in an isolated room that had an attached bathroom.

The room was so small that Dianne decided it must have been a storage closet at one time.

They thought they were lucky to have their own bathroom, but they soon learned it had another entrance, and people kept coming and going from the other side. That was tolerable until a patient who evidently had some kind of stomach virus kept coming in and throwing up. Since Dianne could not be exposed to germs, they asked for a maid to come and disinfect it. They thought the other patient had left, but she came back again, so their efforts were all in vain.

Dianne was sent to radiology for a sonogram on both her legs. It was even more painful than the first one had been because her lymph nodes were swollen and sore. She felt almost like she was in a torture chamber. The technician complained because Dianne kept moving.

"I can't help it; it hurts so much," Dianne told her.

After what seemed like almost an eternity, the process was finally completed. A short time later, she was wheeled back to her storage closet/room. A doctor came by and said she had a large blood clot in her left leg. Dr. Halawani had been summoned, but he was tied up with another patient who was in intensive care. By that time, it was past lunchtime, so Rick went to the cafeteria and got himself a sandwich. Dianne hadn't had anything to eat all day after breakfast, so a nurse had a tray of food delivered to her, and she managed to eat some of it.

When Dr. Halawani arrived, he informed them that Dianne would have to be re-admitted to the oncology ward because of the blood clot. Unfortunately, there were no rooms available, so they would have to remain in the ER until one of the oncology patients was discharged.

Their wait was approaching the ten-hour mark, and since it was nearly Christmas, they began to compare themselves to Mary and Joseph with "no room at the inn." The only thing they had to distract them during that time was a TV set in the room.

Dianne definitely was not happy about having to go back into the hospital, especially so close to Christmas.

"I can't believe this is happening to me," she lamented. "Besides that, I think I may have beaten my fruit baskets to the hospital. They haven't been delivered yet."

Finally, just when they thought they couldn't hold out any longer, a nurse came by and told them a room had become available and Dianne would be wheeled up immediately. She sighed as she rode through the halls, up the now-familiar path to the oncology ward.

"I'm back," she announced, as she rolled by the nurses' station, waving as she passed.

Because of the danger from the blood clot, this time Dianne was positively forbidden to take even one step out of bed, so she became completely bedridden for five days. She received shots of heparin to try to dissolve the clot. She kept thinking about Dolores's problems with blood clots and how she had passed away from a pulmonary embolism. She was actually afraid to go to sleep at night, wondering if she might not ever wake up. The thought that she might actually die was foremost on her mind.

The doctor finally gave permission for her to sit in a chair, but the tendons in her legs had drawn up from lack of use, and she couldn't even put her weight on her feet without excruciating pain. They had to lift her from the chair to the bed and then back again, so the second day they brought in a chair that was the same height as the bed.

Since she couldn't get out of bed and needed assistance in bathing, she got help from an aide named Fredna. Upon learning that Dianne had taught at Pineville High School, Fredna remembered that several of her children had taken classes under her.

Dianne was impressed with Fredna's skills as an aide.

"Fredna is one of the best aides I've seen since I've been in the hospital," she told Rick.

By that time, she was ready for physical therapy once again. The therapists informed her that she couldn't go home until she could walk. She finally got to the point where she could put her weight down on her feet and legs again, and she managed to take a trip down the hall using a walker.

After seven days in the hospital, Dr. Halawani told her she was being discharged. It was December 21, just four days before Christmas. She was so weak from the additional hospital stay that she and Sallie decided to cancel their plans for the Christmas dinner, so she phoned the Piccadilly Cafeteria to let them know she wouldn't need the food after all.

Jonathan managed to finagle an invitation for a Christmas dinner from one of his friends. Working together, Dianne and Rick managed to prepare a simple Christmas meal consisting of roasted chicken, macaroni and cheese, broccoli, rolls, a bought apple pie, and tea. It was the first real home-cooked food they had eaten since Dianne was admitted to the hospital in November. Jonathan came home shortly afterwards and announced that his Christmas dinner hadn't been as good as he had hoped it would be.

"Something was wrong with the turkey, and nobody ate any of it," he told them.

"Well, I guess we came out better than he did, after all," Dianne decided.

Christmas that year was a pretty bleak affair. They had no tree, no lights, and no decorations. Since Dianne was unable to do any Christmas shopping, she told Rick and Jonathan to use the Christmas money to buy their own presents. Rick got a chair to go with the desk for his ham radio station and Jonathan decided on a gun cabinet. Dianne got zilch, but she really didn't want anything. At that point, just being alive was enough of a present for her.

Dianne continued gradually regaining her strength, although she still couldn't walk without the aid of a walker, and walking was still painful for her. She finally got to the point where she could cook a little, and Rick and Jonathan scattered like leaves in the wind where the kitchen was concerned.

Rick did help out by doing the housecleaning, and he also had to buy the groceries, as Dianne didn't have enough stamina to make it around the grocery store. She learned that she had to make out a very detailed list, specifying exactly what amounts and which brands to buy, but once he got the hang of it, he did pretty well.

"I know how to buy groceries. I used to shop for my Mam-Ma Tumminello when I stayed with her," he informed Dianne.

Because of the holiday season, Dianne's second round of chemo treatments was scheduled for the second week in January. She didn't really know what to expect when she reported to the doctor's office for an appointment before the treatments. She was told to go to the blood lab for tests before she could see the doctor.

She was still using the walker she had borrowed from Jerrine. Because she couldn't get her feet into any of her shoes, she had to wear her bedroom slippers. It was a long way down the hall to the lab and she barely made it down there and back. It was the longest walk she had made since she had been diagnosed with cancer.

After the doctor's appointment, she was sent across the hall to the chemo lab. When Rick found out the treatment was going to take at least four hours, he announced that he was going home and Dianne could call him to come and pick her up when she was finished. She was left all alone, wondering what she was going to do about getting food, since the treatment was going to run through lunch time.

The lab consisted of a long room with six green leather recliners, each of which formed a station for a patient's treatment. Each recliner had its own curtain and a table for the patient to set things on. Several TV sets were located high on the wall facing the recliners. There were also two rooms with beds for patients who might be unable to sit for their treatment. Dianne was assigned a room, and she was glad because each room had its own TV set.

There were three nurses in the chemo lab. She learned that their names were Jerry, Mary, and Belinda. Jerry was a male nurse, and he was apparently the head nurse for the lab. All the nurses were good, but Belinda quickly became one of Dianne's favorites because she was so kind and friendly and showed a genuine concern for each patient. Pink ladies who volunteered for hospital duty assisted in the lab by picking up items from the pharmacy, running errands, and also getting food for the patients. Dianne was surprised when one of them came by with a pad and pen and took her order for lunch. She ordered a hamburger and French fries, but she could eat only a few bites of food, as her stomach was still shrunken from her hospital stay.

She was still worried about losing all of her hair and she asked Jerry about it when he came around to start the IV for the chemo treatment. She had brushed it when she got home from the hospital, and the hair that came out filled up an entire wastebasket. Now her hair was so thin she could see through it.

"Am I going to go completely bald?" she asked Jerry.

"You probably are going to lose some more of your hair. Whether or not it will all fall out, I don't know," he told her.

Getting the IV's inserted was the worst part of the treatment. Having such a large needle stuck in her veins was very painful, but once it was done, the pain subsided. As promised, she was given anti-nausea medicine before the treatment, so she felt no ill effects as she watched the bags slowly empty while the medicine entered her body.

Since she would have to come for treatments for four days in a row, Jerry suggested she might want to leave the IV in until it was all over with. She agreed, and he wrapped her arm with an Ace bandage and told her not to let it get wet. She had finally graduated to taking showers at home, but during the four days of chemo, she had to revert to taking only sponge baths.

One side effect of the treatments that nobody had told her about was hot flashes followed by chills so severe she started shaking and her teeth started chattering. She was still sleeping on the couch because she was afraid she would roll over on her bad leg if she slept in the bed. It was just as well, she concluded, because she would have kept Rick awake all night with all the hot flashes and chills she was experiencing.

Her leg went down a little after the chemo treatments, and she could walk somewhat better after that. She graduated to a cane, but she still couldn't move very fast. She made it through the three weeks between treatments, and then the whole process started all over again. The second time she reported for her treatments, she noticed that her left leg had turned red again and felt hot to the touch. She asked one of the aides in the doctor's office if the doctor could look at it. The aide replied that she couldn't see the doctor because she didn't have an appointment.

"Just have Jerry check it whenever you get over to the chemo lab," the aide told her.

Jerry took one look at the leg and notified Dr. Halawani, who came almost immediately. He sent Dianne back to radiology for another sonogram on her leg.

The prognosis was that she had developed another blood clot in the leg, and she would need even more blood thinner to dissolve it.

"Please don't put me back in the hospital," she begged.

"Okay, I'm not going to put you in the hospital. Here is what we are going to do. You will have to get an injection of heparin in your abdomen for five days. Starting today, Jerry can give it to you when you come in for the chemo treatments," he decided.

"Thank you so much. I really don't want to go back to the hospital!" Dianne exclaimed.

———

Dianne continued the traditional chemo for three more months. Then, on her next visit, she was informed her blood count was too low and she had to wait before getting any more treatments. Several trips back to the blood lab over the next month showed the same results. Her body had simply not bounced back the way it was supposed to, and giving her any more treatments could be very dangerous.

It was then she had another appointment with Dr. Halawani, who had come up with an alternate plan.

"There is another drug called Rituxan we can give you. It doesn't have the same side effects as traditional chemo, and it doesn't affect your blood count. It contains 'smart molecules' that seek out and destroy the cancer cells. They are then excreted through your kidneys," he told her.

So, she began a new regime. Her treatments consisted of a once-a-week round of chemo for four weeks. Then she skipped three months before having another month's worth of treatments. She felt almost as if she had been let out of prison.

The only bad thing about the new treatments was their side effects. She began to have severe hot flashes immediately after the treatments. She also had to be careful about not getting overheated because that caused her to feel as if she were about to break out in hives. On the other hand, her swollen legs began to return to their normal size, although her left ankle and foot were still somewhat swollen.

When she finally reported for another doctor's visit, she began to quiz the doctor about her legs.

"When is my leg going to get back to normal? Why is it still swollen?" she asked.

"I'm afraid your leg is about as good as it's going to get," he told her.

She sat in shock, barely able to keep herself from screaming, although she was screaming inside her head. As good as it's going to get! I thought my leg would be okay after all the chemo treatments. Now it's going to be messed up for the rest of my life!

The doctor did recommend that she start wearing a special anti-embolism hose to keep the swelling down. She and Rick managed to find them at the pharmacy located on the bottom floor of the hospital. Dianne hated them at first, but she finally got used to wearing them and began to put them on the first thing every morning.

As if that news wasn't bad enough, she learned two more things she would have to face. She had been told she would be on blood thinner for only six months to a year. Because she had developed several blood clots in her leg, she would now have to take blood thinner for the rest of her life, Dr. Halawani informed her.

The doctors seemed to be in some sort of competition to see who could give her the worst report. A conference with the urologist, Dr. Lowentritt, had produced more unexpected news. Originally, she had been told that she would have to keep the urinary stents for just a few months. Further tests showed that her urinary tubes were partially blocked due to scar tissue formed as a result of the tumor. So, she would have to keep them for the rest of her life. Even worse, they would have to be changed out every six months to a year, which meant she would have to have day surgery once or twice every year.

Dianne was beginning to get depressed again. Here she was in her retirement years, and this time was supposed to be the prime of her life. Instead, she was facing months of more chemo treatments, along with a lifetime of taking blood thinner and having day surgery every six months to change out the urinary stents. Once again, she began to feel that life just wasn't fair! Why were all of these horrible things happening to her?

Her walking had improved as her legs began to return to an almost normal size. Plus, she was able to drive again, and she even drove herself to the hospital for the chemo treatments. But she still didn't get around as fast as she used to. One day when she was going through the hospital entrance she got behind a man in a wheelchair. She wasn't in the best of moods because she was still mulling over her unfortunate situation. The man seemed to be taking all day, and she couldn't wait to get past him and get on down the hall for her blood test. Finally, he made it through the door, and she was right behind him. She maneuvered around his chair, dodging the crowd of people who were also navigating down the narrow entrance. Then she glanced down at him as she passed. She was shocked to see that the man had no legs.

In that moment her life was changed. She realized how lucky she actually was to have two legs and still be walking on them, despite all she had been through. She walked more slowly down the hall, as a thought formulated in her mind.

Well, God, I guess you just opened my eyes. I have been complaining and blaming you for all my problems, but now I see that a lot of other people have bigger problems. I'm going to make the most of what I have and stop complaining. I will make it through all the chemo treatments, and maybe someday I will get the chance to tell my story so that I can help other people.

Chapter 15

*A*s Dianne continued her chemo treatments every four months, she began to feel well enough to tackle the remodeling project she and Rick once again had discussed. They contacted several remodelers who advertised in the Alexandria paper and finally decided on which ones to use. Before the remodeling could begin, they had to have additional work done on the foundation, which left their yard in a complete mess and totally demolished almost all their shrubs bordering the house.

Their first priority was getting the carport enclosed and installing an electric garage door in order to provide more security. The man they selected for that job was an excellent craftsman, and they were so pleased with his work they also hired him to build a screened-in porch on the back of the house.

After they had the brick work done on both the carport and porch additions, the yard had to be sodded to prevent it from washing away before the winter rains set in. Dianne hired a landscaper named Eric Myers, who turned out to be a former Pineville High student. He made her a special deal on planting replacement shrubs around the house and making a circular flower bed by the driveway in a spot where they had previously cut down a large pine tree.

They then replaced the carpet in Jonathan's bedroom and the radio room but decided to postpone any more remodeling until after the Christmas holidays. Dianne knew it would take quite some time to pack up all the items from the kitchen and bathroom cabinets, so she felt that was the best thing to do. As soon as Christmas was over, they took down the tree, and she immediately started emptying the kitchen and bathroom cabinets. She had been collecting boxes and newspapers for quite some time in preparation for the project.

It took her almost two weeks, and they had to stack a lot of the boxes in the living room and radio room, but they managed to get it all done just before the remodeling crew showed up right after the first part of January. She thought she was being organized by labeling each box as to its contents and keeping out items she would need to cook with. But she soon found herself digging through boxes, trying to find something she had forgotten she would need. Some items she never located, even though she remembered packing them. So, they just learned to live with the situation until the remodeling project was finished about five months later.

In the end, they had replaced all of the original flooring and repainted or re-papered all the rooms except the den, which was paneled. The kitchen and bathroom cabinets and countertops had been redone, and all the appliances had been replaced. Dianne ordered new draperies and curtains for all the windows, and they had some new bookcases custom-made to accommodate their book collection. In short, it looked like a completely new house, inside and out.

When they could finally unpack and get everything back in its place, she began to rest easy. It had been a long, messy undertaking, but a worthwhile one. She and Rick thoroughly enjoyed all the improvements they had made and felt that their home was now up-to-date.

The cats had not adjusted well to the remodeling and all the noise it created. One morning Dianne awakened to the sound of hammering while the back porch roof was being built. She walked into the kitchen and discovered both cats were hiding. They came out when they saw Dianne, but they were still nervous, with ears back and tails twitching. As Dianne continued her regular routine of eating breakfast and reading the paper, they relaxed somewhat and sat by their food bowls, waiting expectantly to be fed.

At the end of October, Dianne realized something was wrong with Annie, so she carried her to the vet. Annie was going into renal failure, the vet decided. She recommended several procedures to help prolong Annie's life, and Dianne agreed because she wanted to keep the little cat around as long as possible. Annie seemed to rally for a while, but she had her ups and downs for the next few weeks. It was almost time for Thanksgiving, and Annie loved roasted turkey, so Dianne wanted to keep her alive to enjoy one more Thanksgiving.

It was not meant to be. Annie lost her appetite and began losing weight rapidly. She grew weaker and weaker and was barely able to stand. Dianne knew it was almost the end, but she still held out hopes that Annie would last a few more weeks. Then Annie began falling down when she tried to walk, so Dianne realized there was nothing more she could do. It was one of the hardest decisions she had ever made, but she felt the kindest thing would be to have Annie put to sleep.

During Annie's last night at home, Dianne picked her up and held her in her lap, petting and stroking her.

"Annie, you're the sweetest cat ever," she told her, blinking back tears as she spoke.

The following morning she carried Annie to the vet's office and told them what needed to be done. She walked down the hall into one of the back rooms with Annie, the vet, and one of the vet's assistants.

"Her name is Orphan Annie. She's been orphaned twice, and I'm not leaving her alone now," Dianne declared.

It was the first time she had actually witnessed a euthanization. She watched as the vet administered the lethal injection, and then the light of life died out in Annie's eyes. That was it. She had lost the last living contact with Dolores, except for her sister Sallie.

She carried Annie's body back to their house where Rick was

waiting. He had dug a hole beside the large oak tree in their back yard. That was the best place to bury Annie, he had decided.

Dianne slowly lowered Annie's body into the ground. "She made it to twenty-one. That's a lot longer than most cats live," she said.

They each ceremoniously tossed a spade of dirt over the grave. Rick finished the task, tapping down the dirt and replacing the sods of grass.

"They say pets don't have a soul, but, somehow, I think Mother and Annie are together now," she told him.

Kitty Snowball seemed to know something was wrong. She appeared to be looking for Annie over the next few days. Then she settled back down into her routine, happy to be the sole center of attention in the household. Dianne was petting her one night when she noticed she could feel all the cat's ribs and also her backbone.

"Why is Kitty so skinny? She was always eating her food and Annie's, too. I can feel all her ribs and almost every bone in her body," she exclaimed.

The following day she took the cat to the vet's. The diagnosis was that Kitty had either pancreatic cancer or intestinal lymphoma. There was no way to predict how long she would live, but the vet prescribed some medications that would prolong her life and make her more comfortable. She was also put on a special diet.

The medications made the cat hungry all the time, and she ate every few hours, but she never gained any of her weight back. In fact, she continued losing weight to the point where she looked like skin and bones.

Dianne was spending $100 a month on medication and food for the cat. She had spent $500 on Annie the last month of her life, so she felt it was the least she could do for Kitty. She loved her pets and wanted to keep them around as long as possible.

But Kitty started growing weaker and weaker. Her body had used up every ounce of fat, and now it was using up the muscles and other tissues. It became apparent that the cat was not going to make it much longer. Dianne debated on whether or not to have her euthanized, also, but decided to wait awhile.

One morning she got up early to get her son off to work. She fed the cat, as usual, but could see she was weaker than ever.

"Son, you had better pet Kitty before you leave for work. I don't know if she will still be alive when you get back," she told Jonathan.

She went back to bed but was awakened several hours later when Rick came into the room.

"You'd better get up. I think Kitty is about to go," he announced.

Dianne rushed out into the hall where Kitty's bed was located. By that time the cat had gone into a coma, and there was nothing more they could do for her. They just had to wait it out. Within thirty minutes, she was gone.

Dianne called Jonathan and gave him the bad news. Kitty had officially been his cat, since he was the one who had brought her home.

Jonathan wanted them to wait until he got off work to bury the cat. Rick went ahead and dug a second hole under the oak tree, right beside Annie's grave. When Jonathan got home, they carried Kitty's body out to the burial spot. After they placed her in the grave, they each spaded some dirt over the body. Then Rick and Jonathan finished filling the hole.

"Poor little Kitty. She gave it a hard fight, but she's gone now," Dianne lamented.

"I don't think we'll be getting any more pets," Rick noted.

"No, I don't think so, either," added Dianne.

Dianne still had three major tasks ahead of her. First and foremost, she had to finish her chemo treatments, which would take a total of two and one-half years to complete. She also wanted to get started writing on her book. She had already written the first two chapters mentally some years ago. Now it was time to get her ideas down on paper. The third thing that remained was selling the ten-acre Hollis pasture in Rocky Branch. The girls had never gotten around to selling it, and they weren't in a big hurry. After all, when it was gone, all their ties to Nip 'n' Tuck would be severed.

They had several chances to sell the land, but it had never worked out. While F. D. had owned the property, he had used the pipeline that ran from the highway to his pasture as an access road. Now that both their parents were gone, Dianne and Sallie learned that they did not actually own the right-of-way to the property, and that presented a problem. The neighbors who owned the land over the pipeline decided they didn't want anybody else crossing their land, so they put up barricades to keep everyone off.

After searching through old land deeds, Dianne found that F. D. had reserved a right-of-way to the pasture for himself through their original two-acre lot across the road from their new house. She checked with Sybil Brantley, the lady who had bought the Hollis property, and found she had no objections to them going through on her land to get to the pasture.

The only problem was the right-of-way came to a point and did not have enough width to actually allow a vehicle to pass through to the pasture. Dianne contacted another lady who owned the piece of property adjacent to their right-of-way and offered to buy a small triangle of land large enough to finish out a driveway. The piece of property they needed was worth only about one hundred and fifty-eight dollars at its estimated market value, but the lady and her son also refused to sell.

The only choice left was to take the parties to court because according to Louisiana law, landowners are entitled to access their land from the nearest public road. Dianne contacted a lawyer in Farmerville, and he agreed to handle the case for them. Several months later, just before the case was scheduled to go to court, Dianne received a phone call from Jerrel Gates, one of her former classmates who lived in Rocky Branch. Jerrel and his wife, Judy, were interested in buying the pasture and building a house on it, he told her.

She explained the problem about the right-of-way to him, and

Jerrel told her he thought he could get a way in from the other side of the pasture. Dianne agreed it would be a good idea to check because there were actually five different ways to get to the pasture across other people's property.

Luck was with them, and Jerrel secured his right-of-way and phoned Dianne about the results. She and Sallie were jubilant about not having to go to court. They were also excited about Jerrel buying the property, since he had been one of Dianne's classmates for twelve years and had also been Dolores's student in the seventh grade. They learned in a later conversation that he had worked as F. D.'s "top boy" during the summers of the peach orchard days, so he was quite familiar with the pasture.

Dianne and Sallie met Jerrel and Judy at the lawyer's office in Farmerville to sign the papers. They exchanged a few stories about their childhood days while waiting in the lobby.

"I remember one time when Mrs. Hollis paddled me at school," Jerrel told them. "I got mad about something at recess and climbed up into a tree and wouldn't come down. She told me she was going to the mailbox to get the mail and I had better be down by the time she came back. I climbed down while she was gone and she paddled me good when she got back."

Dianne and Sallie both laughed. "That was a rare occasion," Dianne said. "She didn't paddle very many people."

The girls agreed that their parents would have been pleased with their choice of who got the pasture. Both parents had liked Jerrel and thought he was a "good boy."

"We just have one request. Call us whenever you get your house built on the property, and we'll come by and take a tour of it," Dianne told them.

"We'll sure do it," Jerrel assured them.

Dianne drove back to Pineville, both elated and relieved that the property was finally sold. At the same time, she was a little wistful because she had lost the last piece of property that connected her to her childhood years. Still, it had to be done, she reasoned. There was no use in keeping a piece of property they weren't going to use again. Hopefully, it would be made into a beautiful house place, and Jerrel and Judy would enjoy living on it.

———

Through all the chaos, Dianne had continued with her chemo treatments. Some of the faces at the Cabrini Cancer Center had changed. All of the three original nurses had left and were replaced by Cindy and Blake, along with some other temporary staff members. Dianne's former student, Dewanda, moved from the sixth floor into the cancer center to become one of Dr. Halawani's nurses. She was glad to have somebody there who took a special interest in her progress.

Other people who were especially nice to her included Carol, the receptionist; Linda and Vicki, two of the aides; a nurse also named Linda; Ruby, the receptionist at the blood lab; and Bonnie, one of the Pink Ladies in the chemo center. Janet, the social worker for the cancer center, and Susannah, a nurse who worked in the research department, always had a kind word for her whenever they saw her walking through the center for a treatment or blood test. All in all, she was impressed with how well she was always treated by the staff members.

Having a three-month break between treatments allowed her to work towards her goals. She began to reflect on her life, counting off the things she had accomplished.

Well, I made it through thirty-three years of teaching, and now I have a retirement check coming in every month for the rest of my life. I got married and raised a child who has now become a responsible adult. I took care of Mother while she was sick and helped to make her last years as comfortable as possible. Rick and I remodeled our house. Sallie and I sold all the property in Rocky Branch. I still have one more thing I have promised myself I would do, and that is to write a book about my teaching experiences I need to get started on that, but just when and how, I don't know.

She wrote out the first two chapters by hand. They had been formulating in her mind for years, so it wasn't too hard. Then she began brainstorming, jotting down all the events she could remember, sorting them into categories. Still, she was at a loss as to how to continue on the writing process. English had always been her best subject, and she had been good at writing while she was in high school and college. But would it be enough?

It was about that time she spotted an advertisement in the Alexandria paper listing some continuing education courses for the fall semester at the LSU-Alexandria campus. One of the courses was on novel writing. She stared at the paper, almost in disbelief. It seemed almost too good to be true. Was God intervening in her life again? she wondered.

After completing three college degrees, she had vowed to never take another class, never take any more notes, and definitely never take any more written tests. She was through with all that! But, here was her chance, staring her in the face. She couldn't let it go by, she decided.

She enrolled in the class and reported for the first session, which was held at the Red River Bank in Alexandria. Not knowing what to expect, she walked into the room and took her seat. There were only seven class members, all ladies, each of whom had an idea for a different kind of novel. The teacher, Debbie Hancock, was a certified English teacher who had written and published nine historical romance novels under the pen name Elizabeth Leigh, she learned.

She found the class to be both entertaining and informative. Attending class was something she looked forward to each week. Towards the end, each student had to write the first chapter of their novel and furnish copies to all the other students in class. Dianne typed hers out on a typewriter, as she had never mastered the art of composing on a computer. She handed out her copies to the other class members with the hopes they wouldn't be too critical of the project.

Aside from recommending that she change the order of the first few paragraphs, the other ladies, along with the teacher, seemed to think she was on the right track. She was delighted to finally be writing the novel she had talked about for so many years.

A second course on novel writing was offered during the spring semester, and Dianne signed up for that one, also. Five of the seven original members continued with the class. When it was over, Debbie offered to hold a critique meeting every two weeks at her house where class members could attend and bring ten pages of their novel for everyone to read.

Dianne and one other lady, Becky Jemerson, were the only two who took her upon the offer. They began meeting every two weeks, and their work began in earnest.

Dianne finally mastered the computer enough to use it for writing her manuscript, and she was glad because it allowed her to make corrections without having to re-type the entire thing.

They continued meeting whenever they could over the next few years. They were eventually joined by another lady, Norma Franklin, who was working on a novel set in during the Civil War era. All three ladies were eager to finish their novels and try to get them to a publisher.

Throughout the project, Dianne had run into a lot of her former students and co-workers. She had told them all about writing the novel and promised to let them know when it was published. Some of them wanted her to mention them in the novel, and some didn't. Some went so far as to request their names be changed if she decided to write about them.

"Oh, don't worry. I'm not going to say anything bad about anybody," she always assured them.

Often she would come home and tell Rick about running into some of her former students or co-workers. It seemed to happen in spurts. She would go out on errands for months and not see a single person she knew. Then, suddenly, in a single day she would cross paths with two or three acquaintances. She might be at the grocery store, at Wal-Mart, buying gasoline, or even shopping for clothes. Wherever it was, she was always surprised.

But the biggest surprise happened one day when she went to vote.

One of the ladies checking voter registration saw Dianne walking towards her table and exclaimed, "Mrs. Lundy, didn't you use to teach at Pineville High School?"

"Yes, I did," Dianne replied.

"I used to be one of your students." The lady then proceeded to tell Dianne her name, and it sounded like she said "Karen Rockett."

Dianne was puzzled because the name just didn't ring a bell. "I taught some Rocketts, but I don't remember a Karen Rockett," she admitted.

"Oh, that's my married name. I used to be Kerri Sullivan," the lady explained.

"Kerri, of course, I remember you," Dianne told her. "You had short hair back then, but you still have the same smile."

Dianne's former students usually recognized her, although sometimes they didn't. Her appearance had changed, partly due to a change in her hairstyle and color. One problem she had encountered during chemo was dealing with her hair loss. At the rate it fell out during the first few weeks, she expected to go totally bald, and she even purchased two turbans to wear should that ever happen. She was forced to cancel several appointments to have her hair cut because she was just too ill to make it to the beauty salon. Although it was thin, her hair grew out to almost shoulder length, longer than it had been in over twenty-five years. She finally resorted to parting it in the middle and pinning the sides back, just to keep it out of her eyes.

She had decided to follow in Dolores's footsteps when gray hair had first appeared, and she had begun dying it years before. One of the no-no's during chemo was having one's hair dyed or bleached, so she was forced to let the gray grow back in, resulting in hair that was at least three different colors. Not a becoming situation, she decided.

When she was finally able to go back to her regular beautician, Khang, at Creating Self Images, she was still unable to have anything done to it other than getting it cut and styled. She had to wait until the chemo treatments were over before she could do anything about the color.

Her hair began to grow back, and she was finally given the "okay" by Dr. Halawani to change her hair color. She wanted something different. Originally, she had planned on having it frosted, but upon learning that it would have to be first dyed and then bleached, she decided against that.

"Just make me a blonde," she told Khang.

She looked at the sample swatches and chose a platinum blonde color. Everybody liked her new look except for Rick, who informed her it made her look older.

"I don't care. I like it, and I'm the one who counts," was her response. "Besides, you know what they say—blondes have more fun!"

———

Despite the fact that Dianne had apparently bounced back from the depressed state she faced when diagnosed with cancer, there was still one more serious matter weighing heavily on her mind. It had been there all along, sometimes just a niggling feeling, but something she could not shake. She had given up going to church while caring for Dolores over the last years of her life, but she had not forgotten the promise she had made to Dolores about going back to church.

Dianne had attended church all her life. While she was growing up, her family hardly ever missed a service, going three times a week and also attending all the gospel meetings held in the Rocky Branch Church of Christ, as well as those of neighboring churches.

When she had attended Harding College, she had received additional instruction in bible classes and studies, to the point where she felt almost supersaturated with biblical knowledge. She could not and would not leave her roots.

She had planned to go back to church several times, but it had never worked out. During her battle with cancer, she had begun to compare herself to Job, wondering just how many more trials she could withstand. She had asked God why He had bestowed her with such a fate. She felt there was always a reason for everything, but why she had to endure such pain and torment was a puzzlement.

God, I know you have a reason for everything you do, and maybe someday I'll fully understand it all. Maybe I'll know why these terrible things had to happen to me. Please set my feet on the right path and show me the way, was the prayer that had echoed in her mind, over and over.

She hadn't forgotten about the man in the wheelchair who had no legs. No, not at all. Every time she thought about him, she knew God had not forsaken her. She had health problems that would follow her the rest of her life, but she was still blessed. Of that, she was totally convinced.

Now it was time to pay God back, if there was such a thing as paying Him back.

She had to make it back to church. She just had to.

The Pineville Church of Christ had changed locations since she had last attended. The congregation had moved from their building by Cheek's Marine on Military Highway in Pineville to a new facility on Highway 28 East. She had passed by their grounds several times while running errands.

She called her cousin Jerrine and asked her about the times of services and also about the layout of the building.

"I sit on the third row from the back in the middle of the auditorium," Jerrine told her. "If you come, be sure to sit with me and my family."

Dianne walked into the church the following Sunday. She spotted Jerrine, sitting right where she had said she would be, along with her daughter Donna and Donna's twin girls, Jerrianne and Jennifer. Dianne took a seat beside Jerrine and settled in to wait for the service to begin.

Things had changed a lot since the last time she had seen the other members of the congregation. Some she recognized, and some she did not. She wondered if any of them would remember her.

The preacher was inspiring, and she went home in a good mood, especially after hearing some of the old gospel songs she had grown up with, along with some newer ones. Some of the members remembered her when she had talked with them after the services. Several of her former students, including Khristi Battistelli Thomas, Norm Blackburn, and his wife, Lea Doss Blackburn, were now members of the congregation. And, of course, there was Mike Roach, the brother of her former FHA president, Vickie Roach Cofer. He had opened the door for her and handed her a bulletin when she first entered the building. But making a commitment to become a member of the congregation again was something she had to think about.

Dianne knew it was her mother's steadfast faith and guidance that had continued to influence her life, even into adulthood. Dolores's faith had never wavered, even in the worst of times. She and Sallie had felt it and witnessed it on many occasions. There was no doubt about it. Their mother had been a strong, Christian woman.

She attended the Sunday morning services several more times before she made up her mind. The time had come for her to make a decision one way or another. Then one Sunday, during the invitation song she went forward and reinstated her membership with the Pineville church.

She walked out to her car after the service, totally at peace with herself for the first time in years.

Well, Mother, you finally got your wish. I know you're happy now. I'm back in the church and we'll be together again someday, she thought.

She hit the button on her key ring to unlock the car then opened the door and climbed inside. After closing the door and fastening her seatbelt, she reached up to adjust the rearview mirror, catching a glimpse of herself in the process. Her green eyes, still as bright as they had been in her younger days, stared back at her.

Well, Dianne, you've come a long way since you left Rocky Branch. The road hasn't always been an easy one, but you always gave it your best shot. Sometimes you made the right decisions, and sometimes you didn't. In the process, you touched thousands of lives. Some of your students went down the wrong path, it's true, but the majority of them turned out to be worthwhile citizens who made good lives for themselves and their families. A few of them became rich and some even became famous figures who are recognized nationwide. Not too bad for someone who started out as a girl from Nip 'n' Tuck. Not bad at all.

She started the car, put it into gear and eased out of the parking lot, humming softly as one of the old gospel hymns came to mind.

O, they tell me of a home far beyond the skies,

O, they tell me of a home far away;

O, they tell me of a home where no storm-clouds rise;

O, they tell me of an unclouded day.

She had to smile when just for an instant she was, once again, back in that little white wooden church in the woods where she had attended worship services during her childhood days. She was, and always would be, a girl from Nip 'n' Tuck.

The End

www.ingramcontent.com/pod-product-compliance
Lightning Source LLC
Chambersburg PA
CBHW021613120626
46545CB00001B/203